THE GREATEST ESCAPE
A True American Civil War Adventure

DOUGLAS MILLER

Liberty!

LYONS PRESS

Essex, Connecticut

An imprint of Globe Pequot, the trade division of
The Rowman & Littlefield Publishing Group, Inc.
4501 Forbes Blvd., Ste. 200
Lanham, MD 20706
www.rowman.com

Distributed by NATIONAL BOOK NETWORK

British Library Cataloguing in Publication Information available

Library of Congress Cataloging-in-Publication Data Available

ISBN 978-1-4930-7185-2 (paperback)
ISBN 978-1-4930-5183-0 (e-book)

♾™ The paper used in this publication meets the minimum requirements of American National Standard for Information Sciences—Permanence of Paper for Printed Library Materials, ANSI/ NISO Z39.48-1992.

For Janet and Andy, my wonderful parents

Contents

CONTENTS

Prologue

Interesting news cannot grow stale; time cannot destroy that interest;
it cannot even fade it; the eye-witness's narrative which stirs the heart
to-day, will as surely and as profoundly stir it a thousand years hence.
—MARK TWAIN, *AUTOBIOGRAPHY*

IN 1893, CHICAGO BECAME THE CENTER OF THE WORLD. IN AN ERA OF train travel, millions rode the iron horse to the city, journeying for days at a time so they could experience the great American World Fair. They went to be thrilled by the latest advancements in science and art, to witness the mechanical marvels they'd only read about, and to see if Americans could top the marvelous Paris World Exposition, which four years earlier had premiered the Eiffel Tower.

Many of America's finest architects had worked to create a brilliant "White City," with entries from around the world. The Chicago Fair was an enormous success, exposing patrons to an amazing range of inventions—from the movie theater to the Ferris wheel, which many patriotic Americans thought grander than Eiffel's tower. The splendor and massed humanity, richly described in Erik Larson's book *The Devil in the White City*, still linger in the collective memory of Midwestern America.

One of the city's most popular attractions, not part of the fair but erected near to the fairgrounds, was the Libby Prison Civil War Museum. In a city crammed with curious exhibitions in unusual buildings, this museum was perhaps the most curious of all.

A massive brick-and-stone structure, Libby had actually been brought to Chicago from its home in Richmond, Virginia, some eight hundred miles away. Decades earlier, it had been constructed as a tobacco warehouse. During America's Civil War, the Confederate states chose Richmond as their capital city, and they converted the warehouse into a prison for Union officers. In the fourth year of the war, Union officers confined at Libby made the building world famous by staging the greatest prison escape in US history.

In 1888, almost 25 years after the war, a group of entrepreneurs bought the old building with the audacious goal of moving it to the city of Chicago. Thousands of bricks and beams were disassembled and carefully labeled. The totality was massive enough to fill 132 rail cars, each of which could haul 20 tons. The Chesapeake and Ohio Railroad won the high-profile contract, and was greatly embarrassed when their train wrecked near Maysville, Kentucky, scattering the contents along the right of way. But everything was carefully collected, reloaded, and safely delivered to the Windy City.

The four stories of Libby Prison were reconstructed on Wabash Avenue between Fourteenth and Sixteenth Streets and ringed with a massive stone wall, which gave it the aspect of a giant castle. Some $200,000—a veritable fortune in those days—had been spent by the time the museum opened in December 1889.

Flyers, pamphlets, and newspaper advertisements quickly followed. *"Attention! No Stranger Should Leave Chicago without visiting Libby Prison, the Great National War Museum,"* said one. The famous chaplain C. C. McCabe, who had almost died of disease and vermin infestation while imprisoned there, proclaimed that he had seen the Libby exhibit in Chicago *"and pronounces it the grandest and most instructive museum in the world."*

The new museum was filled floor to ceiling, in the cluttered Victorian style of the day, with photographs, documents, oil paintings, and a sprawling collection of the war's remains: cannons and cutlasses, Confederate postage stamps and newspapers printed on wallpaper, military proclamations and recruiting posters, Jefferson Davis's love letters to his wife, and—from Appomattox—the very table on which Grant and Lee had signed the surrender. Also on display were ragged battle flags, tiny bone scrimshaws carved by POWs, and a collection of what were described in

the museum catalog as *"War Logs: the collection of tree stumps in this room, filled with shot and shell, is the finest in existence."*

The Rebel surrender at Appomattox, less than three decades in the past, was within easy memory; many visitors who paid the fifty-cent admission fee (children twenty-five cents) had a personal connection to the war. For long after the fair had closed, the Libby Museum continued to pack in the crowds that came to see one of the Civil War's most famous locales—a battlefield all its own.

The most popular part of the exhibit, the one everybody wanted to experience, lay deep in the dark cellar of the old building. During the war, this dank space contained the rooms that served as punishment dungeons for men unfortunate enough to cross Rebel authorities. Those windowless rooms, in their day, had been suffused with the foulest of human and animal odors. One of the basement chambers had been so disgustingly filthy that imprisoned officers had tagged it with the nickname Rat Hell.

In the new museum, of course, these rooms were so clean that the most prim and proper ladies and gentlemen would gladly visit them. And for an extra 25 cents, visitors could see that monument to human perseverance, the "Great Yankee Hole." Many thousands of people poked their heads into the entrance of the tunnel that had led 109 Union officers out of this "Rebel Bastille" in February of 1864.

The men who had actually entered that hole, and had made the difficult passage through the tunnel that led from it, were then pursued by Confederate hunters across 50 miles of freezing swamps; without food or warm clothing or maps, they passed through a series of extreme trials and adventures—none of which the exhibit could more than hint at. Along their perilous journey three decades earlier, many of the Union officers had been helped by slaves and members of the "Union Underground," all of whom risked their lives by sheltering and shepherding the escaping Yankees.

Since Libby had been one of the first prisons established by the Confederacy, its worsening conditions were the subject of anger and consternation throughout the war. And as the Rebels had taken care to place the vaunted prison smack in the center of their capital city, it naturally became a focus of strong emotions on both sides.

So when more than a hundred Union officers vanished from the Confederacy's "escape-proof" building—and when the escape played out over the following weeks in newspapers North and South—the public was riveted. Each day brought new stories and revised numbers of officers escaped or recaptured. In a civil war of mass slaughter, where tens of thousands of young men were expected to stand in rows and shoot each other to pieces, here was an uplifting tale in which ingenuity, perseverance, initiative, pluck, and luck had won the day. Brutally imprisoned, completely on their own, facing a slow death from starvation or disease, the young men in Libby had stood up and prevailed.

The tale of Libby Prison soon grew even more popular, thanks to the POWs themselves. Officers of the Union Army could read and write. And write they did. The more famous the escape became, the more the escapees wrote about it. The first accounts were published within months of the event. They continued to come out for decades—and for long after the Libby exhibit in Chicago had closed.

These prisoner memoirs were published with provocative titles like "Forgotten in the Black Hole," "What I Saw and Suffered in Rebel Prisons," "The POW and How Treated," "A Thrilling History of the Famous Tunnel Escape from Libby Prison"—to the more leisurely and Victorian, "Extracts From My Diary and My Experiences while Boarding with Jeff Davis in Three of his Notorious Hotels."

These young Yankee officers wrote well and clearly, even though many of them modestly started their tales with "I'm not a writer *but* . . . ." Americans were more literate back then, and even young men like these—most in their twenties—had plenty of writing experience, along with a vocabulary broad enough to include words like "cerements," "adamantine," "fugacious," "renitent," or "unpomatumed."

Their histories were very personal, with strong points of view. Many of the men, particularly those whose accounts appeared immediately, were furious at the treatment they'd received at the hands of the Rebels. As with most military memoirs, those written decades after the fact carried a mellower tone. Still expressing anger, they had been tempered by time and by the reconciliation the entire country was experiencing.

These first-person accounts were as diverse as the men who made up the Union officer corps. Some were only a few pages long; some were entire books filled with unique illustrations; some were from lectures; some were written days after the fact, while others weren't recorded until a half-century later. One memoir was written in German. Another was written by a future hero of the Cuban Revolution; another by a Sardinian immigrant who would become the first head of New York's Metropolitan Museum of Art; another by a Romanian soldier of fortune who had served with Garibaldi; and another by a POW chaplain who would carve out a lifelong career on the Chautauqua circuit by delivering, again and again, his one-of-a-kind sermon on "The Bright Side of Life in Libby."

What follows in this book is the story of the Libby Prison escape and its aftermath, truer than it's ever been told. The story is based on primary sources: the four dozen eyewitness accounts that, along with more than forty historic illustrations, took more than two decades to locate. The POWs who went through the tunnel considered it a supreme trial; for most, it was the greatest event of their lives. Their personal stories are front and center in this volume, each memoir adding a unique point of view about the escape and about the minds of Americans in 1864.

These personal accounts, in effect, are interviews with people who are speaking to us direct from the nineteenth century. These eyewitnesses were personal, passionate, funny, and often very sarcastic. The quotes have sometimes been shortened, because writers of that time were notably long-winded; and the spelling of names has been made uniform. Otherwise, original texts are unaltered; spelling and phrasing have been left intact, including racial language and various attempts at dialects and swearing. For the first time, a century and a half after the events, all the Libby memoirs are together in one place.

On April 4, 1865, one day after Richmond fell to the Union Army and ten days before he was assassinated, President Lincoln arrived to tour the fire-ravaged Rebel capital. One of the first sites he stopped at was Libby Prison. A boisterous crowd of soldiers and ex-slaves cheered, *"We'll tear it down"*—to which Lincoln replied, *"No, leave it as a monument."*

The American Civil War was the largest, most destructive conflict of its age. It was the greatest war in the Western Hemisphere. It was

Lincoln in Richmond, April 1865.

the most important event in the history of the United States. Its key triggers of race, states' rights, and militarism may have evolved, but they still define us. More than any event since the Revolution, the Civil War made America what it is today. And the Libby Prison escape is one of its pivotal stories, as well as one of its greatest adventures.

Chapter One

Captured

ALL SOLDIERS GO INTO COMBAT THINKING OF BEING KILLED OR, PER-haps worse, of being maimed. They question their own bravery and worry whether they will let their comrades down.

However, a soldier seldom imagines becoming a prisoner of war.

Infantrymen in the Civil War would have witnessed the horrific consequences of being hit with the large, soft bullets of the era, but they really had no way to imagine life as a POW. For most of the war, guidelines for captives were nonexistent, while penal systems were in a state of constant flux. Treatment varied widely from prison to prison and from year to year.

Virtually all the memoirs written by Libby prisoners expressed their total surprise at being captured. What will happen now? Where will I be taken? Will I be forgotten and die far from home? Each capture was unique but the questions were the same.

Union Lieutenant Clay MacCauley was only 20 when, during the *"ugly give and take"* of the battle of Chancellorsville in May 1863, he came upon a dying soldier begging for water.

"I was about to give him my canteen when I discovered the rebels rapidly coming through the brush. I saw one of the oncoming skirmishers take a sudden interest in me. He jerked his musket from charge to direct aim. I was his mark.

"Perhaps some of you understand just what it is to look into a loaded gun, its trigger under the finger of a man who would just as soon pull as not. Naturally, I remained where I was. For several seconds I looked into the muzzle of that advancing musket. He came upon me swifter than my speech of him now.

I

With the bayonet at my breast the man yelled, "You ——— of a ———, give me that sword."

"I was a prisoner, and doomed to—I could not tell what."

Second Lt. Edward Tobie of the First Maine Cavalry was shocked to realize he'd stumbled into the hands of Rebels after a series of hard charges at Brandy Station, Virginia, in 1863. *"Never was the transition from the wildest excitement and the highest inflation of spirits to a feeling of thorough despondency and heartsickness more sudden and complete. A thousand thoughts crowded through my mind at once. Visions of Libby Prison, with attendant miseries, passed in mental review."*

Three Rebel cavalrymen grabbed Capt. Emeric Szabad while he was on a scouting mission in October 1863. *"I had no choice but to give them my sword, the only weapon I had with me. In other words, I became prisoner, and that for the first time in my life, and a curious feeling it was!"* wrote Szabad.

This was his third war, as he had fought in the 1850s for Hungarian independence and then alongside Garibaldi in Italy. Well educated and multilingual, Szabad had written books analyzing the history of warfare.

At the moment of capture, a Confederate snatched his beloved horse and silver spurs. *"I remonstrated with the man, but all in vain."* Led before a Confederate captain, *"I bitterly complained of the spoliation, but his only reply was 'that he could do nothing, and that I must put up with the laws of war.' It was no use telling him that I understood the laws of war differently."*

Lt. James Fales began his Libby Prison memoir with the bloody ambush of a column of Rebels on the night of June 17, 1863. Expecting an attack, he had dismounted his First Rhode Island Cavalry behind a stone wall that bordered a country lane. *"It was so dark that the enemy could not see us, and so they charged up in the road in column of fours, and the first notice they had of our location was the discharge of sixty carbines. The slaughter was fearful. Horses and men went down in wild confusion, while our men, drawing their six shooters, opened a deadly fire."*

Fales and his men became separated in the dark. When they reorganized and rode out the next morning, *"a charge in our rear forced the regiment to break over a wall and then, as my horse was jumping over the wall, my saddle slipped off over his tail and left me on the ground. I was summoned in the usual form, 'Surrender, you damned Yankee son of a bitch!'*

3

"Under the circumstances, I was obliged to accept the invitation, and a red whiskered gentleman from South Carolina kindly took charge of my sabre and started me to the rear saying, 'I believe your regiment is forming to charge; if there is any prospect of you being re-captured I shall put a bullet through you.' I made no answer, but thought it was pretty rough business."

The officers sent to Libby Prison were often the best men the Union Army had. That's because the officers most likely to be taken prisoner were the ones closest to the action. *"None are captured at the rear. It is generally in the front rank, struggling manfully, the soldier falls into the hands of the enemy."*

These men were what we today would call type-A individuals: driven, aggressive, physically hardy, and almost fearless. They were the officers who led from the front, who showed initiative and courage, and were reluctant to retreat.

Both North and South had begun the war short of all things military, and the paucity of qualified mid-level officers was especially acute. Not only was the US Army quite small in 1861, it hadn't been at war since the invasion of Mexico 15 years before.

Throughout history it's always been difficult to predict, or even to define, what makes a great field officer. No one can really foresee how a man will react to the stress of being under fire. And officers face the added burden of having to order other men, whom they know well, to death or dismemberment. To lead men toward enemy guns goes against every human instinct. Few men can do it. Fewer still can do it well.

Of necessity, a large number of the lieutenants, captains, majors, and colonels who fought in the Civil War received their promotions based on performance in combat. Unlike the case of a peacetime army, these promotions weren't based on test scores, family connections, or a senior officer's guess.

Good junior officers were the grease that made the entire army machine perform, and many soldiers found themselves suddenly promoted (or demoted) immediately after a battle. In practice this was an efficient system because it was shaped by the crucible of combat. Initiative, bravery, and leadership could be instantly rewarded. At the same time, cowardly, overly cautious, or by-the-book soldiers could be quickly demoted or transferred behind the lines, where they'd cause less harm.

The best generals found their officers wherever they could. Formal military training was not a factor, nor was academic standing or even proficiency in English—some foreign-born officers could barely speak it. Same with age; most of the men captured and sent to Libby Prison were in their twenties, and a handful still in their teens.

Lt. A. B. White had just turned 21 when he was captured by the Fourth Virginia Cavalry at Warrenton, Virginia. The young Yankee was surprised by a sudden encounter with two of the most renowned Rebel generals. *"Within two minutes I saw Jeb Stuart pass by, and in ten minutes more I was taken before General Lee. After salutations had passed, he said, 'I see you are a cavalry officer.' In the blandest tone imaginable and as if he were asking the most ordinary question he said, 'I suppose* [Union general] *Meade is across the Rappahannock River?'*

"I replied that if he would keep moving up that way he would probably find out. After talking for a few minutes on other matters, he repeated his question in a different form. I again said the only way I knew to get the information he sought was to keep marching in that direction. He laughed heartily at this, and said, 'well, you are such a boy-ish looking fellow I thought perhaps you would tell me.'

"I was then rapidly hustled to the rear, where I joined, I should think, at least 300 of our men." It was October 12, 1863.

Maj. Sam Byers's tale of how he ended up in Libby begins with an attempt at humor but concludes with a somber reflection.

"I was now between two lines of the enemy and among the rocks. I picked up a copy of Bonner's Ledger [a Unionist weekly], *which one of the boys had dropped, and waved it in surrender; but they 'didn't read the Ledger,' and fired on me immediately. I then ran down toward the line below me; but I was a 'goner'!*

"'You Yankee son of a ——— ! Come out of that sword and run to the top of the hill,—or we will blow you to h——l!' exclaimed one of the grey-coats.

"The day was ours, but I was a prisoner in the hands of a more than barbarous foe. In a hollow behind the mountain I found the remainder of my captive

*comrades. There were eighty of my own regiment, of whom only **sixteen** lived to return from prison."* (emphasis in original)

In mid-1863 Confederate general Robert E. Lee, on his way to Gettysburg, overwhelmed Union general Milroy at Winchester, Virginia, and captured three thousand of his men. Among the prisoners was Chaplain C. C. McCabe of the 122nd Ohio, an irrepressibly upbeat pastor known by his men as "the singing chaplain." Earlier Civil War protocol had dictated that surgeons and chaplains were to be released after battles. But such humane traditions were fading away as the war's death toll continued to rise. Rev. McCabe had the misfortune to run into Rebel general Jubal Early, whom Gen. Lee liked to call his "Bad Old Man."

"I addressed him thus, 'General Early, we are a company of surgeons and chaplains who have stayed behind to look after the wounded; and would like very much to be sent back to our regiment.' He smiled, and turning to me said 'You are a preacher, are you?' I answered that I was.

"'Well,' said he, 'you preachers have done more to bring on this war than anybody and I'm going to send you to Richmond. They tell me you have been shouting On to Richmond for a very long time—and to Richmond you shall go.'"

Chapter Two

On to Richmond

Once the rebels had set up their capital of Richmond, Virginia, as the central clearing point for POWs—more by default than by any grand design—they had to deal with the problem of transport. Getting thousands of prisoners moved hundreds of miles created huge logistical difficulties for the Confederacy. They had no official protocol, so it was up to each commander in the field to figure out how to get his captives to the capital. They had to improvise food and transportation, then detach their own soldiers as temporary guards and escorts.

The first step was to count and organize the POWs during the strange, sad calm that followed most battles, when the wounded were given what treatment was available and the dead were buried.

Yankee cavalry captain Willard Glazier, who was knocked unconscious during a cavalry skirmish, awoke to find himself lying among fellow prisoners behind Rebel lines. *"Here we witnessed an amusing exhibition of Rebel bravery. The woods in the vicinity were full of skulkers and, in order to make a show of having something to do, they would make their appearance in the rear of the fighting columns and devote themselves sedulously to guarding the prisoners. Privates, corporals and sergeants in succession, until some sneak of higher rank came along, and said in a tone of authority, 'Gentlemen, your services are needed at the front; go and do your duty like soldiers.' This was said with chattering teeth and anxious glances in the direction of our cavalry. Thus we passed under the notice of one coward to another."*

For most soldiers, POWs were the first live enemy they had seen face-to-face. They were naturally curious about their foes, especially about their regional accents, which were much more pronounced in the America of 1863 than they are today. Capt. Glazier recorded this confrontation with a Rebel:

"REB: 'Yank, hand me that ar hat, and come out of that overcoat, and them ar boots, too, you damned blue-jacket.'

"FED: 'The articles you demand are my personal property, and you have no right to take them from me.'

"REB: 'We have authority from Gen Stuart to take whatever we d——n please.'

"FED: 'If you are a gentleman you will not be guilty of stripping a defenseless prisoner.'

"REB: 'I'll show you my authority, you d——d blue belly' (drawing his revolver). 'Now take off that ar coat, or I'll blow your brains out.'

"FED: 'Blow away then, it's as well to be without brains as without clothing.'

"Johnny Reb was not quite disposed to fire upon me, and, giving his head a shake, walked away thinking, no doubt, that he could supply his wants in another direction without wasting ammunition."

After any battle, soldiers were exhausted, dehydrated, and famished. Union corporal Tobie remembered the excitement when a little food finally arrived, helping relieve *"the sense of gone-ness in my stomach,"* and after they had finished:

"A young rebel who had been quietly listening to the various discussions, took me a little aside and said in a serious manner, 'I want to ask you a question; don't you believe that the side that is right in this war will win in the end—not the side which you think is right, or which I think is right, but the side which is right in the sight of God?'

"'Most assuredly I do,' I replied.

"'So do I,' said he, 'and that's about all the consolation I can get out of it.'

"For an hour, I had a good conversation with him about war matters, which I have no doubt did us both good."

It was natural for soldiers to speculate about the motivations of the enemy. Since each believed his own cause was totally just, they wondered: How could anyone fight on the other side and still have a clear conscience?

Chatting around a fire on a cold night, Capt. Szabad's guards asked what state he was from, and were surprised to hear he'd come all the way from Eastern Europe.

"This filled my captor with a sort of astonishment; he found it incomprehensible, how a Hungarian could fight with the d——d Yankees against the Southern people, who were fighting for what the Hungarians had fought for in 1848. However, I told him roundly, that I came to America, to fight for the Union, the destruction of which would cause joy to none but tyrants and despots. We continued to chat as long as our eyes kept open."

Cavalryman Edward Tobie was taken at Brandy Station, June 9, 1863, and as he sat with the prisoners he spotted his horse being ridden by a Rebel. *"I made bold to approach him with a request that I might take some things from my saddle-bags, which he granted I thought with surprising readiness."* And when Tobie produced a *"liberal quantity of good old army coffee"* from the bags, the two agreed to split the valuable item equally.

"The Rebel soldier, that is, the real fighting men from the front, treated us, as a general thing, kindly and with true soldierly courtesy. But the bummers, the coffee-coolers and dog-robbers, the thousand and one hangers-on around the army, plundered the prisoners at every opportunity, from which the better men and officers protected us as well as they were able."

In their memoirs, many prisoners were quick to acknowledge that their treatment could be surprisingly kind, particularly when their Rebel guards were fellow infantrymen. Lt. Wells, for instance, recorded what happened after he'd given up his beloved boots and most of his uniform:

"It is pretty severe on a cavalryman to be dismounted and compelled to make a prolonged march on foot. Only for the extreme kindness of a guard near me, who, during the night (when unobserved by the command), got down from his horse and permitted me to get into his saddle and ride until thoroughly rested, I should have fallen by the way."

When his column stopped at the blackened remains of what had been a bridge over the Hiwassee River, Lt. Wells held his tongue—because his own unit had set it on fire in an earlier raid. Both grey guards and blue prisoners were forced to wade through rushing waters up to their waists: *"Having ourselves destroyed the bridge, we could not well complain."*

Maj. Tower's first experiences after capture were unusual. Taken at Gettysburg, he was one of the few Yankees who began his imprisonment in friendly Union territory.

"All through our march in Pennsylvania and Maryland, people along the route gave us provisions, which our guards allowed us to receive . . . in fact, during our long march in charge of the men who had seen service, we received no unkindness.

"Our rations, after we entered Virginia [Rebel territory], were scanty, and our march a hard one, as it rained very hard most of the time, and when it did not rain the heat was almost unbearable." It was July 1863; they had to hike two hundred miles over muddy roads, soaking wet, barely fed, and sleeping where they could. Despite the conditions, most of the prisoners were suitably passive because they hoped to be exchanged soon after arriving in Richmond. Naturally, the Confederates encouraged this hope. But the ranks were full of special cases like Maj. Tower, who looked for every chance to sneak away.

"Once I tried it. While marching along a railroad one rainy night I managed to slide down an embankment, and thought I had succeeded, when a voice said to me, 'If you feel rested you better join the other fellows.'"

A second time he tried to sneak off, and for a second time was caught and put back in line. It was officers like Tower, men whose constitution could never accept confinement, who would later be part of the great Libby escape.

Lt. Byers and his men were also sent on the long road to Richmond: *"I had scarcely slept for a week; and now, tired and hungry, I must walk all night. But I slept some; yes, strange as it may seem, I would sleep as I walked— and if we stopped for a few moments' rest, nothing but kicks and curses would compel us to start again.*

"We were placed in dirty stock cars and started for Atlanta. The prisoners huddled together and kept warm, but two of the guards froze to death on the top of the train."

Remembered POW Drake: *"The engine was like an old wind-broken horse. There was a great lack of oil or grease to lubricate the running-gears. The screeching was earsplitting. Our coaches were old, rickety freight cars, some of them filthy in the extreme, having been used to transport stock and never been cleaned."*

The exhausted prisoners were so jammed they had to take turns sitting down. They seldom got any food, and when they did it was awful. The trains of the overworked and declining Rebel rail system could barely make fifteen miles an hour, so these horrible trips could last for days.

Sgt. Sam Boggs of Illinois wrote: *"We were put on board of some freight cars and run to Atlanta, Ga, where they turned us into a large slave pen, a table was brought in, a blank book placed upon it; then a Rebel major called out, 'Attention Yanks! If thar's a-r-y sergeant among you all, what kin write, I want him to come and write you all's names in that ere book.'"*

One of the Yankees suggested that his men write their own names, as that would ensure correct spelling. According to Boggs, a Confederate major agreed, and after watching twenty-five of the new prisoners sign the roll, the Rebel officer remarked with surprise: *"'Well, I'le swah, you-all's got book-l-arnin.' We's-kotched a hull passel of schoolmarstahs; they kin all rite by gosh!'"*

"Our column must have seemed more like a band of condemned criminals than a body of honorably defeated soldiers," wrote Lt. Clay MacCauley about being marched from the battlefield after Chancellorsville. When they passed a small farmhouse, *"A little woman came running down to the roadside. She raised her little fists and shook them at us, her black eyes sparkling. With a sort of scream she cried out, 'Kill 'em all, colonel, right here for me!' . . . Negroes at times came out of their cabins to look, but never a word said they."*

Enduring rainstorms that alternated with blazing heat, they hiked on for three days with nothing to eat until finally, *"In the afternoon a wagon was driven into our camp with rations, so we were told. This was the way of the distribution: the barrel of flour was tumbled from the wagon to the ground. The barrel burst open where it fell. At the side of the flour the beef was dropped. Now, hungry as we were, what could we do with either the flour or the beef? We had neither kettles nor fire. There lay the two gifts of food. Some tried to eat the pasty flour but soon had to give over the effort."*

As the POWs marched deeper into the South, many of the captured Yankees were paraded through Southern towns where the local populace was allowed, even encouraged, to insult and threaten them. Capt. Caldwell wrote, *"We arrived in Staunton, (VA) around noon, where we found the sidewalks thronged with citizens, soldiers, women, children, and negroes—in short, all ages, sizes and colors, anxious to see the live Yankees.*

"We were necessitated by our unfortunate condition to submit to the most contemptible treatment, and outrageous insults, that an enraged and diabolical enemy could heap upon us. The citizens far outrivaled even the soldiers in the exhibition of hate and virulence. They seemed to take intense delight in hurling their anathemas upon us with unmitigated fury, such as 'd——d Yankees,' 'thieves and robbers,' 'black abolitionists,' 'every one of you ought to be hung,' etc. Having been robbed of our arms and every means of defense of course we had to make the best of their vile insolence."

In Caldwell's case, the men in blue responded by singing patriotic Union songs as loudly as they could, hoping to drown out their attackers. But this *"had the tendency to only increase their fury and intensify their malignant curses, which were heaped lavishly on our heads."*

"We were paraded through the streets of town as if we were wild animals. A Rebel Major who had been imbibing the spirits cursed us and said we had come there to deprive them of their niggers, but in a few months we would all be keeping the Devil and old John Brown company in a warmer place than the South. Once he fell down, but jumping up and balancing himself, he shouted, foaming at the mouth like a dog possessed of the hydrophobia, 'We'll burn New York and Philadelphia next week!' The citizens cheered the drunken orator and cried 'good, good!' He was a 'gentleman' who labored to prove the black man was an animal, who had no rights, and for punishment should be put to death; one of those who spoke of the 'last ditch,' but run when danger threatened."

"There is a great rush among men, women, and children, to see the 'hated Yankees'. Barnum, with all his monkeys and bears, could never draw such crowds of inquisitors," wrote Capt. Byers of his treatment in Columbia, the capital of South Carolina. *"This is the finest town and the most heartless people I have seen in Dixie. We were taken through the streets and received the jeers, taunts, and curses of a bitter enemy. We bore their insults in silence, but did not forget them."*

Nor did he forgive. Writing of his treatment by the citizens of Columbia in "What I Saw in Dixie, or, 16 Months in a Rebel Prison,"

Byers paused for a stinging aside. Jumping ahead to two years after his men had been marched down the streets, he told of entering Columbia a second time—as a soldier in Sherman's conquering Union Army. *"After-wards, when I had escaped, I saw them in their grief. I saw their city burn to ashes, and their proud spirits laid low in the dust. Their great men were fallen, and their proud men were beggars."*

The men also saw exceptions to the hatred that was hardening both sides. Maj. Tower remembered what happened when, after two weeks of a grueling march, his group of POWs and their Rebel soldier-guards arrived in Staunton, Virginia, to be put on trains for the final miles to Richmond:

"A large crowd was at the depot to meet us; our reception was very loud if not very warm. Here we were to say goodbye to our guards, and to be handed over to the tender mercies of the 'Stay at Homes.'

"Captain Patterson, of the 61st Virginia, had been in command, and he bade us goodbye saying, 'I and my boys have treated you as well as we could. When you get to Richmond everything will be taken from you; the rubber blankets, haversacks and canteens you have will be of great use to my men.' Instantly almost every man handed them what he had, the guard then left us, but soon came back and loaded us with pies, cakes and cold meat, and when the cars started for Richmond gave us three cheers, which we returned.

"This was goodbye for a long time to any considerate treatment."

CHAPTER THREE

Fresh Fish

THE AMERICAN CIVIL WAR WAS THE FIRST WAR IN WHICH RAILROADS played a crucial role, and Richmond was one of the South's most important railroad hubs. Troops and weapons could be dispatched in every direction; most POWs arrived in the city along these same tracks.

Once at the local depot, prisoners were separated into groups of officers and enlisted men. The enlisted men were sent to Belle Island in the middle of the James River, while the officers were marched to Libby.

The guards were always in a hurry to accomplish this transfer, since once they handed over their POWs they were free to rejoin their units in the field. This meant prisoners could be delivered at any time, twenty-four hours a day.

Willard Glazier, one of the best of the Libby chroniclers, described his 8 a.m. march through a gauntlet of Richmonders:

"*As we passed along we were saluted with innumerable questions, the general character of which may be inferred from the following specimens, 'How are you, blue bellies?' 'Why didn't you'uns all come to Richmond with your arms on?' 'What did you'uns want to come down here to run off we'uns niggers and burn we'uns houses for?'*

"*Mrs. Johnny Reb remarked: 'If these are the officers of Lincoln's army, what must the privates be?' Another sensitively delicate matron chimed in with a tragic shudder, 'Oh, what a pity that our noble sons should be murdered by such miserable vagabonds!'*

"*The usual southern epithets for Federal soldiers were vigorously showered upon us, 'Hirelings,' 'Mudsills,' 'greasy mechanic,' 'Northern vandals,' etc.*

15

"A troop of boys followed in the rear, hooting and hallooing and as is generally the case, they surpassed the older ones for smartness and venom."

Union POWs were curious to see this capital of the Confederacy. Their view was cursory, but they couldn't help but notice that the roads and buildings were in disrepair, and that the clothes of the inhabitants were threadbare. So many of the South's men were in the military that almost all the people they saw—slaves aside—were women, children, or the very old.

By late 1863, the war had been going on for nearly three years and the South was suffering severe shortages of everything. Its plantation economy was based on exporting cash crops such as cotton, tobacco, and indigo; the payment was then used to import manufactured goods. But the Union Navy was successfully blockading Rebel ports, and little was getting out or in.

Medicine, hardware, salt, tools—from pencils to penknives, all manufactures were running out. Worse, the Confederate dollar was plunging in value. Widespread use of paper money was new for both North and South, but the Union's "greenbacks" held their value while the Rebel "greybacks" fell to trading five for an American dollar, then ten, then more.

The Confederate government's response was to ban Union currency, but everyone used it anyway. The result was the creation of an underground economy. Extreme inflation wiped out Southerners' personal savings and began to push basic foods out of reach. In late 1863, when Rebel privates were paid eleven dollars a month, Libby POW Sam Byers recorded Richmond's food prices: *"potatoes, $18 a bushel; turkeys, $25 each; whiskey, $75 a gallon. This was in the money of the Confederates."*

On April 2, 1863, hundreds of Richmond's hungry women held a protest rally that quickly turned violent as they smashed their way into shops and looted food supplies. The melee was only stopped when Confederate president Jefferson Davis turned out with the militia and literally "read the riot act," ordering the women to disperse lest they be fired on. Reluctantly the ladies went home, but they left the city shaken. Women in the Confederacy were subjects of veneration, revered for being hard-working, loyal, quiet, and removed from politics. This surprising, destructive bread riot seriously disturbed the Rebel leadership.

Such was the capital of their young nation. Obviously, things were much worse than the authorities realized. They tried to keep the outbreak secret, but the story quickly made its way North. *"I know there was a riot and a serious one, for even part of the guard of Libby Prison was taken up*

The Richmond bread riot.

town to aid in quelling it, as I heard them telling of their exploits after returning," wrote POW Capt. John Kreidler.

The riot was symptomatic of a much larger problem. Though the Confederates didn't realize it at the time, their country was already in a downward economic spiral from which it would never recover. The South was a rural nation of farms, small towns, and plantations; yet it couldn't grow enough food to prevent malnutrition from undermining the war effort.

These food shortages would have particularly severe consequences for Union POWs, who would be last in line for food or other supplies. Who in the South could justify giving anything to these "invaders" when so many citizens were starving? Union prisoners were feeling the brunt of the South's inability to feed itself.

The Rebels had two problems with food production. First, they had mainly grown cotton before the war and even into the first years of the conflict. But you couldn't eat cotton, and Lincoln's navy soon made sure it couldn't be shipped overseas for cash either. Plantations shifted to growing food as best they could, but it was too little and too late.

A second problem was even more intractable: a shortage of farmers. Most able-bodied white men were in the military, not working their fields. With war casualties depleting their ranks, Rebel recruiters scoured the countryside in order to force ever more men into the service, compounding the problem.

The Confederacy was forced to rely more and more on its traditional farm workers—Black slaves. But the slaves were not as happy and compliant as their owners imagined. Once they got the chance, slaves took off in large numbers, escaping to the Union Army whenever it came near. To the surprise of many white masters, whole Black families fled, leaving behind everything. Charlotte Forten, a teacher in Sea Island, Georgia, reported speaking with a plantation wife who insisted that she and her husband *"had devoted themselves to the good of their slaves, and lamented their ingratitude in all deserting her."*

At first Union Army leaders felt conflicted about taking thousands of slaves into their ranks; but once they realized the impact it was having on the South they encouraged it. "Contraband" is what the fleeing slaves were called, and as contraband of war their flight to freedom would obviously be a key to the Union victory. Instead of growing food for the South, they began laboring for the Yankee army as everything from cooks to teamsters. Particularly infuriating to their ex-masters, they were soon being armed and trained for combat.

Most Union officers would have had little contact with African Americans before the war. In the 1860 census, only 226,000 Blacks were counted out of a total Union population of 19.5 million. In areas like New England and the so-called Middle West whites made up 99.2 percent of the total.

By contrast, the Confederacy had 260,000 free Blacks, 3.5 million slaves, and 5.5 million whites. Blacks were more than a third of the South's total population; in many rural areas they constituted the majority.

Few Yankees would have visited the South before the war, much less seen a working plantation. Photographs were in their infancy and newspapers couldn't reproduce them, so what Northerners knew about slavery came from second- or third-hand descriptions. And mostly what they'd heard was that while slavery might have some bad points, it was also normal and eternal. Southerners argued that slavery had always existed, was still thriving around the world, and was no more likely to end than dueling, or war itself.

Then came *Uncle Tom's Cabin*, the most popular book in the country's history and one that forced every reader to confront slavery viscerally. It inflamed all the passions, enraging the North and outraging the South. When Abraham Lincoln met its author, Harriet Beecher Stowe, he famously remarked: "So you are the little lady who started this big war." After *Uncle Tom's Cabin* had swept the nation, it was practically impossible for anyone to be neutral about slavery.

The more Union soldiers actually saw of the South's "peculiar institution," the more radical their feelings grew. What Capt. Sam Byers witnessed in the South led him to write in his diary about Southerners: *"Slavery has brutalized these men. They think it no harm to burn a nigger or starve and kill a Union prisoner. They don't even treat the privates of their own army decently, so the guards told us on our way here."*

Union colonel Thomas Higginson was an abolitionist who raised one of the first regiments of Black troops, but even he was unprepared to see slavery up close. Stationed in Sea Island, Georgia, Higginson went to visit the same plantation wife who felt she'd treated her slaves so well she thought them "ungrateful" for running away. One of her escaped slaves was now a soldier in Col. Higginson's regiment. *"So, calling up my companion, I said that I believed she had been previously acquainted with Corporal Robert Sutton? I never saw a finer bit of unutterable indignation than over the face of my hostess, as she slowly recognized him. She drew herself up, and dropped out her answer as if so many drops of nitric acid, 'Ah' quoth my lady, 'we called him Bob!'. . . Bob simply turned from the lady, touched his hat to me, and asked if I would like to see the slave jail."*

Entering the tiny jail, Col. Higginson didn't understand the devices inside and was appalled to learn they were punishment stocks with small holes—*"evidently for the feet of women or children. In a building nearby, we found a machine so contrived that a person once imprisoned could neither sit, stand nor lie, but must support the body half-raised in a position scarcely endurable. I remember the unutterable loathing with which I leaned against the door of that prison-house; I had thought myself seasoned to any conceivable horrors of slavery."* Stories like these quickly made the rounds in the Union Army.

In 1863 Southerners still considered the loss of some of their slaves, along with other shortages, to be temporary. They were totally, defiantly sure of success. They didn't doubt that Gen. Lee, with God's help in a righteous cause, would find a way to defeat the hated Yankees.

Exhausted after their weeks of difficult travel, the Yankee POWs entering Richmond looked around with grave uncertainty. Libby Prison was famous, or infamous, and all dreaded the prospect of confinement there.

"I was ill, had a raging fever, and was famishing for a drink of cold water. While on the street, I could see water dripping from the eaves of the buildings. I borrowed a cup, and watching my chance stepped a little aside and tried to catch some. As I did so one of the guards ordered me back in emphatic terms, enforcing it by prodding me with his bayonet, the scar of which I carry to this day."

"A concourse of darkies followed us to the prison, who evidently pitied our condition and knew we were the true friend of their race. One of the colored men was knocked down for giving some tobacco to a prisoner."

Lt. Wells's column entered the city from the south, crossed the James River, and was marched in twos down Cary Street to Libby. The POWs were excited by a rumor that they would soon be going home. *"Our column halted under a dark and frowning wall of brick and mortar, looking up, there over the entrance to a jail-like structure I saw painted on a board in large black letters 'A. Libby & Sons, Ship Chandlers and Grocers'. And immediately the thought came to me that despite the promises that an exchange of prisoners would take place on our arrival in Richmond, we had now reached our final destination, and that the building before us was the notorious Libby Prison of which we had heard so much, and instinctively the familiar quotation came to my mind: 'All hope abandon ye who enter here.'"*

Libby Prison sat next to the James River and Canal, at the corner of Cary and Twenty-First Streets. It was in the city's warehouse district, and by being close to the water provided easy access for traders and travelers.

Libby Prison. Drawing by Lt. Col. Cavada.

The rectangular building was four stories high, with the guards and dungeons on the bottom floor and the POWs on the upper three. The site sloped down to the river so that, on the upper Cary Street side, only the top three floors were visible.

The building, constructed in 1852 as a tobacco warehouse, was acquired by the Libby family a few years later and converted into a chandlery, or provider of shipping supplies and wholesale groceries.

Early in the war it was not overcrowded with prisoners. Most were exchanged a few weeks after they arrived. The original plan had been to house up to five hundred men there, but by the time the POWs of 1863 arrived, more than twice that many had been shoved inside.

Guards occupied the basement floor, which was divided into rooms for offices, storage, a carpentry shop, and filthy dungeons used for punishment. Immediately above this was a floor divided into guards' quarters, prisoners' kitchen, and hospital. The upper two floors, where the prisoners slept, were further divided into three large rooms each.

Lt. Tower, who spent many months in Libby, described it simply: *"Built of brick and roofed with tin; the building has a front of about 140 feet, with a depth of 105, there are nine rooms, each 102 feet long by 45 feet wide; the height of the ceiling is about 7 feet, except the upper story, which is better ventilated owing to the pitch of the roof."* The building completely filled a city block; the wide streets around it could easily be patrolled by Rebel guards 24 hours a day.

Lt. Col. Federico Cavada was one of the more fascinating of Libby's denizens. A Cuban American raised in Philadelphia, he served in the Union Army Balloon Corps. It was his job to go up in the basket and use his artistic talents to sketch Rebel positions. Captured at Gettysburg, Cavada would later pen the volume *Libby Life* and add his original drawings: *"Had we known that we were entering this loathsome prison house not to leave it again for many, many weary days and months, more than one heart would have grown faint, for there were among us some who were doomed never to recross its threshold again as living men."*

On arrival, the POWs got their first introduction to jailer Dick Turner, the twenty-three-year-old in charge of day-to-day operations. Before the war Turner had been a plantation overseer. He treated Libby's inmates the same way he'd treated slaves—with extreme brutality and mocking abuse. Libby's memoirists were unanimous in their hatred of the man.

Commandant of the prison was Thomas Turner, a man even younger than Dick Turner and also despised for his cruelty. Lt. Glazier wrote of him: *"He not only deprives us of little comforts which would greatly mitigate our woes, and cost him nothing, but he heaps barbarities upon us with Herculean and fiendish strength."*

The Libby POWs were often confused about which of the two Turners was which, and commonly mixed them up in their accounts. Dick Turner was a private with little education, while Thomas Turner was an officer who had risen to the rank of major. They were equally despised, and with good reason.

Dick Turner would place a desk at the prison entrance and sit there, surrounded by bayonet-toting guards, with an open ledger book. He'd tell the entering prisoners to deposit all their valuables with him, saying that they would most likely be robbed once inside. He'd also declare that all Yankee money was illegal and must be handed over as well. Turner promised to enter all in his ledger, and claimed that the confiscated items would be returned to prisoners when they left Libby under the terms of an exchange.

The POWs sensed this was a lie, and it was. After Turner's opening speech, the arriving prisoners gave up no more than a few token items. That was a cue for each prisoner to be searched more deeply.

"Dick Turner demanded our pocketbooks, (how thankful I was to know that I had extracted the three twenty-dollar bills and that he was only going to get about three dollars) and very deliberately opened them, counted out the money, gave us credit for it in his book, then told a sergeant to search us. Up stepped the sergeant like a man of business, thrust his thumb and finger into my watch pocket and fished out the three twenty-dollar bills. Alas! How soon my joy was turned to sadness!"

Before the prisoners' arrival in Richmond, the robbery had been haphazard. At Libby it was methodical. Turner had the last and most thorough shot at taking anything the POWs still had. Since the beginning of the war, he and his guards had been fleecing Yankees by the thousands,

Turner searches the men.

and they were very good at it. Still, a surprising quantity of money and valuables made it into the building, where it formed the basis of lively underground trading that went on with the guards until the war's end.

"*Yankee ingenuity, as was often the case, became more than a match for Rebel cupidity. Our 'greenbacks'—the object of their closest scrutiny—had been folded between our toes, or concealed in the lining of our garments, or solidly packed in our hollow regulation buttons, the caps of which could easily be removed and replaced; and in some instances men had their money in their mouths with a quid of tobacco. Many of our valuables also were saved by slyly passing them to those who had been previously examined. In this way I retained my journal.*"

Col. Louis Palma di Cesnola had been captured at the battle of Aldie in June 1863, after leading a charge that would make him one of the first recipients of the new Medal of Honor. A Sardinian aristocrat and professional soldier, he wasn't about to be intimidated by the common guards at Libby:

"A Rebel sergeant searched me from head to foot in the roughest manner possible. He took away from me every possible trinket I had, my penknife, eyeglasses, Meerschaum pipe, matches and a bunch of small keys, and was angry because he could not find any greenbacks. He ordered me to take off my boots for inspection; I answered him that I had a servant to perform that service for me. He insisted, but I refused until he took them off himself and searched them very minutely. He began to abuse me, using very abusive language and denying my veracity. I entered the gates of a Confederate prison stripped of everything."

At least their long travel was over. In their starved and exhausted condition, anything that offered a roof was an improvement over what they'd been through. Almost every Libby memoir focuses on that single moment where the writer himself crossed into the unknown life inside:

"The gloomy and forbidding exterior of the prison, and the pale, emaciated faces staring vacantly through the bars, were repulsive enough, but it was at least a haven of rest from the weary foot-march, and from the goad of the urging bayonet."

"We were escorted up a flight of stairs, at the head of which was a door secured by ponderous bolts. These were thrown back, and between the points of two bayonets in the hands of stalwart soldiers on either side we crossed the dreaded portals and found ourselves at last secure within the famous BASTILE OF THE CONFEDERACY." (capitals in original)

They had still one more Libby ritual to endure, as the new POWs were instantly overrun by an earnest surge of the veteran prisoners screaming, *"Fresh fish! Fresh fish!"* Hearing this cry, hundreds descended from every room to mob the new arrivals, anxious to hear the latest news from the war and home:

"What army are you from?"

"Any hopes of an exchange of prisoners?"

"Where were you gobbled?"

"Oh yes, we know how it happened. Overwhelmed by superior numbers."

"How are we doing in the West?"

"Did the Rebs get your greenbacks?"

Such frantic scenes might occur day or night as everyone was swept up in the excitement of new faces, new stories, of anything at all to interrupt the tedium:

"Our guard tried to reason with the mob, but it was no use. We could not budge an inch until we had told them who we were, where captured, when, and how the battle went."

"But in an hour's time we had shaken hands all around, said 'how d'ye do,' and told the news from 'God's land,' to unlucky representatives from every state in the Union. Maine was there, California, and even North Carolina."

"The prison veterans called themselves the 'old fish' or 'old rats.' Turner's methodical robbing of the 'fresh fish' they called 'the scaling process,' which always takes place before they are packed away for safe keeping."

The frenzy would die down to scattered conversations, and then a thousand young men would begin to lie down on the hard floor:

"Lighted lathe sticks added a grotesque weirdness to the scene. Our next step was to get into camp; in other words, to hunt for quarters for the night. We discovered no bunks, no chairs, or seats. We soon found we had to stake out our own sleeping claims, and to recognize it by our neighbors on either side. Every new-comer deprived the aborigines of just so much ground, and every candidate for a fat man's club was looked upon with aversion as encroaching upon territorial rights."

The officers typically ended up in rooms with others from their own units. One room was for men from the Army of the Potomac, another for the Army of the Cumberland, etc. Others were named for the senior officer in that part of the prison, such as Milroy's room or Streight's room. The guards had no overall system. Surges of prisoners came and went in ways they could neither anticipate nor control.

All the prisoners had arrived in Libby totally worn out by hard marching and poor eating. The only thing they wanted was to sleep, and sleep some more. The prison quarters had barely enough space for all the inmates, who were forced to lie on hard, greasy wooden floors. Their coats had been taken from them; only a few had blankets. They had no idea what they would see upon awakening, and they were too exhausted to care.

Night prison.

Yankee lieutenant Drake had been captured in Tennessee; he had spent almost a month of hard marching and riding on screechy railroads before he got to Libby. At least now he would have a roof over his head:

"It was with a feeling of relief that we passed through its portals, cold, hungry, exhausted, so mentally depressed that many were perfectly indifferent; we knew we would have a chance to lie down and rest."

The Prison and the City

Libby Prison was unique in the same way so much of the Civil War was unique. The facilities there were improvised by patriotic, hard-working men who had almost no idea what they were doing.

North and South, officials in charge of enemy POWs had never managed prisons, much less a gigantic prison bureaucracy. They never had close to adequate funding. They had no specific "rules of war" to define what was and wasn't allowed; what was an atrocity and what was considered acceptable behavior. No real preparations had been made to house prisoners because everyone had thought the war would be over quickly.

In 1861 the American Civil War was sold to the public as most wars are sold. Citizens were told, and leaders convinced themselves, that a short, sharp fight would define things, after which everyone could go home and sort out the new realities that resulted. Lincoln's first call for recruits specified they were enlisting for ninety days—this from a belief that three months would be enough to crush the rebellion. Most Confederates couldn't wait to begin the war, so sure were they of victory because *one Southern man could whip 500 Yankees.*

All these people were wrong, blinded by their own jingoism. It turned out that both sides were tough, brave, bloodthirsty, resourceful, and terribly dedicated.

At any rate—with all convinced they would quickly win the war, why spend time planning for POWs? Each side could scarcely see to the basic necessities for its own army.

With no guidance, experience, or precedent to fall back on in the matter of war prisoners, vast networks of prisons, guards, and supporting bureaucracies had to be quickly improvised and then reimprovised throughout the war. It was a system that did not so much evolve as lurch from crisis to crisis. The victims of this bad planning would be the young soldiers themselves. An astounding fifty-one thousand men would enter these Civil War prisons and not leave them alive.

With the addition of Virginia to the Confederacy, the Rebels had established their capital in Virginia's capital, Richmond. The city became the locus for almost everything Confederate. It was not only the political and military center of their new nation; it was also a transportation crossroads, a fortress, and most crucially the center of weapons production. In 1861 Richmond had almost forty thousand residents; the war would increase it to triple that size.

When the Rebels won the war's first major battle at Bull Run, it was logical to bring the fresh POWs to the city, only sixty miles away. Right from the start, Richmond was overwhelmed with a thousand-plus Yankee prisoners. At first the POWs were locked up in the city's slave pens—the dungeons where human chattel were held for sale. Those were considered "the appropriate accommodations" for Yankees; almost at once, they were overcrowded.

Forced to act quickly, authorities commandeered a number of warehouses and other industrial buildings, pushing out the tenants to create instant prisons. One of the first was called Castle Thunder, an ugly stone pile that was set aside for, and quickly filled with, politically "disloyal" civilians. Other holding places were scattered around Richmond for disparate groups of common criminals, women convicts, runaway slaves, and the like.

Rebels herded Union-enlisted men—privates, corporals, sergeants— onto a muddy spot called Belle Island. It was a flat space with no amenities, just a few windblown tents. The prisoners were forced to live outdoors and sleep on the wet ground. Through most of the war, and through every season, the people of Richmond were able to look out on the river at this teeming mass of miserable Yankees; the good citizens were able to see that their enemies were slowly dying of starvation, disease, and exposure.

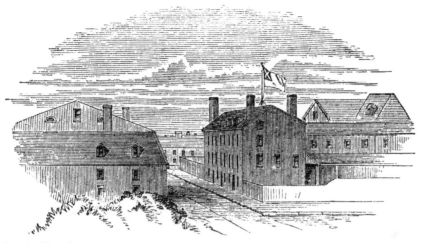

Castle Thunder

To process Union officers and put them in pens, the Rebel regime apportioned a large brick building originally built as a tobacco warehouse and later owned by "Libby and Sons, Ship Chandlers and Grocers." It was solid and relatively isolated. It had running water and was close to the rail lines.

The structure was conveniently large, four stories tall, and virtually empty. With the addition of a few sinks and toilets, Libby Prison could reasonably hold five hundred men. At night, with Rebel guards occupying the ground floor and prisoners confined to the top two stories, the building would be "escape-proof."

Withal, it was a miserable place for human habitation. Each of the upper floors consisted of three huge, vacant rooms, with no furniture of any kind. The prison's water, coming straight from the James River, was full of mud, waste, and disease. Prisoners had to sleep on hard, filthy floors without any bedding, and were never let outside. Ever.

In the early days of the war, when the battles were relatively small and prisoners numbered in the hundreds, a system of "parole" was established. Any man captured could sign a document stating he would no longer fight against the enemy, and he would simply be let go. If a "parolee" was caught again in uniform he could be executed, but this was hard to enforce in an era before photo IDs and fingerprints.

These soldiers were officially "bound by their parole" to drop out of the war until they could be exchanged for an equal number of enemy parolees. The South and North would "trade" parolees, often on paper; a private for a private and an officer for an officer. Those paroled men could then rejoin the fight.

The parole system worked well because neither side wanted to house or feed enemy prisoners. It was considered better to let them go and get equal numbers of your own men back in the ranks. So even if conditions were bad, the average POW was likely to be sent home after a brief spell of confinement. This system had the added advantage of taking away most of the incentive for escape. Why risk your life when, by doing nothing, you were likely in a short time to cruise home on a comfortable steamboat?

It was an extremely simple, efficient, and humane system. But as it relied on trusting one's enemies and treating them as equals, it was doomed to failure. Extremists on each side began accusing the other of cheating, and newspaper editors realized how popular it was to whip up hate against an evil enemy.

In an attempt to gain control, both sides set up central facilities to process the prisoners and get official counts. But neither authority could anticipate having to hold onto tens of thousands of enemy soldiers permanently.

As the war went on, both sides grew increasingly embittered. At first the parole system was dropped in favor of confinement, even though one-for-one exchanges with the enemy were able to continue.

Then the newspapers and politicians got involved, and that spelled the end of any humane treatment. Opinion-makers couldn't bear to watch the hated enemy sitting out the conflict, eating food that might have been given to their own fighting soldiers. Newspapers railed at the miserable POWs, arguing that they were being treated much too nicely.

On December 7, 1863, the *Richmond Enquirer* ran an article announcing a *"splendid dinner"* for the Libby inmates, *"served up on the table d'hôte of the prison, and embracing a bill of fare unequaled in Richmond since this cruel war commenced."* Of course it was all a lie, but that fact didn't stop the article from being circulated throughout the South.

Endless details, bureaucratic infighting, and general incompetence were allowed to hold up prisoner exchanges. So the well was already full of poison when the final deal-breaking issue arrived: how to deal with Black Union prisoners?

Libby POW Lt. Fisher observed: *"History hardly records a more bitter hatred than that which was manifested by the Southern people towards the colored soldiers. The confederate authorities refused to consider the colored soldiers when captured as prisoners of war, refused to parole them, and treated them with exceptional harshness and indignity."*

How could Southerners treat them otherwise, with their entire society based on slavery? As Confederate vice president Alexander Stephens declared in his infamous "Cornerstone Speech" of 1861: *"[Its] cornerstone rests upon the great truth, that the negro is not equal to the white man; that slavery—subordination to the superior race—is his natural and normal condition."*

So once the US government announced plans to bring Blacks into the army—and they were already in the navy—Southerners lost all reason in their outrage, and, with it, their fear. Soon entire regiments of ex-slaves were fighting for the Union. Well trained and armed, they proved to be as tough in battle as any white soldier. It was the Southern whites' worst nightmare.

The Confederacy responded by announcing that any captured Black soldier would be sold into slavery. Further, the Rebels declared that any white officer captured while leading ex-slaves would be executed by hanging. The South would never consent to exchange Black prisoners one-for-one.

Inmate Sam Byers reflected in his Libby diary: *"The Johnnies [Rebels] say that they won't exchange men found commanding darkies, in fact, they propose to kill all such at sight; that's the way Richmond papers talk. So nobody knows when we will get out of here, if ever."*

Byers was typical of many Union officers in that, even as he called African Americans "darkies," he was ready to lay down his own life in the war against slavery. In this same diary entry, Byers speaks up for Gen. Benjamin F. Butler, the controversial Union officer who demanded racial equality in prisoner exchanges: *"The Johnnies have good reasons for not liking Ben Butler. He believes them to be traitors, and handles them accordingly. If we prisoners were to stay here 10 years, our prayer would be for more Ben Butlers."*

The Union refused to back down on its demand for equal treatment of Black prisoners. It was an impossible impasse. The prisoner exchange program stalled, then stopped.

Lt. Fisher knew that the end of exchanges might lead to his own death in Libby. Even so, he said, *"There was but one honorable course open to the [US] Government. Its soldiers, whether black, white, or red must be protected. The south stood firm, and the result was that the cartel regulating exchanges was deemed cancelled."*

Tens of thousands of young POWs realized that instead of going home in a few months they could expect—what? Ten years? They began to lose hope, and as they did, the death rates in the prisons rose.

Paroled. Drawing by Lt. Col. Cavada.

Hundreds of deaths became thousands. It seemed to the POWs that no one cared or even noticed. On both sides men sensed abandonment by their own governments, and to a degree they were right.

This was the situation officers confronted when they entered Libby in late 1863. After two years of use as a prison, the building was more filthy than ever, and grossly overcrowded. Food allotments were decreasing, the hatred of the Richmond populace and guards was increasing, and the hope of exchange was fading. Union soldiers began to discuss whether it might be preferable to be killed in battle than to die slowly of starvation as prisoners of "Johnny Reb."

Chickamauga and Colonel Rose

CHICKAMAUGA WAS THE SECOND-BLOODIEST BATTLE IN THE CIVIL War. For two days in September 1863, more than 120,000 men shot it out in the rugged wilderness of northwest Georgia and almost a quarter of them became casualties, an astoundingly high percentage. Like many Civil War battles, Chickamauga was a melee of massed charges, counter-charges, odd decisions, fatal miscommunications, full-on blunders, cowardly collapses, and heroic final stands.

When the fighting ended on September 21, the Union's main army in the West had been driven back and almost destroyed. Almost. The

Confederates had scored a major victory, but the Union remnant was able to withdraw behind impregnable defenses in the city of Chattanooga. The Rebels laid siege to the city, hoping to starve the Union force into surrender, which would give the Confederacy complete command of the American West.

"The West," to Americans of the 1860s, basically meant anything beyond Pittsburgh. Tennessee and Ohio were the West. Arkansas and Texas were the Far West. It was a vast wilderness of few roads and fewer cites, where farmers cut their fields out of virgin forest.

The soldiers in these Western armies were different from their fellows in New York and Virginia. They were men who, almost universally, grew up outdoors; they lived a life of open spaces and personal freedom. This new land had few traditions; people believed in practical things, things that worked. They tended to be suspicious of any authority, whether preachers, bankers, or politicians. Officers in both the Blue and Grey Western armies complained about how hard it was to discipline these men, but they never faulted their bravery or fighting ability.

With the Rebel victory at Chickamauga came almost five thousand new prisoners of war, of whom 250 were officers destined for Libby Prison. The core of the Libby tunnelers would be made up of these Western men.

Capt. I. N. Johnston of the Sixth Kentucky Volunteer Infantry was typical. Born and raised on a small farm, he described himself as *"a plain, blunt man."* He worked his land, learned the three "R's" in a log schoolhouse, courted locals by penning *"sundry epistles to the fairer portion of creation,"* and felt mildly patriotic.

But when, on April 12, 1861, the Rebels fired the first shots of the war on Fort Sumter in Charleston Harbor, Johnston suddenly saw *"the very life of the nation threatened by armed traitors."* He joined with hundreds of young men in his county to form the Sixth Kentucky Volunteer Infantry, which soon elected him as their captain.

It can be argued that the worst military decision made by the Confederacy was its very first. By firing on Fort Sumter, the regime of seven seceding states in the Deep South had ended decades of debate and started a war. The shock of this direct attack on a US Army garrison cannot be overestimated. It galvanized a divided North and unified an irresolute South. The fence-sitters got off the fence and chose sides. The simmering conflict had become a war to the finish.

Millions of formerly ambivalent Northerners suddenly became focused militants. Johnston spoke for them when he wrote: *"I felt that in such a cause, and for such a country, it would be sweet even to die."*

It was men like Johnston who ultimately would win the war—common farmers, men of natural intelligence, dogged determination, and general cussedness. In Libby Prison, Johnston would become one of the most dedicated diggers, having already had a bellyful of war. He'd served in the three biggest Western battles and become a casualty each time. At Shiloh he was shot through the face and lost consciousness. Surgeons stitched him up and he returned to his unit with an ugly scar. Eight months later, at the battle of Stone's River, he was hit three times—*"but not severely,"* he said.

At Chickamauga, Johnston was sick but still determined to fight with his men. On the second day of battle his Kentuckians had to retreat, and Johnston couldn't keep up. He was caught by two Rebel lieutenants who treated him well, even warning him to hide his watch and his money. Then he joined a huge throng of prisoners—all starving and shivering in the nighttime cold—and was surprised to learn how bad conditions were for his enemies in grey: *"The men guarding us were very kind, and said they would gladly give us food, but they were as destitute and as hungry as ourselves. To prove their sincerity they marched us to a sweet potato patch, and all hands, prisoners and guards 'pitched in.' We then made fires and roasted the potatoes, and often since have made a worse meal."*

Col. William McCreery of the Twenty-First Michigan Volunteer Infantry, who would also escape through the Libby tunnel, begins his first-person account with waking up on the field at Chickamauga behind enemy lines, having no memory of how he got there.

"Recovering consciousness, I found myself within the rebel lines, three times wounded and unable to move, my dead and dying comrades lying thick around me. A throng of rebel stragglers soon began to make their way to the front. Calling to one of them, I asked, 'will you not give me a drink of water from your canteen? I am very thirsty.' He finally gave me a drink and asked if

I had a jack-knife. I told him to put his hand in my pocket and if he could find one he was welcome to it. From that moment he was my friend.

"He left me and soon returned with a rebel chaplain, and a stretcher on which they carried me some half a mile to the rear. The chaplain was very kind, and after a little time, placed me upon his horse, taking me almost two miles farther. I was deposited under an apple tree, and after receiving what I supposed to be good rebel advice from the chaplain and a hearty 'God bless you,' I was left to my own thoughts."

It was now after dark. McCreery estimated seven or eight hundred Union soldiers at this place alone. All lay on the cold, damp ground, with no food or treatment for the wounded. Finally, a man he knew brought him two ears of corn and water, which McCreery readily pronounced *"the best I ever drank."*

Thoroughly exhausted, he did not wake until daylight and was delighted to find a fellow named Mead from his own unit; he *"had already built a fire at my feet and was making a cup of coffee from the last he had. He proved to be a most excellent provider. I don't think he would steal, even from a rebel, but he had what the old soldiers used to call a 'terrible long reach,' which proved to be of great benefit to me personally."*

The surgeons finally appeared. Unable to move from his prone position, McCreery watched them work. Amputation was the quickest and safest way to treat most limb damage in this era; the doctors had plenty of chance to perfect their technique. After every battle they set up amputation assembly lines to treat thousands of ghastly wounds. The resulting piles of severed limbs have entered our lore as a shocking visual that no Civil War movie seems to omit. But to McCreery these body parts belonged to men he knew—fellow patriots who had offered themselves up to the slaughter—and he expressed this sentiment in the language of the nineteenth century:

". . . faster and faster, lying here, lying there, each awaiting his terrible turn. I see pale faces, bloody garments. True right arms that had offended by reason of their loyalty to that old flag are lopped like slips of golden willow. Feet that never turned from the foe, forever more without an owner, strew the ground.

"I did not hear a moan—the very silence oppresses me—no sound save the gnawing of those terrible saws."

Charles Earle was to become the youngest of the Libby escapees. Only eighteen years old when captured, he was already a lieutenant with two years' combat experience. The surrender of his small company after Chickamauga was particularly tragic because it was the result of officer incompetence, or perhaps outright cowardice.

The Ninety-Sixth Illinois Infantry Regiment had fought bravely until it was almost wiped out, losing two-thirds of its men. Earle himself was twice hit by bullets but stayed active with his unit until ordered to retire. On returning to bivouac and seeing the stacked rifles of the men who had been lost, Earle *"threw himself down upon the ground and burst into sobs and tears."*

He and the dozen-odd comrades left to him were ordered to *"reinforce the pickets in front of the regiment, and remain there until you are relieved. The Command will retire towards Chattanooga, and if you are attacked, retreat in the direction of that place."*

The entire army was withdrawing; Earle's small company was positioned on Missionary Ridge to warn of any Rebel advance. Numerous times he distinctly heard the command *"in retreat march"* as, one by one, the units around him fell back. *"I expected every moment to hear the same for my command, but it did not come. The anxiety which we experienced at this time can hardly be described."*

They were doomed. At two in the morning a staff officer was sent to order the unit's retreat. That officer never arrived. Even so, he later reported to his superiors that he had delivered the order. This omission was the same as laying a death sentence on Earle and his fellows.

"Our orders were imperative—to stay where we were posted, and although we could see nothing to be gained, it was unanimously agreed to hold our ground." By 11 a.m. they had been discovered by Confederates and forced to surrender. They knew conditions in Rebel prisons would be bad; but none imagined that, of the fourteen men captured, only five would survive.

"These companies were sacrificed, were allowed to be captured, and went through all the horrors of Libby and Andersonville, a large majority of them meeting their deaths in these places, because a staff officer had not the courage to do his plain duty."

Thousands of POWs were jammed into cattle cars for the long, slow journey to Richmond. Col. McCreery's untreated wounds began to fester. He became feverish. Then luck intervened in Augusta, Georgia, where he learned of a hospital staffed by the Sisters of Charity. Anti-Catholic prejudice was strong at that time, but McCreery would have none of it. *"I shall never forget the kindness with which I was received, and the tenderness and care with which my wounds were dressed. May Heaven Bless the Sisters of Charity!"* He would have plenty of time to reflect on their grace during the coming months in *"that prison-house of torture and slow death, familiarly known as the 'Libby Prison.'"*

Also riding by train from Chickamauga to Richmond was the formidable man who would initiate, plan, and ultimately lead the Libby breakout—Col. Thomas E. Rose of the Seventy-Seventh Pennsylvania. Among the twelve hundred or more prisoners who dreamt of escape from Libby Prison, the red-haired Rose would turn out to be the most obsessed of them all.

Rose was not a colorful figure. He was not especially articulate. He certainly was not artful. He had the nuts-and-bolts personality of a career army officer, which he remained after the war. In the words of Lt. Thomas Moran, who knew Rose well in Libby and afterward, *"He was a brainy, cool, and intrepid man, coined for just such a daring enterprise."*

Indeed, Rose made his first escape attempt before he even got to Libby, somehow slipping off the POW train and away from the guards. When the Rebels caught up to him, he was by himself, 500 miles from any Union help, without food, a compass, or a map.

His straightforward manner is easily seen in his self-effacing memoir. Written twelve years after the war, Rose refuses to consider himself a hero and never veers from the basic facts: *"On my way thither, I escaped at Weldon, North Carolina, and after wandering about for a day, I was recaptured by some rebel cavalry that came upon me accidentally. I was suffering at the time from the effects of a broken foot, which caused me to be too slow in reaching a place of concealment."*

The broken foot is a fact he mentions almost in passing.

Colonel Thomas E. Rose.

In late September 1863, the POW trains from Chickamauga began arriving in Richmond, followed by the usual separation of officers from enlisted men, many of whom had served together for years. Army units in the Civil War were often made up of men from the same region. In many cases they'd known each other from childhood. Lt. Earle was familiar with every man in his company, and his memory of their final moments together is evocative.

"Almost a quarter century has passed since that night of parting, yet its memories are as vivid as if it was yesterday. I see the dimly lighted streets of the capital; the lines of determined yet dejected men; those heroes of Chickamauga, now prisoners of war; I hear the measured step of the soldiers at that midnight hour, and their quiet, yet earnest conversation, as the possible fate of the morrow is discussed."

Earl arrived at Libby alone and full of apprehension. *"We found men here who had been incarcerated for 12 months, and it was thought advisable to commence a residence which might be extended for years, by attending a prayer meeting."* Earle particularly appreciated the sermon from army chaplain C. C. McCabe, *"whose cheerful example did everyone good."*

Col. Rose's memoir contains a single sentence about entering Libby, then goes right to business in the next: *"I soon set about devising means of escape."*

CHAPTER SIX

Libby Life

To enter Libby Prison in late 1863 was to enter bedlam. Usually prisons are places of isolation, of small cells and lonely confinement. Libby was the opposite—a once-empty stone warehouse, reconfigured to hold a few hundred men on a temporary basis, and by late 1863 bulging with more than twelve hundred.

Men had barely enough room to turn around. At night every square inch of floor space was occupied. The odors, the noises, the irritation

of being continuously surrounded by a swarm of starving men, gave no respite.

"Perhaps the most repulsive feature about Libby was the lack of privacy. There was a constant jostle of one man against another. Confinement in private cells for a few hours would have been a boon!" complained Capt. Starr of the 104th New York Volunteers.

Most of these officers had never been confined in their lives. They were men of action, energy, and basic intelligence—otherwise, they wouldn't have become field officers.

"The prison is crowded to its utmost capacity; we jostle each other at the hydrants, on the stairs, around the cooking stoves. Everywhere there is wrangling and confusion. You are in a whirlpool, and you must keep whirling around with the merciless eddy in a sort of diabolical gyration. Some of the prisoners here have not once stepped outside the prison door during more than eight months!" wrote Lt. Cavada.

The rooms were barren of everything but humans; no cots, no chairs, no tables. Some of the long-term veterans had ersatz furniture they'd built out of boxes and barrels, but it always ended up in the stoves of winter. Most of the men had no choice but to sit on the floor and eat meager rations with their fingers. Few had anything to keep them warm during the long winter nights.

The low seven-foot ceilings on Libby's middle floors added to the claustrophobia. The top floor was just as crowded, but at least the angle of the roof added a little more headroom.

The windows were barred and had no glass, so it was freezing in the winter and blazing hot in the summer. The Confederates even denied prisoners the chance to stand near these open windows; anyone who dared pop his head out for fresh air could be shot by the guards.

If these men inside the prison were some of the best in the Northern army, the guards outside Libby were some of the worst in the Southern one. Guarding POWs was a job no one volunteered for. Who wanted to patrol a prison when they had a war to be won on the battlefield? The job was so tedious, and utterly devoid of glory. You would hardly want to tell your grandchildren about it. At the same time, prisoners were trouble and

Shot by guards.

could be dangerous. Shifts were long, pay was poor, and the food almost as terrible as what the prisoners got.

Things kept getting worse. As the war went on, any Southern male who was the tiniest bit able was sent into the fighting army. Truly scraping the bottom of the barrel to find anyone who could hold a rifle, the Rebels sent their prison guards to the fronts and replaced them with the very old, the sick, or the very young.

In the lower middle of the prison were the kitchens and the toilets. Both were fed by water running directly from the James River, muddy and foul. At least they had plenty of it. But they never had enough toilets, especially with so many of the prisoners suffering from digestive diseases and the "Tennessee Two-Step," or diarrhea. *The thirst caused by the salty food and quenched by drinking this muddy water—it was this or nothing—gave us all the diarrhea, and those who escaped were the exception,"* wrote N. A. Drake of the Twenty-Second Wisconsin. *"Imagine, if you can, 300 men with a diarrhea standing in line waiting their turn on the water closet, where six only could be accommodated at a time."*

If a soldier got sick he was sent down to the hospital on the first floor, even if the so-called hospital had little medicine and scarce medical personnel. At least they gave men filthy cots to lie on, but most of those who went to the hospital never came back. They just slowly wasted away. *"As a rule the men all fought going to the hospital. It was reported that if they went there they were pretty sure to die. But when one got so ill he could not attend roll call he was taken to the hospital, willing or not."*

Men died every day, their bodies stacked like wood until they had enough for a cartload. The dead were stripped of everything they had before being thrown into unmarked graves. A few intrepid souls managed to escape by hiding among the corpses. Rebel authorities caught on to this, and even the dead had to be guarded until they were finally in the ground.

Libby's food was not only sparse but of the worst quality. Former farmers among the POWs averred that their pigs back home ate better. Rebel officials declared the prisoners were being given the same rations allotted to their own soldiers, but this was not true. In some instances the food may have been similar, but the prisoners always got the very worst of every commodity. Their corn was ground up with the cobs, the soups were full of maggots, and nobody ever figured out where the infrequent pieces of meat came from; they speculated about mules that had died of disease or old age.

Many POWs wrote home that the short rations left them so starved and dizzy they never could have been up to the demands of active army life. Further, Confederate soldiers were paid wages and could supplement their diets through buying, bartering, and even begging from the local population. None of these alternatives was available to the POWs, though some were able to buy food with the greenbacks they'd smuggled inside. Many pooled their money and bought fresh produce, causing Richmonders to complain that they were driving up local prices.

Essentially the men ate the same things every day: a small chunk of hard corn bread a few inches square, full of husks and unground grains, and a kind of gruel so thin that the men liked to joke about *"going diving for a bean"* or asking a friend, *"Might I borrow a bean to dip into my soup?"* Occasionally they got bacon or some other meat. The corn bread was so hard and the bacon so salty they usually had to be soaked in water before eating. *"We ate it, bugs and all, and wanted more,"* wrote N. A. Drake.

Conditions were onerous enough during the era of prisoner exchanges, but by late 1863 the transfers had slowed to a crawl. The POWs had no idea when they'd ever get a decent meal or even feel the sun again, much less go free.

Despair drove up the mortality rate. The term "having the blues" was much in use, and many witnessed the decline to death that could overtake those who just gave up.

Some officers made extensive and ever-changing efforts to occupy the men, give them something to do, create hope and distraction. Classes were set up in French, Spanish, German, and Latin. *"Dancing was taught to large classes, and it was truly refreshing to see grave colonels tripping the 'light fantastic.' The doctors endeavored to enlighten audiences by lectures on gun-shot wounds, amputations, the effect of starvation on the human system, and other cheerful topics,"* remembered Capt. Moran, who published one of the best memoirs. *"It was not infrequent to see a lively 'break-down' at one end of the room and a prayer meeting at the other and to hear the loud turn of the banjo mingling with the solemn doxology."*

Capt. Caldwell found many prisoners who shared his faith. *"Oh! How often in Christian fellowship, with dear brethren whom I met in prison, did my heart burn with the pure love of Jesus? How often did we embrace each other, and walk the floor of that old prison for hours, relating the joys and experiences of other days? And O, blessed thought, we could feel that it was good even to be in prison, while Jesus reigned with us there."*

Religious and Bible discussion groups formed. The men could hear orations on the issues and sciences of the day, including the exciting new disciplines of phonology, phrenology, and mesmerism. Speakers gave sermons that promoted the growing religion of Spiritualism, which promised communication with the dead and thereby grew very popular.

Philosophical debates were held: *"Resolved, that the Fear of Punishment has a greater influence upon mankind than the Hope of Reward." "Resolved, that men ought not to shave their faces."*

Gen. Neal Dow of Maine, already famous as America's greatest advocate for Prohibition, lectured about the evils of demon rum. He was also a dedicated abolitionist and must have been a spellbinding speaker, as the crowds he drew were always large. Of course, even the general himself joked about how easy it was to take the temperance pledge while living in a building devoid of alcohol.

The usual social tensions prevailed. Prisoners took to carrying small Bibles in their breast pockets to demonstrate their religiosity, while others countered by carrying a deck of cards in the same way. Some carried both. Others used their breast pockets to flaunt possession of an item that life in Libby had made luxurious: a toothbrush.

The prisoners had a weekly newspaper, the *Libby Chronicle, Devoted to Facts and Fun.* In the absence of printing facilities, the journal was written on loose scraps of paper and read aloud at 10 a.m. every Friday. In the words of editor Louis Beaudry, it was *"issued weekly from the Prisoner & Co's steam press of thought. Price of admission, one moment's good attention."*

Beaudry was a minister who tried to keep the contributions upbeat and lively.

The first issue featured a 100-line Homeric ode to vermin, "The Libbyad":

"If old poets wrote of battles 'twixt frogs and mice,
Why not I write of skirmishes 'twixt men and lice?
And while thus these verses rude we are inditing
Look 'round to see the different styles of fighting"

Alongside, the editor sprinkled some vintage 1863 humor:

"Why is our soup in Libby like the stuff of which dreams are made?
"Answer. *Because it is a body without substance."*

"How does Libby differ from another public institution in Philadelphia?
"Answer. *That is a northern home for friendless children—this is a friend-less home for northern children."*

"If you don't want corns on your feet, don't wear tight shoes. If you don't want to get corned all over, don't get tight."

The *Chronicle* featured announcements of the latest distractions: *"All will desire a good hearing of the lecture on 'Life and Manners in Cuba' by Lt. Col. Cavada."* A mention of *Major Henry's series of lectures on 'Mesmerism'* concludes with the editor's hope that the major can mesmerize enough of the prisoners *"as to make us believe that we are amply fed and clothed."*

Libby Chronicle editorials called on officers to treat each other with more courtesy and professionalism. *"Nothing is more revolting than to witness the owner of shoulder straps playing the vulgarian—indulging in any kind of obscenity."* Editorial writers complained about too much swearing and smoking—tobacco being the one commodity the Confederacy had in plenty—and made much comment about prison's two most popular topics, food and prisoner exchanges.

The September 4, 1863, edition announced that *"all who desire to exhibit their worked bones will have an opportunity to do so."* This "bone fair" was to highlight the best examples of Libby scrimshaw—the laborious craft of carving leftover beef bones into brooches, crosses, finger and napkin rings, etc. Recommended as the competition judge was Col. Cesnola, the Sardinian aristocrat who had refused to remove his boots—and would become, decades later, the first director of New York's grandest art museum, the Metropolitan.

Mock trials were a popular entertainment. Many of the inmates were lawyers and judges, so along with humor their proceedings had an authentic feel. Witnesses *"were required to raise their left foot and subscribe to the following oath: 'You do pompously swear that you will tear, tatter, transmogrify, and torture the truth, the whole truth and everything but the truth, so help you Jeff Davis.'"* To increase the amusement, foreign-born officers who barely spoke English were cast as accusers and defendants, bringing howls of laughter as they worked to decipher the proceedings and make their arguments.

Libby was a miniature North America, with all immigrant groups represented. But the normal animosities between religions and nationalities tended to fade in prison. Not only were the men sharing the same fate for the same cause; it was plain to see that ethnic strife, or any kind of strife, would spell disaster in such a crowded place.

Even the Germans, considered by many to be the "job-stealing, filthy immigrants" of the mid-1800s, found a peace of sorts in the big building. *"Some Americans' venom for the Germans flourished. The American, despite his many excellences, finds it hard to free himself of nativistic prejudices. Gradually, such harsh injustice mellowed and friendly relations formed."*

But from the beginning, any Black soldier captured by the Confederates was treated as the lowest category of slave. *"There were attached to the prison about twenty 'native Americans of African descent' who had been cooks and officers' servants in the Union Army."* *"Captured, they now suffered under Turner's thumb: scrubbing floors, cleaning stairways, carrying wood, etc."* Local slaves were already doing much of the menial work in the prison. *"Every morning a Negro came round. He told us he had been sold seven times in his life. His was always the same cry on entering the room: 'Great news in the papers.'"*

Known as "Old Ben," this man was a much-loved character in Libby and was praised in nearly every memoir: *"You are glad to leap to your feet when you hear the stentorian voice of 'Old Ben,' the black news-man who cries: 'All fo' copies of de mornin' papers! Great news in de papers!' But nothing stirs the sleepers like the call 'full statement of exchange of prisoners!' Then there is a general resurrection of bodies, and a large patronage is enjoyed by the poor slave who has often cheered the inmates of this doleful place by his well-intended jokes and musical, pleasant laughter."*

"'*Great tallygraphic news in de papers! Great fightin' in de Souf-west!*' *It is astonishing how the cry thrills us. It has a home sound, and we forget for the moment we are prisoners in Secessia.*"

Each of the four Richmond dailies—the *Enquirer*, *Examiner*, *Dispatch*, and *Sentinel*—could be purchased for Confederate small change. Often only a single sheet and printed on the cheapest brown paper, these journals were "*filled with the most exaggerated falsehoods of 'Yankee barbarity,' and imbued with the most uncompromising hate of the Union and all who remained loyal.*" Still, any distraction was a good distraction; the men passed the papers around until they fell to pieces.

"*Whenever they are full of bluster and abuse, we know it has been going ill with the Rebels. When the tone is mild and reasonable, we believe that things go on swimmingly with them. Thus we interpret their accounts, as gypsies interpret dreams.*"

Another elderly slave, known as "The General" or "Old Smoke," passed through the rooms every morning, carrying out a nineteenth-century notion of disease prevention. "*The 'General' was quite an original, and one of the peculiarities of Libby, never to be forgotten. It was the 'General's' duty to go through the prison with a kettle of burning tar, fumigating the rooms. He would inform us on each occasion that the smoke was 'bery benewicial to the gemmen, kase it was a good Union smoke.*'"

"*How long he had been doing this only he knew. But really he was the only ray of brightness we had. He did his best to cheer, telling us it would not be long ere we would be sent home. How we did ply that old fellow with questions. He looked at that time to be near a hundred years of age,*" wrote POW Drake.

When Drake's unit was exchanged, "*We asked him if he would like to go North with us to freedom. The old fellow's eyes glistened as we told him the end of the war meant freedom to all slaves. We found he knew it as well as did we. He said he prayed the good Lord to let him live till he would see all the black men free.*"

All Blacks—even those who had been freemen in the North—were subject to extreme brutality from their new Southern masters: "*For the most trifling offenses they were stripped and tied over a barrel when Dick Turner, to gratify his devilish nature, would give the poor fellows on the bare back from thirty to forty lashes with a horsewhip.*"

Old Smoke. Drawing by Lt. Cavada.

Two Libby chroniclers, Capts. Lodge and Chamberlain, wrote passionately about a beating that awakened them on the night of July 24, 1863: *"Those of us on the 2nd floor were aroused by the cries for mercy of a poor darky who was being whipped. A barrel was laid on the floor, he was laid over it, and received on his bare back 250 lashes by actual count. This was done, we supposed, for exchanging money but the negroes said it was for attempting to escape."*

"Several officers [were] *at the windows, one of whom explained that they were whipping a negro downstairs. Between each beseeching cry for mercy I could distinctly hear the 'whack' of the lash on the negro's naked back. Presently he said that 'if they would stop he would tell all.' An officer beside me said 'They gave him 38 blows that time.' Some talk ensued, then the lash was plied; again the pleading and screaming rang out upon the midnight air. 'whack, whack, whack,' the terrible howling of a strong man in his agony, until the man's voice grew hoarse and faint, the shout descended into a wail, the wail subsided to a moan. . . . At last the brutal beating ceased. The officer beside me announced 'one hundred and twenty nine that time.'"* The POWs were even more upset when they learned the victim *"was a free man who had been serving with our men and is being held here as a prisoner of war."*

"Today I saw the man who was so unmercifully whipped," wrote a still-furious Capt. Lodge. *"He is a bright mulatto (Clarence Miller), a native of Philadelphia, and was captured on the gunboat Sciota. He was just as much entitled to protection of our government as any man on board. His features are good and even handsome, and his appearance is as much more intellectual and gentlemanly than that of the man who whipped him as can possibly be."*

The Yankees increasingly saw the slaves as their allies in the war. Abolition was an abstract cause in the North, but marching through the Confederacy made it real. The prisoners loved taunting the Libby guards by singing the most abolitionist version of "John Brown's Body"—called "The Kansas Brigade's Version"—at the top of their lungs:

"They hung him for a traitor, themselves a traitor crew,
His soul is marching on.
John Brown was John the Baptist to the Christ we are to see,
The Christ, who of the bondmen will the liberator be,
Until throughout the land the slaves shall all be free,
As we go marching on."

Of course, basic ideas about race in the nineteenth century were far distant from our own. Nearly everyone took for truth what we see today as racist. The churches taught that God had created the races to be distinct and unmixed. Minute measurements of physical characteristics were held as proof of the supposed hierarchy. And those who made the studies always believed their own race to be the "superior" one.

For instance, Samuel R. Wells in his massive 1866 volume, *New Physiognomy, or, Signs of Character*—weighing in at 760 pages, with more than a thousand illustrations—used skull measurements to "prove" that: *"Foremost among the races, by right of the largest and best-formed brain, stands the Caucasian."* Then he went on to subdivide every race into smaller groups, and then subdivided them again. Wells identified almost a dozen different racial "types" in Great Britain alone: English, Gaelic, Cymbrian, Julian, Saxon, Welsh, Irish, Highland Scot, Lowland Scot, and others, all the while specifying their distinctive "natural" traits. The Irishman, for example, *"is fond of stimulants,"* while the Gaelic suffered from *"deficient reasoning power and foresight."*

With so many "scientifically proven" racial differences just on the islands of Great Britain, it's easy to understand why everyone saw an even bigger gulf between races of different colors.

The words "racism" and "racist" didn't exist in the 1860s and wouldn't for decades to come. Those terms wouldn't have made sense to people of the nineteenth century, since nobody called for social equality or integration. Major questions about race had to do with divining whether one was a "quadroon" or an "octoroon" or a "mulatto"—each term carrying major consequences; and most minorities—Mormons, Jews, Utopians, Amana colonists, free Blacks, Quakers, Shakers—didn't care to join a "melting pot," they just wanted to be left alone. Asking a thousand Northern officers for their opinions about slavery would have elicited a thousand different answers.

Then on January 1, 1863, Lincoln issued the Emancipation Proclamation, and the covert cause of the war became overt. Preserving the Union and destroying slavery were now the same cause, inseparable from each other. The Union officers in Libby saw this clearly, and it inspired them. They were ready to fight for the cause—to kill and, if need be, to die for it.

In October 1863 the inmates of Libby Prison made their first plans for an escape. It was a big, audacious scheme that aimed at nothing less than victory for the Union. The idea was to stage a simultaneous uprising of all Yankee POWs in Richmond. Some 15,000 enlisted Union men and 1,200 officers were prisoners at nine different sites throughout the city. A force of this size easily outnumbered the Rebel guards in the capital. A massive revolt could overwhelm the guards, grab arms from the city's arsenals, and create a new force of army units. The planners even hoped to *"take prisoners Jefferson Davis and his Cabinet, and other leading Rebels, and then march en masse until we should arrive in our own lines."*

The plan was highly ambitious but not beyond reason. The plotters had thousands of desperate, battle-hardened men to draw on. They also had outside help. Lt. Roach was in on the scheme from the start. As he later explained: *"From a Union lady with whom communication was had through a negro, who was allowed access to the prison for the purpose of scrubbing the floor, we had the most correct and reliable information in regard to the number of troops in the vicinity of the city, the number and kind of arms, and amount of ammunition in the arsenal and other places in Richmond."*

Col. Abel D. Streight, one of the highest-ranking officers in Libby, was chosen "chief in command" of the escape. A Council of Five was secretly appointed to serve under him, and then a burgeoning group of lower officers.

Col. Streight was a leader known for his energy and combativeness. Earlier in 1863, on his own initiative, Streight had launched a cavalry raid deep into Rebel territory in northern Alabama and Georgia. It was an action both brave and foolhardy. Destroying everything military and engaging in constant skirmishes with the Rebels, Streight and his band pressed on for hundreds of miles into the Confederacy.

Streight was an outspoken abolitionist who had written antislavery tracts before the war. On his raid he not only encouraged local Unionist farmers to join him—which many did—his band also encouraged any slaves they encountered to escape.

One Sgt. Briedenthal recorded what happened when Streight's men overran the Round Mountain Iron Works, a major Confederate war plant *"for manufacturing a variety of the munitions of war, such as cannon, shell, etc. But through the agency of fire, applied by us, with the hearty cooperation of the*

Colonel Abel Streight.

negroes, who threw the first brands into their own sleeping berths, we soon had the conflagration of one of Dixie's most valuable establishments."

His force was finally run down by the vaunted Rebel cavalry officer, Gen. Nathan Bedford Forrest. By constantly moving his men and telling them to stir up dust and noise, Forrest tricked Streight into believing he was outnumbered. Streight actually had twice as many soldiers as Forrest, but they were exhausted and far from home. The Yankees surrendered on May 3, 1863.

The raid had caused damage and even more excitement, so Confederate authorities decided to make an example of the captured officers. While the enlisted men were marched to Richmond and quickly exchanged, Streight and his officers were informed they were to be sent to Alabama for trial on the charge of "inciting slaves to insurrection." That crime carried the death penalty. Even though slave revolts were extremely rare events, nothing terrified Southerners more. *"They call Streight the 'Yankee Raider,' and both fear and hate him,"* noted Capt. Byers in his Libby diary.

Union authorities immediately vowed to retaliate if Streight was singled out in any way. The trial never occurred but the Rebel authorities refused to exchange Streight or his officers, and this controversy marked the beginning of the end of prisoner exchanges.

The POWs in Libby were slowly realizing that if the exchange system broke down, they were on their own—and would have to save themselves.

CHAPTER SEVEN

Elizabeth Van Lew

FROM THE GARDEN OF HER MAGNIFICENT HOME ATOP CHURCH HILL, Miss Elizabeth Van Lew could look down on the grim POWs staggering into Libby Prison a few blocks away. Church Hill was where many of Richmond's wealthy lived, and it provided commanding views of the city below. For decades the columned Van Lew mansion had been a social and political destination for the South's elite. John Marshall, chief justice of the Supreme Court, had been a regular visitor. Elizabeth had seen Edgar Allen Poe read "The Raven" to guests in the drawing room. Just a block away stood famous St. John's Church where, fourscore and seven years earlier, Patrick Henry had declared: "Give me liberty or give me death!"

Elizabeth's father had been a successful hardware merchant; she grew up amid splendor and slaves. The family rode about Richmond in an expensive carriage pulled by six white horses. Elizabeth never married—she was said to have been betrayed by a faithless lover—and after her father passed away in 1843, she lived in the giant house with her elderly mother, a few relatives, and half a dozen slaves. Everyone in Richmond knew the Van Lews.

When the war began, Elizabeth was in her forties, short, scrappy, and full of energy. In her youth she had been considered a beauty, but that was fading. Her neighbors knew her as an intense, independent soul. They also remembered that, before the war, she had not been afraid to declare her opposition to slavery and secession. They knew she had gone so far as to deliver food and books to the hated Yankee POWs in the city.

As a result she was shunned by upright Southerners, but was otherwise left alone with her eccentricities. Who cared what some aging spinster thought about politics or the war?

What the Confederates in their capital city did not know was that, by the middle of 1863, Elizabeth Van Lew had already developed the underground network that would make her the most effective spymaster of the Civil War. From her estate overlooking Libby Prison, Van Lew ran an intensely loyal group of informers, spies, slaves, ex-slaves, and saboteurs. Like her, they were lifelong Richmonders who had refused to give up their faith in the United States. They lived among slavery, and they hated it.

In his 1996 study *The Secret War for the Union*, Edwin Fishel called Miss Van Lew's efforts "the most productive espionage operation of the war, performed by either side." By the end of the war Van Lew's ring was so efficient that her encrypted reports were being delivered across Union lines almost daily, often wrapped around a fresh rose cut from her garden.

In the fall of 1863, Miss Van Lew was deeply involved in Col. Streight's massive uprising and escape plan. She was the "Union lady" that Lt. Roach had boasted was feeding the plotters "the most correct and reliable information" about local Confederate forces.

Because Col. Streight's raid had destroyed so much Southern property, and because he was accused of "attempting to raise a negro regiment," he was easily the most hated man in any Southern prison. Which is precisely why Van Lew wanted to help him escape.

It would not be easy. Even if the planned uprising should succeed, large Confederate forces were only a day or two away on foot. The POWs would have to fight them and cross 50 miles of wet, cold, open country to reach the Union Army to the east. But they were military veterans and spoiling for a chance to get back at their captors, or at least the opportunity to die on their feet. According to one of their company: *"Some were in favor of trying to rush down the staircase, kill the guards if necessary,—be killed themselves if so it should chance. Why not? They might as well die that way like men as to rot to death like vermin."*

The only Confederate forces permanently stationed inside Richmond were units of city and military police, a few hundred prison guards, and

Elizabeth Van Lew in the garden of her mansion. Photo taken after the war.

an *ad hoc* local militia that could be assembled from government bureaucrats. Miss Van Lew's spies were able to keep the Libby plotters informed about these or any other Rebel forces that could threaten the uprising. Her operatives also made it possible for plotters in the city's different prisons to communicate with each other.

Lt. Roach, who had been captured while serving with Col. Streight, explained that their plan was to suddenly overpower the Libby guards, *"proceed to the arsenal, arm ourselves; then release all the prisoners in Richmond, form them into companies, regiments, and brigades"* and grab any

Rebel official they could find. This huge mob of starving men would then attempt a multiday march to the closest Union lines.

But the plan was simply too big to remain a secret. Lt. Roach charged that even though all had sworn *the most solemn oath to preserve the strictest secrecy, [the plot's] existence was discovered by some inmates of the prison, and by them treacherously revealed.*

The revolt was just days away, and Confederate authorities reacted quickly to head it off. The guard was doubled, cannon were brought to bear directly on the prison buildings, and the battle-hardened division of Gen. Pickett was ordered to camp close to the city. *"The project was at once abandoned as impractical,"* wrote Roach.

Elizabeth Van Lew was disappointed, but she didn't give up trying to free Col. Streight. Spies know the virtue of patience, and she was willing to await other opportunities. As she wrote in her secret diary, *"We have to be watchful and circumspect—wise as serpents—and harmless as doves, for truly the lions are seeking to devour us."* Besides, her underground network was growing in size and in effect.

Miss Van Lew and her comrades continued to take great risks to aid individual prisoners. Almost every Sunday she went for a walk beside Libby, careful not to look directly at the prison or its inmates. Slave laborers working inside Libby discreetly let the POWs know, *"That is Miss Van Lew. She will be a friend if you manage to escape."*

One of Van Lew's main contacts in Libby was Robert Ford, a Black teamster who had been captured while working for the Union Army. In Libby he was forced to do menial labor, which brought him into contact with slaves who worked at the building. One of them came from the household of Abby Green, a white Unionist and member of the Underground; through that slave, Ford could pass information into and out of the prison.

The Van Lew spy ring was especially effective for being made up entirely of Richmonders. They did not have to infiltrate businesses or government institutions because they already worked in them.

Samuel Ruth, for example, was superintendent of the Richmond, Fredericksburg, and Potomac Railroad, a crucial part of Virginia's infrastructure. This secret Unionist did all he could to delay military trains, allow bridges to go unrepaired, and make sure his maintenance crews were undermanned. No less a personage than Gen. Robert E. Lee complained about Ruth doing his work *"without zeal or energy,"* prompting Ruth to pick up the pace just enough to keep his job—and his cover.

Later in the war, Ruth would come up with the idea that the North begin actively advertising for skilled Southern workers. When newspapers printed that premiums were being paid to defecting "machinists, blacksmiths, molders, and other mechanics," large numbers of them deserted, and Ruth had another excuse for why his railroad was performing so sluggishly.

The key ingredient of this strong Unionist Underground was unwittingly supplied by the Confederate leaders themselves. Early in the war they had rounded up every man in Richmond they considered a "Union sympathizer" and locked them all away in grim Castle Thunder Prison. When no actual evidence of spying could be found, the authorities let the prisoners go back to their lives, confident they had put the scare into them. But the Rebels had miscalculated. By confining those men together for weeks, they had enabled them to connect with each other and take their mutual measure as Union sympathizers. Once released, they were part of a loyal group who knew each other as only fellow prisoners do.

Van Lew wrote, *"When the cold wind would blow on the darkest and stormiest night, Union people would visit one another. With shutters closed & curtains pinned together, how we have been startled by the barking of a dog, the blood rushing to our hearts, as we would perhaps be tracing on a map Sherman's brilliant raids, or glorying in our Federal leaders. Then to follow the innocent visitor to the door, to lower the gas as they said good night and the last words often were, 'Do you think I am watched?' Such was our life, such was freedom in the Confederacy. I speak what I know."*

A few times during the war, Elizabeth herself was approached by strangers who assured her they were fellow Unionists. She reacted with feigned ignorance. Those earnest men let her know they wanted to help the Union cause, or that they had important information she might like to hear. But she didn't bite.

"[I] have turned to speak to a friend and found a detective at my elbow. Strange faces could sometimes be seen peeping around the columns and pillars of the back portico."

Her spy ring stayed intact by refusing to admit anyone they didn't know. To this day, no one knows which enquirers were sincere and which were Rebel detectives.

The North's Pinkerton Detective Agency tried to infiltrate spies into Richmond. Timothy Webster, an experienced Pinkerton man, went undercover but was caught after only a few months. In April 1862 he became the first American since Nathan Hale to be hanged as a spy. The public executions of Webster and later spies graphically reminded Van Lew and her fellows of the terrible risks they were taking. She recorded the executions in her diary, writing that she was inspired by them and not deterred. It has been said that nothing focuses one's mind better than the prospect of hanging; Miss Van Lew *always went to bed at night with anything dangerous on paper beside me so as to be able to destroy it in a moment. Written only to be burnt was the fate of almost everything of value."*

Elizabeth Van Lew's mansion in 1866.

Just two months after the mass POW uprising had been abandoned, Col. Streight tried to escape again. According to Lt. Roach, Streight received a note from a guard saying that *"we were fools for remaining in prison,"* and that for a bribe of $100 in greenbacks and two silver watches, Streight and a companion would be allowed to escape. According to the Confederate version of the story, published in the *Richmond Enquirer*, it was Streight who approached the guard about a bribe. However the plot had begun, Streight was able to find the greenbacks and watches quickly.

On December 18, 1863, at the agreed time of 3 a.m., Col. Streight and Capt. Read of the Third Ohio squeezed their way out a Libby Prison window and used a blanket to lower themselves to the ground. They handed the money and watches to a guard and began walking up one of the barely gas-lit streets of the city—probably heading for a safe house where they could await further help.

They had gone only a few paces when they heard Rebel guards screaming at them to halt. Before the two Yankees had time to react, the guards fired on them. It had been a trap. Luckily the shots missed, but Streight and Read were surrounded by a squad of seven guards and hustled back to Libby. According to Lt. Roach, Libby jailer Dick Turner knew Col. Streight had been the leader of the foiled uprising and had personally hatched this plan to have him killed. Capt. Read and Streight were put in irons and sent to the dungeons, *"where their situation and suffering was most horrible."*

In this attempt as well, it is all but certain that Streight had received help from Elizabeth Van Lew, and that her group arranged for a safe house as well as transportation out of the city. The spymaster was so generous with her own money that by the end of the war she was destitute.

Apart from buying books and food for POWs, Van Lew secretly paid lawyers to defend accused Unionists; she also slipped cash to Rebel government officials when favors were needed; she might even have bribed slaves in the local munitions factories to sabotage their own work. But the full truth about Van Lew and her work will probably never be known.

That's because one of the most exceptional things about this woman was the way in which she destroyed her own legacy. After the war, determined to stay on in Richmond, she covered her former activities in a shroud of darkness.

In 1866 Van Lew was discreetly given permission to go into the National Archives in Washington, D.C., and withdraw all papers concerning her activities. Documents regarding the information she sent North had surely run into the hundreds of pages, each carefully encrypted in her own hand. After her visit to the archives, all the documents disappeared. It is assumed she burned them.

Of all the messages she received, only one piece of paper survived. It was found among her effects, and demonstrates the value of Miss Van Lew's spy ring, in that the commander of the North's largest army could expect such a specific request to be promptly answered by "Mr. Babcock" (one of her code names):

Head-Quarters, Army of the Potomac
2PM, February 4, 1864

Mr. Babcock—
Have you any confirmation being over what roads the enemy move their supply wagons from Battlefield?

Geo. G. Meade
Major General

Along with that single sheet of paper, Van Lew saved her personal diary, but half of those papers or more were lost in the chaos that followed the collapse of the Confederacy.

As a result, nearly everything about Miss Van Lew and her activity is still subject to debate. A crucial question, for example, is whether Van Lew ever managed to place a spy inside the Confederate White House.

We do know that Van Lew had raised in her household a particularly bright slave girl named Mary Elizabeth Bowser. Since it was illegal in Virginia for slaves to learn to read and write, Van Lew arranged secretly for Mary to be freed and educated in Philadelphia at her own expense. When barely twenty, Mary went to Liberia as a missionary educator in the new nation that was supposed to welcome ex-slaves back to Africa. Mary, however, did not take to Liberia and asked to return to the Van Lew home. She made the long journey back across the Atlantic and was arrested in Richmond, as Virginia law forbade any freed slave to return to the state.

At her trial Mary *"declared that she had never been given her freedom but had only been permitted to go away on a visit."* The judge handed her back to Van Lew. Sometime later, Varina Davis, whose husband was Confederate President Jefferson Davis, asked Van Lew for help in obtaining a house slave. Good servants were especially hard to find during the war, and Southern aristocrats frequently helped each other in this regard.

In 1911 *Harper's Monthly* published an article based partly on interviews with Van Lew's niece Annie Hall, who had been ten at the end of the war. The article stated about Mary Bowser that *"in consummation of Miss Van Lew's scheming, she was installed as a waitress in the White House of the Confederacy. What she was able to learn, how long she remained behind Jefferson Davis's dining-chair, and what became of the girl ere the war ended are questions to which Time has effaced the answers."*

According to an account by descendants of Richmond Unionist Thomas McNiven, *"She was working right in Davis' home and had a photographic mind. Everything she saw on the President's desk she would repeat word for word. She made a point of coming out to my wagon when I made deliveries at the Davis' home to drop information."* McNiven was a baker who served the Union Underground by picking up and dropping messages during his deliveries. Historians argue about whether his stories are reliable.

Mrs. Jefferson Davis, forty years after the war, wrote a letter denying she had ever *"had in employ an educated negro 'given or hired' by Miss Van Lew."* Mrs. Davis insisted that *"my maid was an ignorant girl born and brought up on our plantation who would have not done anything to injure her master or me."* But the Confederate White House had many servants, and it was far from a happy household. In 1864 another slave made a successful escape from bondage there, and actually set the Confederate White House on fire before vanishing. The flames were put out before they could do much damage, but this violent defiance by one of their own slaves disturbed the president and his family.

Some commentators have argued that "Mary Bowser" was actually Mary Richardson, another slave in the Van Lew household who was known to have worked for the Underground. Whatever her last name was, Mary married and disappeared after the war. No records of her subsequent life have ever been found, though the newsletter *American Freedman* published an article in 1867 with statements attributed to her. Though short on detail, the article asserts that *"while appearing as a slave, [she] was in the secret service of the U.S. She could write a romance from her experience in that employment."*

In 1995 the US Army's Military Intelligence Corps, after considering all the evidence, inducted Mary Elizabeth Bowser into their Hall of Fame.

The end of 1863 found Col. Abel Streight in one of his favorite attitudes: that of being a thorn in the side to the Confederate regime. Even from the squalor of his dungeon in the basement of Libby Prison, Streight managed to taunt the Rebel authorities.

With one sheet of paper and a purloined pencil, Streight wrote a protest addressed to the US Commissioner for Prisoner Exchange. He passed it through a hole cut in the floor above; other prisoners copied the message and sent it North via a surgeon who went North on an exchange of doctors. The message arrived in good hands and got widespread publicity. In it, Streight wrote:

"We were seized and ironed, and placed in this cell on bread and water. There was no attempt on the part of prison authorities to conceal the fact that they deliberately laid the plan, and seemed to consider it a smart trick. I leave it to you to judge whether it was not a deliberate plot to rob and murder us.

"The cell in which we are placed is in one corner of the cellar of Libby prison. I cannot describe to you the filth, nor the loathing stench. The cellar is filled with old rubbish and has not been cleaned for years, consequently the number of rats and mice is beyond computation. How long the prison authorities will keep us here I have no idea; but it is certain we cannot survive it long. I have stated that we were reduced to bread and water; what we get for bread is of such a quality that we, as yet, have been unable to eat it."

Streight and his companion, Capt. Read, managed to survive in the dungeons for twenty-two days and were then brought upstairs to the

Elizabeth Van Lew.

main prison. Shortly afterward, Streight received information about a secretive new group plotting an escape. This time there was a multistep plan to tunnel into the local sewer lines. The digging had already started.

CHAPTER EIGHT

Colonel Rose Takes Over

JAMMING 250 OFFICERS CAPTURED AT CHICKAMAUGA INTO LIBBY Prison so overcrowded the building that it tested the sanity of everyone involved.

The guards became anxious about controlling so many POWs, particularly since the end of exchanges made the prisoners more desperate than ever. *"In the great gloomy rooms nearly 1,200 men watched the inexpressibly slow passage of time, the days going like scarcely moving tears, the nights like black blots dying out of a dream of horror, seemingly endless in its duration."*

How could anyone get out of a prison like Libby? It was surrounded by open space that was constantly patrolled, and the POWs were never allowed outside or on the lowest floor of the building.

"Scheme after scheme was discussed. It was constantly on our minds during the day and our dream at night. But an escape seemed almost impossible. We were surrounded by a strong guard at every point, and could we escape from the building we were in an enemy's country without food or money or allies, and withal weak from insufficient food and clothing."

Col. Thomas Rose didn't care about such logic. He did not see the point of accepting hopelessness. As fellow inmate Lt. Thomas Moran remembered: *"From the hour of his coming, a means of escape became his constant and eager study; and with this purpose in view, he made a careful and minute survey of the entire premises."*

Rose saw everything in terms of escape. In his memoir, he talks about nothing else. Unfortunately, he arrived just before Streight's planned mass uprising had been exposed, with the result that *"the doors were made more secure, the windows were closed with iron grating, and guard was largely reinforced."*

But Rose was convinced the system had to have a flaw. He studied the guards and their habits, learned about previous attempts that succeeded or failed, and spent hours surveying the activities around the prison.

While making these rounds, Rose found a fellow prisoner as determined as he was: Capt. A. G. Hamilton of the Twelfth Kentucky Cavalry. Like Rose, he saw other prisoners giving in to despondency, sinking slowly into lethargy and death. *"Hope was all that sustained many—to many it was a hope for liberty in any form. Even death was sought. But among us were many* <u>strong minded men</u>*—with a courage of steel. Among these I found Colonel Rose to be in the front rank. Our acquaintance ripened into a mutual friendship, and we soon had the full confidence of each other,"* wrote Capt. Hamilton. These two would prove to be the most stalwart of all the Libby inmates, and would support each other to the bitter end.

They spent their time evaluating any possible route to freedom. Every theory and plan was considered. The only method with even the remotest chance of success, they decided, was to dig their way out. *"During all this time the idea of escape by tunnel was being discussed. There were, however, apparently insuperable difficulties to a plan of this kind. It was absolutely*

Libby Building.

impossible, as far as we could see, to obtain access to an outside wall in the basement, or indeed, to any part of the cellar floor."

The Libby Prison building was four stories tall, with each floor divided into three equal rooms named "West," "Center," and "East." The basement or ground floor was different from the others in that it was cut into the sloping hillside. Only one side of it opened to the street, with the back part below ground.

The floor above the cellar was considered the first floor. Its west room served as the commander's office; the center room was the kitchen where inmates did their daytime cooking; and the east room was the hospital.

The upper two floors were the prisoners' quarters.

The cellar was off-limits to all POWs. Doors and stairways connecting it to the upper levels had been sealed off and nailed shut. The basement's middle room had been turned into a carpentry shop and also contained the dungeons. The prisoners did not know much about the east and west rooms.

The POWs were aware that sometimes the nearby James River would overflow, inundating the basement. *"It was common to see enormous swarms of rats come out from the lower doors and make head for dry land in swimming platoons amid the cheers of the prisoners in the upper windows."*

Rose also noticed that workmen would occasionally descend into a sewer line near the river, probably to clear debris and perform maintenance. He wondered: Might they find some way to enter that sewer and follow it to freedom? At the very least, Rose determined to reconnoiter the cellar. It was risky to try this alone, but one night during a howling thunderstorm he made the attempt.

The center room on the first floor served as the POWs' kitchen. Crowded, raucous cooking went on there all day long, but the space was abandoned at night. Leaking sinks and pipes kept the floor constantly wet, so it couldn't be used for sleeping.

With the furious storm crashing through the wee hours of the morning, Rose worked his way into the dark kitchen. Feeling his way around, he suddenly became aware someone else was with him in the damp room. As Lt. Moran described it: *"The impenetrable darkness made it impossible to determine whether he had met a friend or a foe; neither had a weapon, yet each made ready to spring at the other's throat, when a flash of lightning revealed their identity."*

It was Capt. Hamilton. He was trying to take advantage of the storm too. They agreed the frequent lightning made an attempt hazardous; but if they could somehow get down into the cellar, maybe they could slip by the guards between flashes.

With his penknife, Rose whittled a piece of firewood into a wedge and used it to pry up one of the floorboards. They found a plank long enough to reach the basement below and jammed it into the hole. With Hamilton standing lookout, Rose slid down into the large, dark center basement room.

Waiting silently in the blackness, Rose let his eyes adapt. A dim glow leaked in from the windows that faced the street. It was still too dark to see anything inside the room, but he could hear breathing and realized a few men, probably workers, were sleeping in the carpentry shop. Careful to not disturb them, Rose worked his way toward the street side of the room. To his amazement, he saw that the doorways and windows were wide open. Hidden in the dark, Rose watched a guard march past outside, so close he could have touched him.

Retracing his steps, Rose climbed back up into the kitchen, replaced the plank and closed the hole. Hamilton, waiting anxiously the whole time, was eager to exploit this latest discovery. The two considered attempting to escape right then, but decided the lightning posed too great a risk. Instead they decided to sneak into the basement again during the next storm, and just walk out the doorway when the guards were hiding from the rain. Then they went upstairs to sleep, taking care to avoid notice by either guards or inmates.

"The very next day a rare good fortune befell Rose," wrote Moran. A team of the highest-ranking Libby prisoners, under the direction of Gen. Dow, had been put in charge of distributing bales of clothing sent from the North for shivering prisoners in Richmond. Through some elaborate bit of chicanery, they somehow stole a *"new, fine rope nearly a hundred feet long and an inch thick"* that had been used to wrap one of the bales. After smuggling it into Libby, they presented the precious item to Col. Rose.

Rose and Hamilton used the rope to make more nighttime visits to the middle basement room. Each time they stole a few small tools, including chisels, files, and saws, which they then hid among their blankets. The elderly workers didn't seem to care about the thefts; apparently they didn't report them.

"Once while down there I was discovered by one of the workmen," wrote Rose, *"I seized a broadaxe with the intention of braining him if he attempted to call the guard, but he went to bed, blew out his light, and begged me not to come there again."* The man likely made no mention of it to his fellows; as Rose noted, *"I never noticed any additional vigilance."*

Finally they got the severe nighttime storm they'd been waiting for; but things did not go their way, as Col. Rose recorded: *"There were several in the plot, but I was to make the first attempt. I made the venture one very dark and stormy night. I easily passed the first sentinel, but unfortunately was seen by the second, who happened just at that moment to be facing towards me. He called out to the first, who, on hearing his name, faced about and saw me."*

One guard screamed lustily for help, while the other cocked his rifle and poked it through the open window. He repeatedly demanded, *"Who goes there?"* but did not enter the dark room.

"My only chance to escape being shot or captured was to run back into the shop, which was as dark as Erebus, and climb the rope into the room above. The sentinel called for the corporal of the guard, but before he could enter the carpenter shop and strike a light, I had drawn up the rope and replaced the plank. As there were workmen sleeping in one end of the shop, the corporal must have supposed that one of them had tried to pass, as he soon gave up the search and did not enter the room above."

This was a serious setback, particularly because they had alarmed the guards. They felt they had no choice but to go back to the tunnel plan. And a tunnel could only be dug from the east basement room of Libby, the space known as Rat Hell.

This room was as large as all the others in the building, a bit more than 100 feet in depth. It had some windows in the front but most of the space was deeply dark, even during the day. The room was so filthy it was only used for storage. Two feet of rotten straw covered the floor; hundreds of rats lived there, more likely thousands.

"To gain the carpenter shop required but little skill; but to reach the ground-floor of the eastern division was a very delicate operation. It was evident, however, that if an escape was to be made it must be from this room, as it was at all times dark therein, and it was seldom visited by the rebels either day or night."

How to get into this east cellar? It was completely sealed off, both from the center (carpenter's) room beside it and the east room hospital on the floor above it.

Then Hamilton had the flash of genius that would make everything else possible. The center/kitchen room on the first floor and the east room in the cellar were catty-corner to each other. By cutting a diagonal path through the dividing wall in the rough form of an S, Hamilton saw they would be able to angle down from the kitchen and drop into the empty east basement.

As luck would have it, Capt. Hamilton was a working mason and his expertise was exactly what they needed. At the bottom of the wall they wanted to cut through was a bricked-up, unused fireplace. Two cookstoves stood nearby and used the fireplace chimney for their exhaust. Hamilton borrowed a simple penknife; *"when nearly all the prisoners were sleeping one night I carefully moved one of the stoves aside, and with the aid of the knife dug the mortar out of the bricks."*

They laid out a rubber blanket to hold the debris and Hamilton went to work with quiet precision. Lying in the gloom, he carefully cut out the mortar between every brick, all the while being careful to leave the brick itself undamaged. Through night after night of this tedious work, Col. Rose was his only companion.

"We were obliged to make no noise whatever in doing all this; for one of the sentinels was just outside the door within ten feet of where we were. We were obliged to take out all of the front bricks without fracture so that they could be replaced; for it was through this door that the prison inspector entered every day, and the first object he met on entering was this fireplace and stove."

Lt. Moran described their difficulties keeping the project a secret. *"Rose guarded his comrade against the constant danger of interruption by alert enemies on one side, and blundering friends on the other; and, as frequently happens in human affairs, their friends gave them more trouble than their*

Close-up from an 1880s drawing, showing the S-curve cut that allowed Rose and his men to get from the kitchen down into the east cellar, or Rat Hell.

Fire-place showing aperture through which prisoners escaped.

Fireplace.

foes. Night after night passed, and still the two men got up after taps from their hard beds, and descended to the dismal and reeking kitchen to bore for their liberty."

They used the Rebel guards to time their effort. The guards would call out each hour, so when the men heard "ten o'clock" they slid down to work; and when they heard "4 a.m." they closed up the hole, dumped ashes in the old fireplace, and blew dust over everything. Rose explained: *"As the morning hour approached, we would carefully replace every brick, and then put back the dirt, making the fireplace look as if it had never been disturbed. We would then replace the stove in its proper position, go up-stairs, conceal our tools, and go to bed."*

Hamilton pick-pick-picked at the bricks for twelve straight nights before he completed the path to the east basement. His meticulous and silent work paid off perfectly. For the next three months this old Libby fireplace would be disassembled every night and reassembled every morning, and the guards never caught on.

Lt. Earle, who later joined the escape group, marveled at Hamilton's work. *"So ingeniously were the bricks and stones replaced that one would never notice that anything had been disturbed. After I was aware that this opening existed, I have looked intently for evidence of carelessness in closing this opening, but I could see nothing."*

Every day hundreds of men, both guards and prisoners, would pass by this fireplace or use the cooking stoves attached to it. No one ever noticed anything amiss.

They had to continue with their silence, but both were excited and reinvigorated. Hamilton later wrote: *"I will never forget the satisfaction and relief that our little party experienced when the entrance was completed. It seemed as though half the battle had been won, although in reality our labors had barely commenced."*

Tight Fit

THE OPENING INTO THE EAST CELLAR, RAT HELL, WAS FINALLY READY.
Col. Rose wanted to be the first one down. As instigator of the escape
plan, he was determined to carry success or failure on his own shoulders.
Maybe the Rebels were waiting and would immediately throw him into
the dungeons. But whatever might happen, Rose wanted to get on with
it.

The very next night the two men brought their stolen rope down to
the kitchen where they had secretly dug out the fireplace. They moved the
cookstove away from the opening and discussed the size of the S-shaped
path they had created, knowing it would make for a tight fit. But Capt.
Hamilton was the mason, and he contended that enlarging the pathway
risked collapse of the chimney.

The kitchen was dark and empty. Rose and Hamilton moved the
bricks from the fireplace to open the pathway, attached the rope to a
support post in the kitchen, and Rose began inching his way inside. *"I
entered it feet foremost, at the same time seizing the rope. As soon as my feet
and legs were dangling below, the inevitable law of gravitation forced my body
into the hole as tight as a wedge. The fireplace was so narrow, and my body in
such a position, that I could not use my arms, and of course I could not use my
feet; so that I was perfectly helpless. Of all the tight places that I ever was in,
before or since, that took the lead. I whispered to Hamilton that I was wedged
so tight that I feared the whole Southern Confederacy could not loosen me."*

The colonel was worse than stuck; any movement made him slide
down lower, jamming his chest so tightly that it became ever harder to

breathe. As their friend Lt. Moran described it, *"Each effort only wedged him more firmly in the awful vise. Rose was gasping for breath and rapidly getting fainter, but even in this fearful strait he refrained from an outcry that would certainly alarm the guards just outside the door."*

Rose was suffocating. His torso was caught tight in the middle of the S while his feet dangled over open space. Every move made him stick tighter, as if a python were wrapping itself around him. He struggled to breathe while Hamilton frantically tried to free him. As Rose told it: *"He was a powerful man, and grasped my left wrist with both his hands; while with my right hand I endeavored to help myself. He pulled with the strength of a giant, but it was of no use. I could not be budged an inch. He then left me sticking in the hole and ran up-stairs."*

A panicked Hamilton dashed through the dark rooms and up the stairs to where the POWs were sleeping in endless tight rows. They were so packed together that entire rows had to turn over in unison.

Hamilton ran right over the top of them, trampling heads and hands and backs in his dash to reach one of their coconspirators. Curses and flying debris followed the major as he flew to the sleeping place of a Maj. Fitzsimmons, but he wasn't there. Luckily, Hamilton quickly located a Lt. Bennett; they both dashed over the rows of men and down to the kitchen.

The two grabbed Rose's arms and after some vigorous tugs managed to pull him up enough to catch his breath. *"As they gave another tremendous pull, I came up so light that we all three fell upon the floor with a prodigious noise. The sentinel who walked in front of the door seemed startled and confused. The prisoners up-stairs called to each other to inquire the cause of the crash. We all three lay where we fell perfectly motionless and almost breathless. The corporal of the guard did not come into the room; and as soon as all was quiet again, we rose, replaced the bricks, dirt, and stove as quickly as possible, slipped up-stairs and went to bed, very much fatigued and considerably discouraged."*

But the next morning Rose was back at it. Entering the kitchen by pretending to cook, he carefully studied the fireplace as closely as he dared and thought up ways to expand the passageway. That night Hamilton went to work on the fireplace, removing more bricks to smooth out

Hamilton.

and enlarge it. Rose attached his rope again; this time he dropped easily down into the formerly sealed-off and inaccessible east cellar of Libby.

"*The darkness therein was perfect, but I examined every part of the room by feeling, then climbed up the rope and pulled myself through the hole in the wall without assistance. It was then that the problem was solved and the escape, with reasonable prudence, only a question of time.*"

The confidence that filled Col. Rose after this achievement would come in handy during the long, trying months to come. For now he was content. A tunnel and an escape felt achingly close.

The two men began digging the next day. They had a stolen chisel and a penknife, bits of candles for illumination, and a hat for fanning air into the tunnel. Hamilton refashioned their rope into a ladder with convenient wooden rungs, which helped considerably with getting into and out of the fireplace entrance.

If they found any advantage to working in Rat Hell, it was that they could easily scatter any soil they took from the tunneling. With straw and other filth covering everything, a little extra dirt would never be noticed.

Their plan was still to dig into the local sewer lines, but they soon realized this would be impossible without serious help. Thirteen men considered brave and discreet were sworn into a secret group, with Rose the unquestioned commander and Hamilton his first assistant.

Rose divided the men into three groups of five members. Each crew worked every third night, followed by two nights off. One man would dig, another would fan air into the tunnel, a third would draw out and dispose of the dirt, a fourth would keep lookout, and the fifth would help out where needed.

Yet as Rose later said, *"I found more difficulties than I had anticipated. The men were totally unused to the circumstances. The profound darkness of the place caused some to become bewildered, and, as absolute silence had to be observed, they could not find their way. As the cellar was very large, it was a matter of great difficulty to find them. I sometimes had to feel all over the cellar to gather up the men that were lost.*

"The indescribably bad odor made some of them sick. The uncomfortable positions in which they had to work amid crawling rats was unendurable to some."

The circumstances were awful and the progress glacial. They were trying to dig under the eastern wall of Libby to reach the sewer line, but soon ran into the huge ancient logs that formed the building's foundation. This row of solid timbers almost caused the party to give up right there, but Rose was determined that they press on. Night after long night they sawed and hacked at the logs with the pathetic tools they had. Progress was measured in fractions of an inch.

By keeping at it they finally broke through the solid wall of wood, only to run into something even worse: water. At first the leaks were just a nuisance, but the deeper they dug the stronger the flow became. Then, one night, a giant burst of sewage rushed in, almost drowning Rose and those working with him.

"What a stench!" wrote Capt. Milton Russell, one of Streight's officers. *"So horrible was that it awoke every sleeper about the building, and the detail at work nearly suffocated with sewer gas. The opening in the sewer was finally closed before daylight and the enterprise voted a failure.*

"Bitter complaints were filed next morning with the prison authorities, asking them for humanity's sake not to allow the scavenger wagons to draw their loads of filth past the prison, as it was likely to endanger the health of the inmates. The prison guards joined with us in our request."

The soaked men felt they had no choice but to declare defeat—all except for Rose, a man who acknowledged no defeats, only temporary setbacks. But he understood why others might give up. *"To the unreflecting the scheme seemed impracticable as soon as the first burst of enthusiasm was over. In very short time, this party was disbanded, and Hamilton and myself continued our dreary work alone."*

The two men started a second tunnel, planning to reach a smaller sewer line that carried waste from the prison. They hoped this would lead into the major sewage system. This time the problem was that the sewer was too small for a man to fit in. The pipes were made of wood, and though they tore out the pipes to create more room, they still couldn't make enough space to squeeze through.

Removing the wooden pipes undermined a section of sidewalk pavement next to the cellar, and it began to cave in. One day they heard a crash of bricks and a guard calling for his superior to come and look. Rose *"got away from there as quickly and quietly as possible. The next day we looked through the gratings of the windows from above, and we saw some negro laborers repairing the damage we had done. How it was they did not discover anything wrong I never could imagine."*

Of course, maybe the slaves discovered everything but chose to say nothing. Maybe Robert Ford, Elizabeth Van Lew's contact among Libby's laborers, helped ensure that no consequences followed. Rose thought he overheard those workers *"saying something about rats"* but wasn't sure if they were seriously considering that rodents alone could have caused such a cave-in.

Going down into the cellar the next night, Rose again feared the Rebels might have laid a trap for him. But the room was as silent and empty as ever.

"It was at this time that my friend Hamilton gave up all hope of final success," Rose noted. *"It did seem to be hopeless. I did not despair, but resolved, if possible, to organize another party."*

In his own memoir, Capt. Hamilton remembered it differently. *"Failure was never thought of,"* he recorded. What actually occurred during that nadir of their struggles will never be known, but Rose did have a new scheme and it brought a renewed energy. He was also determined to form a better crew of men, one that would build on what he'd learned from weeks of digging.

Meanwhile, life went on inside Libby. The excruciating grind of boredom and starvation was everyone's reality, though the men did their best

Libby Prison after the war.

to combat it. To Rose and Hamilton, daytime in the overcrowded prison was often harder to endure than the nights spent below in Rat Hell.

At least those labors offered hope, however slight. But so far they had slogged for thirty-nine long nights, with nothing to show for it.

From Skirmishing to Catechism

COL. ROSE AND HIS DIGGING PARTY HEADED FOR THE S-CURVE AS SOON as they heard the sentinels cry out, "4 a.m." It took time to rebuild the fireplace, and then they had to slip upstairs into their sleeping spots before anyone noticed them missing.

Lying on the hardwood floor was so uncomfortable that the POWs tended to be up before dawn. By first light everyone was awake and involved in a unique Libby mass ritual called "skirmishing," wherein the entire inmate population went to war against the swarms of lice, ticks, fleas, and bedbugs that filled the building and bit them constantly. Not particular in their terminology, they called the vermin "greybacks," a term they also used for Confederate soldiers and their currency.

Lt. A. B. White wrote about his first morning in Libby: *"Cavalry-men are used to skirmishing, so when Captain Sawyer, the morning after my arriving, said to me, 'you had better get up and skirmish,' I did not understand him, until he explained that I was to skirmish along the seams of my clothing for greybacks. The spectacle of some 1200 men scanning their shirts with utmost care was a sight that cannot be described as either picturesque or beautiful."*

"The first scene on opening my eyes, was of a kind which I had never imag-ined out of the realms of fiction. I have no wish to describe repulsive things, but I shall certainly not shrink to write down the word vermin in speaking of Libby. I endeavored to turn my eyes away from the scene, but there was no escape," wrote Capt. Szabad, the Hungarian immigrant and aristocrat who often criticized the "common" behavior of many officers in the prison. His was a refined European sensibility; it bothered his sense of propriety

to see lines of Union officers naked and dealing with a scourge that would never be mentioned in polite company.

"The soldier must be a soldier," wrote one columnist in the *Libby Chronicle.* *"In this wretched prison, every soldier sheds blood for his country. The casualties are many. The black flag is raised and no quarters are given to these rebel parasites that swarm as in the plagues of Egypt."*

Once their clothes became infested the men would try turning them inside out, particularly at night. This gave relief for a few hours, until the vermin worked their way back to the insides of their shirts and pants.

"They were the most prolific bugs I ever saw. They were all over us ere we knew it, and at first we would scratch till the blood ran. If we had any before we got to Libby we did not know it. The popular way was to crush them between the thumb nails. The old, large ones would bloody our hands in killing them. The blankets we received from our predecessors were alive with them."

Every morning Libby would be filled with the click-clicking of more than 1,200 men skirmishing simultaneously. Sometimes the POWs would capture vermin and try to drop them onto unsuspecting prison guards. They were particularly angry that the Rebels did nothing to help them battle the pests. The prisoners were never issued soap or cleansers of any sort. Boiling one's clothing worked for a while, but the necessary firewood was hard to come by. The winter cold would slow the greybacks down for a while, but with the spring they would return in even greater numbers.

Capt. Starr took a philosophical view. *"These little fellows would stick closer than a brother. It was not altogether poetic license on the part of the rhymer who said, 'each little flea has a smaller flea upon his back to bite him. This smaller flea, still lesser flea, and so ad infinitum."*

One Confederate newspaper, the *Richmond Sentinel,* explained the situation this way to its readers: *"Although the Northern journals have blazoned forth the fact that the prison is infested with vermin, yet nothing can be further from the truth. The statement is characteristic of their usual mendacity. Every precaution is used by the prison authorities to promote the cleanliness of the persons there confined. There are certainly no vermin in the rooms when assigned to prisoners, and if they exist at all, then it is from the fact that they are brought there by the prisoners themselves, among whom are many whose naturally filthy habits preclude them from being free of such pests."*

Confederate guerrillas. Drawing by Lt. Col. Cavada.

After skirmishing, came the morning count. Erasmus Ross, the prison clerk, counted the prisoners at least twice a day. Twenty-one, short and heavy-set, he was responsible for keeping track of the inmates in all of Richmond's prisons. He carried two pistols and a huge bowie knife, prominently displayed. Two or more bayonet-toting guards accompanied him everywhere. The POWs took to calling him "Little Ross."

Union officers did not like being bossed around by this chubby young Confederate, so they were often surly and slow to cooperate. Ross's answer was to be increasingly harsh and insulting. *"This man was said to be a deserter from our army and was, from the first, and continually and consciously, hated by every man in the prison. He subjected us to every petty tyranny which a normal mind could suggest,"* wrote young Lt. Earle, and most Libby POWs would probably have agreed.

But even if they hated him, they did not fear him. German immigrant Capt. Domschcke saw the clerk as a *"comical little fellow. Ross seemed to be a Rebel only because Virginians were Rebels. He delighted in new and diverse clothes, liked to chat, was pleasant to us, but never could cope with Yankees who teased and played jokes on him whenever they could. Roll call, his main responsibility, often caused him heartache and drove him to desperation after 10, 12, and 15 repetitions yielded the wrong count."*

It was not an easy task to count so many men in the overcrowded prison. The common procedure was for Little Ross to go to each of the six rooms where the men slept, form them into ranks of four, and then walk down the column to produce a total. If Ross was not satisfied with his numbers he could keep the POWs standing in their lines indefinitely.

But some prisoners could not resist the temptation to play with the clerk's equilibrium. They quickly figured out that after the head of the column had been counted a few men could duck down, move behind the others, and reappear at the end to be counted again.

In time the men got bored with this and moved on to a better deception.

Little Ross could only count one room at a time, and it took him a few minutes to travel from one to the next. Acting quickly, prisoners who had been counted would climb up through the roof skylights and drop down into another room. When Ross added up his totals, he was confounded to discover more men in the prison than had been originally admitted.

Lt. Starr recorded his interpretation of the frustrated Ross's Georgia accent, *"Now I am suah there is more than a dozen of you damn Yanks yer, who aint yer,"* which brought thunderous laughter from the POWs.

At first this was just for fun, but Col. Rose realized that by fudging the count deliberately he could keep diggers working in the basement almost 24 hours a day. To make sure the men below would not be missed by Little Ross's crew, Col. Rose assigned five of his men to game the numbers continuously. By a combination of distractions and movement behind the columns, they were able to ensure that the missing men were not missed.

Unfortunately, other POWs not in on the conspiracy decided to join the fun. *"The meddlers' sole purpose was to make 'Little Ross' mad,"* explained Lt. Moran. *"In this they certainly met with success, for the reason of the mystified clerk seemed to totter as he repeated the count over and over."*

Ross calling the roll.

Soon these new "repeaters" were caught red-handed by the guards, forcing Little Ross to switch to the even more onerous tactic of full prison roll calls. All the prisoners would be packed into one room, and as each officer's name was called out he would exit through the doorway to the next room. The process could take hours, with more than 1,200 men jammed shoulder-to-shoulder in the one room.

In response, Col. Rose's team hit on a new obfuscation. The conspirators' five-man team would always know the names of whoever was currently absent. Say the missing man was named "Smith." When his name was called, one of Col. Rose's team ("Jones") would answer "present" for Smith, pass by the clerk, and cross into the next room. When Jones's own name was called no one would reply, so an immediate search would be launched. But Jones was just waiting in the next room, and as soon as he heard the guards were looking for him he would walk up to Little Ross and announce, "I'm right here."

When asked why he didn't answer during roll call, Jones would reply that he *did* respond, and was here to show the guards that they'd obviously made a mistake. Ross usually accepted the explanation and closed his books.

The fact that the prisoners looked so similar helped in this charade. They were almost all in their twenties or thirties, and everyone wore a ragged blue uniform. The greybacks found it hard to tell them apart. *"The prison clerk Ross, after working nearly the entire day to correct his roll, finally gave it up with the remark—'How in the devil can I manage a thousand Yankees when, after counting them all day, I have 24 more men in the prison than ever were here?"*

Having too many men in the building was especially perplexing. Some Libby inmates told Ross that a few Confederates were hiding among the Libby inmates in order to avoid their own military draft. According to POW Caldwell, *"This seemed to be satisfactory, the clerk more than half convinced that citizens made up the surplus—he could not recognize, in counting the second room, that he was counting the same men the second time. Hence, his bewilderment and trouble in accounting for this Yankee trickery."*

Even if the prisoners enjoyed outwitting the guards, it meant they often had to stand in their lines for an entire day of counting and recounting. Wrote Lt. Wells: *"When practical jokes became too serious, and those directly responsible could not be apprehended in any other way, the authorities would reach the guilty parties by shutting off the rations of the entire prison for 24 hours. This treatment generally produced results."*

When Little Ross was finally satisfied, the men were released for their breakfast. In the early years of the war, cooking for all Union POWs took place at a central kitchen in Richmond. Pails would then be hauled across the city to the various prisons. But this became impractical as the POWs' numbers increased, so a new system was instituted in Libby whereby the men would do their own cooking.

"With the Yankee tendency to organization, we were divided into messes of about 20 each. Each man in turn does the cooking for the entire day. In a close, suffocating corner of the main kitchen, we were compelled to burn corn-meal for coffee, and to make rice soup and hash over smoking, broken stoves, it was anything but agreeable labor."

At mealtimes, fifty to one hundred men and more would fill the kitchen, all competing for the same tiny patches of real estate atop the stoves. The moment any cook removed his pot, it was instantly replaced by another. Sometimes arguments would break out and precious food spilled in the hot, smoky chaos. Lt. Col. Cavada, the Cuban Yankee who spent a year in Libby, witnessed this daily human surge; his lively description would be hard to improve upon.

"You find the cook room crowded to suffocation; the stoves are completely covered with all sorts of ingenious contrivances in the shape of pots, skillets, pans, mugs, and cans, and to back this is an army of ferocious cooks, all struggling to look into their 'stews' at the same time—an operation which is utterly impracticable where only three small stoves are to render edible so large a quantity of the most uncookable and undigestible materials.

"So, you advance a few steps and make a frantic effort to wedge yourself in between those fratricidal cooks. In all probability some crabbed fellow lets fall upon your legs a little shower of scalding water; or, an accidental back-hander from some gigantic Hoosier jostles coffee into your eyes. But you must push on bravely, until you have had your toes trodden on for the hundredth time—until you have smutted your nose, and burnt your fingers—until you are half stifled and completely disgusted."

Usually the men would cook any food they had in one pot. They'd boil their rice or corn and then throw in anything available, from crusts of bread to small pieces of (usually rotten) meat and bone, all shared equally by the members in each mess. But the food was the same every meal (except for the days they received nothing at all) and it was never close to enough. Some would gulp down their rations in one sitting, others would spread them out in tiny amounts through the day.

"The meat and soup would be in so rotten a condition that only starving men could eat it. That awful gnawing at the stomach for food can't be expressed in words. It makes an animal of a man. Yes, as you look into the eyes of a

starving man, it makes one think of a fierce, hungry dog. I have seen men—friends—on our floor fight over a small amount of meat. No one can get used to hunger. It is endured because it has to be."

The prisoners had too little food and too much time on their hands, so many took to discussing banquets, feasts, and the greatest meals they'd ever enjoyed. Debates could go on for days about different cuisines, styles, and spices. A New Yorker might minutely describe the fancy dinner he'd enjoyed at Delmonico's. Lt. Roach was surprised to see so many high-ranking officers become obsessed with cooking—*"The avidity with which they would pore over the household department of old magazines and newspapers in search of receipts for preparing various dishes, was no less astonishing than the rapidity with which they became adept in this branch of house keeping."*

Cookbooks were passed around until they fell apart. Men loved imagining every course of the grand table they would set upon their release. While some POWs felt these fantasies made their starvation worse, others found comfort in memories of home and plenty. *"Our mothers were our ideal cooks. Each man would brag about his mother, and would describe in detail how she could cook this and that, and what a feast she would make for him when he got home. Then another would take it up, and so it would go around and round. Often some of the weaker ones would give way and cry like babies."*

These Union officers were young men a long way from home, in an era when few traveled far and family ties were strong. At least they had the mail. The appearance of letters was irregular, but always the high point of any week.

"There is no sound that creates such excitement as 'The Mail! The mail!' A scramble takes place to the room where one of our officers, perched upon a high beam above the crowd, reads aloud the addresses and then flings the missive in the direction of the anxious response. Every one hopes for a letter from the loved ones, though only a few are ever gratified with a message."

Noted Capt. Glazier in his diary for November 27, 1863: *"I was so fortunate as to receive two letters. They were indeed like 'cold water to a thirsty soul.' No one can appreciate the value of a bit of paper crossed with familiar lines and home thoughts until they receive it under such circumstances."*

Most letter writers tried to cheer up their readers. Prisoners not wanting to alarm their mothers would moderate any complaining. Wives and daughters would be told that conditions weren't as bad as they'd heard, and that surely exchanges would be restarted soon. Relatives would try to send upbeat messages to the prisoners as well. But realities crept through. *"The bustle of distribution over, an unusual quiet reigns throughout our dolorous abode. Here a countenance glows with rapture over words of love; there, hidden away as far as possible from the crowds, sometimes with face against the dirty wall, is one whose flowing tears fall upon the page that tells of ominous sickness or sorrowful death."*

Delivery might have been uneven, but it cost only five cents to have a letter sent to or from Libby. At first the POWs could write whatever they wanted, but soon the Rebel authorities decided to read and censor the letters. All prisoners were told to restrict their letters to six lines and to send them in unsealed envelopes. The Confederates could throw away a letter for any reason; only the ones deemed inoffensive would be forwarded to *"the so-called United States."*

To get around the Rebel restrictions on length and subject matter, prisoners and their families had success for a while with good old invisible ink. According to Capt. Russell's memoir, the wife of one of the officers began the practice of filling the open parts of a sheet with hidden messages. Most any organic compound could be used for invisible ink, but lemon juice and onion juice were the most popular. Soon after writing, the juice would dry and leave no trace; all the recipient had to do was heat the page and the words would come out clearly. Northern relatives of the POWs wrote to each other about this, encouraging them to heat any letters received from Libby and to send their own invisible messages.

Rebel authorities might have thought it curious that the six lines allowed were often cramped into the middle of a large sheet of paper. Apparently, they did not realize the rest of the page was filled with invisible-ink messages. But the subterfuge could not last; as remembered by Lt. Fales, *"This correspondence was ended by a foolish man who wrote a letter, and then put in ink the direction, 'When you have read this letter, put it in the oven and read it again.' The rebels baked it and discovered the secret."*

Only one thing elevated the spirits of Libby prisoners more than letters, and that was the distribution of boxes. The boxes Northerners shipped to the ragged POWs were, for many, the difference between life and death.

"There has been great rejoicing of late, owing to the numerous boxes from the North. There is an almost child-like delight exhibited over these timely bounties from home. An officer with a 'box' becomes at once the admired of all admirers, and receives congratulations as hearty as if he had just 'married a fortune.'"

Food was the most popular item but the boxes could include almost anything, and the soldiers needed everything. Libby POW captain David Jones wrote home to his mother in Cincinnati with this list of very specific requests:

"Send me as soon as possible: 1 pr. Pantaloons, 2 pr. Drawers, 2 woolen shirts, 1 pr. Socks, needles and thread, a ham, piece of dried beef, 10 lbs. butter, 6lbs. coffee, 1lb. tea, 10 lbs. sugar, 3 nutmegs, pickles, preserves, late numbers of the Atlantic *and* Harper's *magazines and, if you can, a paper with a list of casualties of my regiment. Box them up well and send them by express."*

Knowing that the boxes would be inspected by Rebels, Capt. Fisher wrote home with special instructions. What no one explains is how he got this letter out of Libby without it being censored: *"You can place money and a letter in a vial and bury it in a can of butter, or sew them up carefully in a needle case. I will find it no matter how concealed. Size of box is of no consequence. Then, if you have room, cakes that time will not injure, cheese, cranberries, pickles, jellies (wines or brandies put in cans and marked 'Worcester Sauce'), and such luxuries as you might suppose would yet tickle the palate of a 'Libby epicurean.'"*

As the months went by and shortages in Richmond became worse, the routine inspection of boxes turned into routine theft by the guards. It took five weeks for Capt. Jones finally to receive his box, and when he opened it his excitement turned to anger, *"I cannot express in words the gratitude it awakened. Unfortunately for me, it had been broken open, and all of the coffee and sugar, and 5 cans of milk besides some smaller articles were taken out."*

At first this lifeline from home was encouraged by Confederate authorities, since the boxes provided food and supplies the Rebels didn't have to subsidize. But before long the shipments became another tool for manipulating and punishing the prisoners. On the slightest pretext, Rebel authorities took to holding up the deliveries for months at a time.

"A new flag of truce boat arrived. The emaciated faces again brightened, though hunger had already produced its results. The question now was, 'have boxes arrived?' Hunger crying out from the mouths of more than a thousand victims, added all its terrible weight to this hope. But again disappointment was our lot."

The boxes were allowed to pile up in the stable yard of a building across the street from Libby, where the starving prisoners could see them. While the guards were not actually encouraged to steal from the boxes, neither were they disciplined when they did so. At night, prisoners could hear the guards breaking into them.

Thanksgiving was a new official holiday in 1863, so *"Major Turner allowed an issue of the remaining few of our boxes this morning, which have been in his possession for the past two months. They were all broken open, and were generally stripped of every thing which could be of any use to us. They were plundered by the common soldiers of the guard here, under the eyes and with the permission of the prison authorities."*

Libby Prison had all the ingredients that lead to such petty corruption. The guards were poorly trained and underpaid. Runaway inflation continued to degrade the Rebel currency, making it ever harder to supplement their meager foodstuffs.

Most importantly, prison boss Dick Turner set the standard by stealing whatever he could from the POWs. The guards followed his lead, but at least in Libby the corruption was not well organized; it was every guard for himself.

"The Rebels, sly foxes, discovered we had something they lusted after: greenbacks. Though the exchange would seem to be by stealth, Turner would know all about it. At first such deals brought us for each greenback [dollar] *$5 to $6 Confederate, and by 1864, up to $16 to $18."*

Capt. Chamberlain recorded how the forbidden trade worked: *"My plan of operation was to station myself at the head of the stairs, and when the right man was pacing his beat, signal to him, and as he walked along with his gun, he would move his bayonet along the wall above his head, writing the number of dollars he would give me for one. If satisfactory, I would roll up my money in as small a wad as possible and quietly drop it near his feet, where he could pick it up without stopping in his walk. If he made the exchange speedily, he would toss a little roll up when he came on his beat again. Sometimes it would be a day or two before the trade was consummated, but in not a single instance did they betray the trust we were compelled to place in them."*

Eventually Capt. Chamberlain was caught and his scheme ended. But the trading was just too lucrative for everyone involved, so it quickly morphed into a new system.

At the same time, the Confederates continued to pass stronger laws in a futile attempt to sustain the value of their currency. Civilians were threatened with prison, and soldiers with execution, to deter them from trading in Union greenbacks.

"Notwithstanding all this," wrote Yankee captain John McElroy, *"in Richmond, the heart of the Confederacy—There was not a day during our stay but what one could go to the hole in the door before which the guard was pacing and call out in a loud whisper: 'Say, Guard: do you want to buy some greenbacks?'*

"There was never any risk in approaching any guard with a proposition of this kind, and if the men on guard could not be restrained by these stringent laws, what hope could there be of restraining anybody else?"

The amazing thing was that the Libby inmates had any money at all. They had been searched and robbed and searched again, yet they still managed to smuggle greenbacks and valuables inside. This trading in cash and goods went on throughout the conflict because it helped both the Blue and the Grey.

German American Capt. Bernhard Domschcke had been a journalist before the war, and was a keen student of how the Libby commerce functioned: *"To the Rebel officers, this business was profitable threefold. (1) They went to brokers and reexchanged the greenbacks for more Confederate money than they had given us. (2) They made 100 percent or more on any goods. (3) They could keep our rations as skimpy as possible.*

"So our money migrated to their pockets without our being able to accuse them of outright theft."

Say, guard, do you want to buy some greenbacks?

By January 1864, Col. Rose and his men were finding it increasingly difficult to dig all night in the dark squalor of Rat Hell, then spend all day enduring the crowds upstairs. The prisoners were not allowed to sleep on the floor during daylight, so the diggers had to catch their rest in small snatches. They had to be constantly on guard against their activities being discovered, or even noticed.

They were also painfully aware that, without adequate food, not only were their bodies deteriorating but so were their minds. Many complained that their thinking and their judgment were becoming foggy.

*"Different minds are no doubt affected to a different degree. The specu-
lative become morbid; the excitable, languishing from the lack of mental
stimulus, sink into stagnation. It is the calm and philosophical who are best
calculated to endure the weary monotony of prison life. But if the bad qualities
of some are so forcibly developed, the good in others are apt to expand in the
same ratio: the amiable become almost feminine in their kindness; the charitable become self-sacrificing."*

So observed Lt. Col. Cavada in his book *Libby Life*, which was published only a few months after his release. He added: *"No place, surely, is
better adapted than the prison-house for the study of human nature. Suffering
develops the real character. This is a crucible to the heart; we live continually as
if in the midst of a crowded street—always under the eye of someone."*

Cavada was an artist, a scholar, and an acute observer of the ways
in which Libby was affecting its inmates. He scribbled on any scrap of
paper he could find and, when released, smuggled the scraps out in his
clothing and shoes.

*"I am repeatedly struck by the fact of how much prisoners become like
children. The importance of momentous events is given to the merest trifles."*

Many of the POWs were closer to their teens than to maturity. And
everyone had to fight his own battle against the overwhelming agony of
nothing but time and more time to fill. Any distraction was a good one.

*"It was the law of Libby that whenever a female was seen looming in
the distance, her presence was announced by the loud call of 'Gunboat'; and on
such occasions there were desperate charges to the windows, which would have
extorted admiration from the most unwarlike spectator."*

The POWs were willing to risk death for the mere glimpse of a
woman. *"The sentinels, pacing their beats outside the building, had orders to
shoot any of the prisoners they could see looking out of the windows, and while
I was there three of our officers were killed and one wounded by bullets fired by
the guards. But only one man of the four was aimed at by the soldier."*

The guards were apparently terrible shots, but as Libby was so packed
with humans any stray bullet could do terrible damage, as witnessed by
Lt. Moran. *"The writer vividly recalls the sight of Capt. Forsythe, of the
100th Ohio Infantry, lying dead in a pool of blood on the floor of the upper*

middle room in Libby. He was shot through the head while reading a newspa-per, and fully 8 to 10 feet from the nearest window."

Moran also witnessed a rare instance of payback, in an incident which gave great satisfaction to the inmates. The ceiling of Libby was pierced by air vents, called scuttles, through which prisoners would risk climbing to gain access to the open rooftop. They were not allowed to be up there, so Lt. Moran savored every moment in the fresh air before having *"to return to the hot human hive that sent up a burning stench through the opening, that seemed like a shaft that led to hell."*

If the men on the roof lay low, guards on the streets below could not see them. But one evening Lt. Moran watched as a fellow prisoner stood to get a better look at a runaway horse, and before the man could get down, a guard fired at him. The bullet barely missed, flattening itself against a chimney and shattering masonry.

The angered prisoner picked up a chunk of jagged brick as *"the enemy was loading his gun for a second shot. He was about to ram home his car-tridge when a cry of 'Look out!' startled him. The alarm came near being late, for that brick descended with a speed that would have done credit to a crack baseball pitcher, as it grazed his head and knocked the ramrod from his hand. In his fright he dropped the gun, as he saw his Yankee assailant detaching another brick."* The guard tripped, fell, and then ran for cover, much to the amusement of both Yankees and Rebels: *"This little incident supplied the guards with mirth for several days, in which the shooter did not join with any enthusiasm."*

Reflecting on the shootings, Lt. Moran decided the reason *"casualties were not greater was due to the fact that by the time a man had lived a few months on the prison rations he was so reduced in physique that it took a good marksman to hit him."*

Toward evening, as the light began to droop, religious leaders held services for the faithful. Small groups would gather around different chaplains while other prisoners quietly ignored them.

The trouble was that often no chaplains were available, as they and doctors were the most likely to be exchanged out. Laymen would conduct services as best they could. An experiment with bringing in Confederate ministers did not go well, as their Yankee "parishioners" could not work up much enthusiasm for reverends who believed in both secession and slavery. Even the more religious prisoners decided they'd rather have no services than Rebel ones.

Historians have long recognized the democratizing influence of serving in the American military, which brought together, and made dependent on each other, groups and individuals who would seldom have crossed paths in civilian life. This was especially true after the South and North passed the first American military drafts, even though both sides allowed the very rich to avoid serving.

Being in prison leveled society further still, since together everyone endured starvation, lice, freezing, sweating, abuse by stupid guards, and every manner of general misery. Despite the great diversity in social class, denomination, ethnicity, and regional background, all the men in Libby shared a common fate.

"A Motley mixture of men," was what Lt. Moran called them. *"Libby prison was a vast museum of human character, where the chances of war had brought in close communion men of every type and temperament, where military rank was wholly ignored and where all shared in a common lot.*

"There were men of all sizes and all nationalities. There were about thirty doctors, a score of journalists and lawyers, a few actors and a proportionate representation of all the popular trades and professions."

Maj. Szabad, being an Old World aristocrat, had a more critical view of this ultrademocratic fraternity. *"Such an uncouth mixture of officers was probably never seen in modern times in any place, either in field or prison. To me, still fresh from Europe, this mixture seemed, of course, most surprising. I could never become reconciled to these exhibitions."*

Cavada added that *"all silly pride and squeamishness must be set aside; the future brigadier must sit, barefoot, with a bucket between his legs, while he washes his own stockings; the dashing cavalry officer must serve his turn at cooking and scouring, and display as much gallantry in charging a row of cook-pots as he did in scattering a battalion of the enemy's cavalry."*

Over time, even Maj. Szabad began to appreciate both the power of democracy and the strength of collective action. The Hungarian wrote about an event he witnessed: a fellow officer secretly joining a group of surgeons who were being exchanged.

"On that very day, Turner, commanding the prison, issued an order that unless the name of the disguised officer were given up to him, the delivery of boxes to the officers would be stopped." This would have been a significant blow to everyone in Libby; yet the POWs not only refused to point the man out, they also rose up screaming and chased Turner's envoy off of their floor. *"'Starve us!' was the unanimous exclamation of the officers in listening to the order."*

Future brigadier. Drawing by Lt. Cavada.

The POW hiding among the surgeons got away without being betrayed, and ultimately Dick Tuner did deliver the boxes, though many were first rifled by the Rebels.

"The ennui of prison life is a great spur to inventive genius, and it was not wanting here. There was no end of amusements. As in high life, the true gayeties of Libby commenced at night, after the usual call of the guards, 'Lights out!' which happened always at 9 o'clock."

Just as every day in Libby began with "skirmishing," so it ended with another unique ritual they called the "catechism." It began after the prisoners, more than two hundred in each of the six rooms, lay down together on the hard floor. If daytime in Libby was a version of democracy in action, at nighttime these officers slid into a barely controlled anarchy.

"Some of the most ludicrous incidents in Libby life occur after all its inhabitants have arranged themselves, each in his chosen spot upon the floor, with his army blanket around him. Then commences a succession of conundrums, questions and replies, technically called the catechism. This embodied a general censorship of the habits, opinions or peculiarities of whatever kink, of any who might attract special attention."

Libby's catechism was not the usual "call and response" one would hear in church services. As they were packed together in sleeping rows and under the cover of darkness, the men could hardly tell who was shouting out the questions and the answers. If the questions were pointed and embarrassing, so much the better:

> *"'Who thinks himself the handsomest man in Libby?'*
> *'McFadden!' would respond a tremendous chorus.*
> *'Who greases his moustache with ham fat?' 'McFadden'*
> *Now McFadden was voted vain, and worst of all, good looking."*
> *"No subject is allowed to escape. The habits, opinions, peculiarities, mishaps of every individual fall under this crucial censorship. Here is a great field for the punster and the jester.*
> *"'Who sold his boots to buy extra mutton chops?' 'Ely.'*
> *"'Who offered to enlist in the Rebel army if he could be released?' 'Goldsboro.'*
> *"'Who hid behind the big gun and was captured?'"*

For the most part, the catechism remained anonymous. The men could yell anything, so they did. Szabad complained: *"Against such hilarities, mixed with traits of vulgar rowdyism, there was no possible remedy. A stranger passing by Libby at midnight, might have imagined himself to be near a lunatic asylum. The place, in fact, was not on the whole, distinguished for refined manners."*

"Who among the colonels has star on the brain?"

"Who has exchange on the brain?"

"Who surrendered for humanity's sake?"

"If any of the comrades displayed irritation, it only served to make matters worse, for there were others determined to keep up a racket and banish sleep. Hardly anyone escaped from some practical joke, or from being dubbed with some slang name or epithet."

"All enjoyed them except the victims at whom they were aimed."

"Who was captured outside the lines, courting the widow?"

"Who plays the spy?"

The Libby catechism wasn't only shouted questions and answers. The entire building could suddenly transform into a wild, cacophonous menagerie. *"The braying of the ass, the cackling of the hen, the hoarse barking of the mastiff, the whining of the new born infant, all contributed to the grand nocturnal chorus, the echo of which must have penetrated high up in the streets of Richmond."*

"Who washed his clothes in the soup bucket?"

"Who is the meanest man in Libby?"

"These questions are endless in their number and variety, while the answers contain jokes almost too severe to be mirthful and facts too startling to be true. Gradually the pounding on the floor with fists and feet dies away, the roars of laughter cease, and sleep comes to drive our cares away and put our sorrows in oblivion."

The process required a grand finish to each night's catechism, so after the men had worn themselves out the event came to a riotous end. *"These highly valued entertainments invariably terminate with a grand bombardment, a finale a la militaire, during which all kinds of missiles, even fragments of stale corn-bread, are rapidly discharged from numberless masked batteries and go whirring all over the room, crashing among the tin-ware and*

Civil War prisoners.

boxes with a continuous rattle, and is not unaccompanied with some serious apprehensions as to the safety of uncovered heads."

"At length all seem satisfied, and sleep and silence—except the sub-base of heavy snoring—reigns supreme until the coming of dawn."

For Col. Rose and his digging crews all this mayhem provided the perfect cover. Under normal conditions it would have been very difficult for them to sneak below to do their work, but this raucous climax to the evenings made it easy. Each night they slipped out of their sleeping spaces and were never missed or even noticed. They had started a new tunnel—one that ultimately held the promise of putting many imprisoned officers on the road back to the Union.

CHAPTER ELEVEN

The Final Tunnel

COL. ROSE NEVER WAVERED, EVEN AS OTHERS DROPPED OUT OF HIS schemes. *"It did seem to be hopeless on account of the difficulty of getting men to work. I did not despair, but resolved, if possible, to organize another party and dig straight through."*

Though his first two tunnels had failed, Rose was learning. He and Hamilton were becoming experts on such esoteric subjects as the construction of Libby's foundation, the regular habits of its sentinels, and who among their fellow prisoners could be trusted for the long haul. They learned about the neighborhood by closely observing the streets surrounding Libby; they already knew more than they cared to about Richmond's soils and sewer system.

All this knowledge went into Rose's third and most ambitious escape plan. For the previous tunnels they had tried to dig their way down into the sewer pipes. This new idea was different; they would still work out of the east cellar but they would start digging in the back of the room, where it was underground. They would bore an escape route at least sixty feet in length, in order to pass under the street east of the room and come up in a fenced courtyard in the next block.

By a great stroke of luck, the block across from Libby was both fenced in and unoccupied at night. During the day this space served as a livery for horses and a storage area for the boxes sent from the North; but no one lived there. The fact of the courtyard being fenced in was especially fortunate since no one standing at street level, including the guards, could see in.

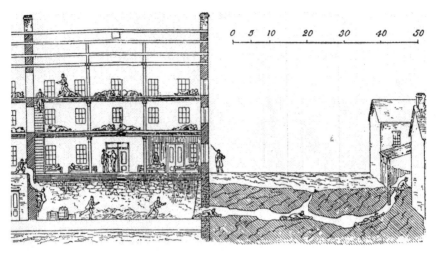

0 5 10   20   30   40   50

Cross-section of Libby tunnel escape route.

If everything went right and the tunnel was oriented correctly, the fence would cover the emerging men from view. The POWs could then hide in this courtyard until they found the right moment to slip away. The guards on their rounds only walked as far as the corner of this block; they would then turn their backs and return to Libby.

The Rebels patrolled all four streets around the prison building, so any tunnel had to go well underneath. Rose's idea was to stay eight feet below in order that *"we would have plenty of earth between us and the surface. It was a drier locality, so that we would not be troubled with water."*

"This plan therefore was the best that I could adopt, the only one that had any promise of success. Accordingly the next day I had a consultation with some of the prisoners. None of them seemed to have much hope, but several of them said they would work if for no other purpose than to 'pass away the time.'"

The first problem was to cut through the blocks that made up the walls of the basement. Chipping their way into the fireplace had taken two weeks because they were forced to work so silently. Col. Rose proposed a radical idea. The next night he took two of his best men, McDonald and Clarke, down into the east cellar and indicated where he wanted to start the tunnel. Then he left the two there and closed up the fireplace. Sealed down in Rat Hell until the next evening, they could work through the day as noise from the prison and the streets covered up their work—or so Rose hoped.

The two men timed their loudest bashes and crashes to coincide with the prison's own workers, who were installing stronger window bars and shoring up parts of the building. As Capt. Johnson recalled: *"This was accompanied by great noise; and while they were thus engaged our boys thumped away with a will, and made their way through the wall without exciting the least suspicion."*

Though the cellar blocks were much bigger than the bricks in the fireplace, McDonald and Clarke were able to remove them in a single day. Capt. Hamilton realized the escape effort was finally making serious progress. *"It was just 38 days after the tunnel project had been conceived that we broke through the wall for the third and last attempt. The mortar was cut with a chisel and the bricks were pried out with a stick of hard wood that had been furnished the prisoners for kindling."*

Col. Rose was as excited as his partner: *"I then went down and found that they had cut a hole entirely through the wall of sufficient size to admit a very large man easily."*

Capt. Johnston, the man who had been shot through the cheeks at Shiloh, started digging that first night: *"Having nothing but a small penknife, our progress was, of necessity, very slow. In spite of all difficulties, however, we made an excavation of about two feet, and felt that we were that much nearer freedom."*

Two feet was great progress to a man like Capt. Johnston. His memoirs from Libby have that straightforward style: *"I have been frequently asked since my escape, how it was possible for a man to be left down in the cellar every day without being discovered. Such a thing seems strange; but the entire work was a marvelous one, and this was a necessary part of it; and though the [Rebel] officers about the prison visited the cellar every day, yet for fifty-one days our company was down there without being discovered."*

The filthiness of the east cellar meant the Confederates loathed this disgusting place even more than the desperate Yankees. No guard ever went into Rat Hell unless ordered to, usually to collect some of the hay or building materials that were stored there. Only a small amount of light leaked in from a few windows on the street side of the room, and any man stepping into the room's deep darkness would quickly be greeted by the screeching squeals of a thousand rodents.

For Col. Rose this was perfect. "To a person coming in from out-doors it was very dark even in the middle of a bright day, so that he could see but a few feet, and as the room was 100 feet in length, a person standing in the north end was secure from being seen. To a person entering this room in the night, however, and staying there all day, as Hamilton or I often did, it was light enough to see.

"Many a time I have seen the rebels come in there and stand and look directly at us. To my accustomed eyes it was nearly as light as day, but to them it was dark as night. If they stayed too long, or came too far into the room, I would lie down behind the straw."

Each of the Libby memoirs has its version of the tunnel-digging, even though only a handful of men actually did the work. In their descriptions, the chroniclers alternately claim the diggers were armed with half a canteen, a broken trowel, a sugar cup, an auger, a small hatchet, or even a busted door hinge. But the specifics don't really matter, since the POWs would have dug the tunnel with their own fingers if they'd had to.

They found that the earth in the area was mostly compressed sand, which is both stable and relatively easy to dig through. However, the men had no wood for bracing the sides and ceiling so that, as the tunnel became longer, the terrible prospect of an asphyxiating cave-in was always in their minds.

Col. Rose, forever the optimist, assured the prisoners that he thought the tunnel safe—and backed up his words by doing much of the digging himself. The others might have been wary, but they followed his lead. *"The tunnel was dry as I had supposed. We made very rapid progress until we had proceeded about fifteen feet, when the air became so vitiated as to support life but a very short time. The flame of the candle would then expire, and the digger would be obliged to crawl out of the tunnel; notwithstanding, one man stood constantly at the mouth driving fresh air into it with a rude fan, constructed for the purpose."*

At first the crew merely waved their hats at the entrance, but as the tunnel became longer they had to come up with better methods of air

Fanning the tunnel.

circulation. Then Capt. Hamilton stretched a rubber blanket over a frame, and this was slightly more efficient. Still, the diggers were never far from oxygen starvation. The tiny candle they needed to work also served them as a warning light that would begin to flame out as the oxygen level dropped. More than once a man stayed too long, passed out, and had to be laboriously dragged by his feet from the narrow tunnel.

But progress led to lifted spirits, which made for more progress. Capt. Johnston was one of the most enthusiastic diggers; he later left a detailed report. *"As the whole process was novel, one in all probability never attempted before, I will describe it for the benefit of the readers.*

"Our dirt car was a wooden spittoon, with holes through each end, and when he had loosened enough earth to fill it, he gave a signal to the one at the mouth of the tunnel by jerking the rope, thus it was kept traveling backward and forward.

"After penetrating some distance the task became very painful; it was impossible to breath the air of the tunnel for many minutes together; the miner, however, would dig as long as his strength would allow, or till his candle was extinguished by the foul air; he would then make his way out, and another would take his place—a place narrow, dark, and damp, and more like a grave than any place can be short of a man's last narrow home."

Many of the Libby diggers made the comparison between their tunnel and a tomb. They could never avoid thoughts of being buried, smothered, and forgotten. But conditions upstairs were so bad they were ready to take the chance.

Acts of Cool Daring

OBSESSION IS THE MODERN TERM, BUT IN THE NINETEENTH CENTURY people preferred "monomania" to describe fixation on a single thing. In Libby, the inmates who fixated on escape were called "monomaniacs." They chewed on every scheme, whether possible or impossible, and chewed on it some more.

During Libby's time as a prison, a few stalwart individuals did succeed in getting out. The majority were recaptured and sent to the dungeons, but those who succeeded were an inspiration to everyone there.

Most ended up like the Connecticut officer who asked Col. McCreery about coming along on his escape scheme. The officer had approached a guard who promised to let him out of Libby for the price of three silver watches.

Col. McCreery, the Michigan officer who had been severely wounded at Chickamauga, was excited until he personally met the Rebel guard who would be accepting the bribe. *"I was not long in making up my mind that this sentinel was not the man into whose hands I would be willing to trust my life. But [the Connecticut officer] seemed to have the greatest confidence in him."*

McCreery refused to go along. The other officer *"invited me to be at the window with him to see him off. Three officers had loosened two of the iron bars so he could squeeze through. He had made a rope out of his blanket which was fastened under his arms. We bade him 'good-bye', and he was lowered one story to the pavement beneath."*

His fellow officers listened from above as he handed over the three watches. Immediately they heard the sentinel yell: *"You d——d Yankee scoundrel, I will give you just two minutes to get back into the prison."*

"There was no mistaking the situation. The rope was lowered, the Colonel again tied it around his body and was drawn up into the prison, greatly to the amusement of the guard." His watches were lost, but at least he didn't end up in the dungeon.

According to Lt. Earle, *"considerable amusement was caused by this unfortunate adventure,"* such that at the next evening's "catechism," public resolutions were passed that included the following provision: *"'Resolved, that although the officers have lowered themselves in the sight of their fellow officers, yet their earnest endeavors under embarrassing circumstances, to rise to their former position, have again placed them on an equal footing with us all.'*

"The resolutions were greeted with immense applause, immediately adopted, and after a few patriotic songs, we quieted for the night."

One of the most celebrated escapades was the ingenious disappearance of Maj. Halstead. This major had trusted in Col. McCreery when both were confined to the prison hospital: *"Before the war he was a tailor in New York. He visited my cot frequently. One day he became very confidential and informed me that he was to start for home the next night.*

*"I inquired if he had been exchanged. He replied, 'It is a special exchange. The surgeon and I are great friends. Indeed, he has been very kind to me but how can I repay him? I said to him a few days ago, "Doctor, I am a first class tailor. If you will bring me a good piece of Confederate grey cloth, together with the trimmings, soldier straps, etc., I will gladly cut, fit, and make the suit with my own hands." I took his measure and have made the finest Confederate major's uniform you ever saw, **to fit my own dear self**. I start for home to-morrow night to see my wife and babies.'"* (author's emphasis)

The major's charade amused every POW in Libby. Most retold the story in their memoirs, among them an admiring Lt. Col. Cavada: *"He coolly walked out of the hospital accompanied by another Federal 'patient' also disguised, and not only walked out of the door, but all the way down the Peninsula into the Federal lines. He had the admirable impudence to adopt his victim's title as well as his coat, and assuming considerable airs, gave himself out as a Confederate surgeon on duty in Richmond hospitals!"*

"The next morning at roll call the Major was missing, and the surgeon was mourning the loss of his new uniform and cursing the 'd——d Yankees,'" McCreery wrote. *"A few days afterward, I received a letter postmarked New York, containing this announcement: 'The tailor is himself again.'"*

A few POWs decided to be ready to walk out of Libby whenever a chance presented itself. These men traded for civilian clothes, then filled their pockets with food and waited for an opportunity.

During the day, Libby could be quite permeable. Not only were guards constantly coming and going, but so were men working on the building. Even curious locals, if they asked the right guard, would be allowed to go inside and view the "caged Yankees."

At least one inmate grabbed up some tools and walked out with the other workers. Maj. Tower witnessed Lt. Kupp disguise himself by soiling his hands and face, putting an old shirt over his uniform, and taking a piece of iron bar in his hands. When the workmen left for dinner he quietly followed them to the street. There he hung back from the group, and daringly turned to approach the prison from the outside. To complete the charade, Kupp pretended to be a Rebel soldier who actually wanted to enter Libby. At the entrance he was confronted by the always-irascible Dick Turner:

"'Hello! What the devil do you want?'

"'Waal,' drawled Kupp, 'I got a furlough to come up to Richmond, so I thought I'd like to drop in and take a look at the Yanks, if you don't mind?'

"'But I do mind; get out of here, confound you, and go to the front, where you will see Yankees enough to scare you to death.'

"Kupp said, 'All right, kernel.'"

He crossed the street and looked at the prison, much to the astonishment of his friends watching from the upper windows. Then he tipped his hat to them and walked away. *"Kupp's escape ranks first in my memory of all the acts of cool daring witnessed during the war."*

The prisoners would do what they could to cover for the escapees and keep Little Ross from noticing for as long as possible. It did not seem difficult to fool him if only a single POW went missing; but then five prisoners escaped at once. *"They were ready for the opportunity precisely at the critical moment, and five of them coolly walked out of the prison one fine afternoon."*

The five missing men were detected by the counters, and when Turner was informed he launched a crackdown. All workers would carefully be watched, the guard was doubled, and visits to the prison were restricted to VIPs only.

But getting out of Libby was only the first difficult step. Escapees still had to reach Union lines, and most didn't make it. Of the five who walked out that day, four were soon recaptured and put in the dungeons. Then Lt. Kupp was caught and brought back, which thoroughly discouraged the Libby inmates. After getting thirty-six miles away, he had still failed to reach Union lines.

The prisoners' problem was that, even if they got out, it was still almost fifty miles east to the safety of the Union Army at Williamsburg. That country was a sparsely populated swamp—a flat land cut with hundreds of creeks and ponds. The area was slowly drained by the Chickahominy River, which also had a tendency to flood. A few plantations and small towns were scattered about, but much of the forested landscape was deserted and always had been, except for swamp animals.

Some Libby escapees headed north, toward the Union lines near Washington, D.C. This route was much more populated, which could be both good and bad, but the distance was double—at least 100 miles.

In whatever direction they headed, the miserable difficulty of escaping was compounded by wet cold in winter and stifling humidity in summer. They also had to contend with an intensely hostile population—Rebel patrols, bloodhounds, guards at all roads and bridges. It was a journey that only the most determined and lucky would survive.

Still, monomania reigned. *"A prisoner, if he deserve the name, is always more or less occupied with the idea of making his escape."* And some ingenious POWs pulled off singular "transfers" from Richmond. *"My resolution was fixed; I longed to be free again and to fill the saddle,"* wrote Col. John Bray, and his detailed account, published in an 1864 edition of *Harper's Magazine*, is one of the best by any POW:

"The first thing necessary was to possess myself of a Rebel uniform. So one day after we had received a batch of new clothing from our Government, I said banteringly to Ross, 'will you trade coats? Mine is bran-new, but I must have some money, so I'm on hand for a bargain.' Ross was an easy, good-natured

Hounds attacking.

fellow, and was particularly ragged, having scarcely a whole garment. He was only too anxious, and soon we struck a bargain, Ross agreeing to give me his coat and thirty dollars to boot.

"Some days after, upon pretense that I was again out of funds, I bantered Ross to trade pantaloons, offering mine, which were new, for his old ones and ten dollars. Making the exchange on the spot, I became, to all appearance, a rebel soldier having a suit of gray."

Bray determined to put his scheme into execution the next day. But suddenly it felt as if all exits were closely guarded. Now that he was trying to get by them, it seemed the sentinels *"stood at all the gates with vigilant eyes."* Days passed until finally, *"On Sunday morning, January 10* [1864] *I made my final attempt."*

Bray disguised his ragged Rebel uniform by wrapping himself in a blanket and joined a group of guards leaving the prison. He handed his blanket to a friend and followed behind as they passed. *"My wits did not desert me. With an air of unconcern, whistling the 'Bonnie Blue Flag,' I sauntered slowly toward the gate—paused a moment to laugh with the rest at some joke of one of the guard; then with deliberate pace, as if passing in and out had been so customary as to make any recognition of the sentinels unnecessary—passed out.*

"My heart throbbed painfully under my waistcoat. An age of feeling was crowded into that moment. But I passed out unchallenged. I was free; and my whole being was a-glow with that thought."

The January afternoon was bitterly cold and snow covered the ground; but Bray *"thought of nothing, cared for nothing but my escape."* By the end of his first day he had walked 21 miles and avoided detection by the Rebels. Exhausted beyond measure, he fell deeply asleep. Daylight awoke him but he couldn't move. He slowly realized he was frozen to the ground. *"I endeavored to rise, but for a time was unable. My feet were lumps of ice, my face smarted with pain, my hands were without feeling. I barely escaped freezing to death."*

With considerable effort he got to his feet and began walking—but he was lost, without food, and chilled to the bone. He still had days to go before reaching safety, but then *"a negro suddenly confronted me. Whence he came I knew not; he stood before me with a look of inquiry in his eyes. I remembered that I wore a Rebel uniform. But he was not to be deceived:*

"'Yer can't come dat game on dis chil',' he said, with a sparkle in his eye. 'You'se a Yankee prisoner escaped from Richmon'. But, Lord bless yer, massa, I won't tell on yer; I'se real glad yer's got away.'

"I saw in a moment this fellow could be trusted—I have never seen a negro yet, in this war, who could not be trusted by a Union soldier; and so I unbosomed myself to him at once.

"'Dis chil' glad to help yer,' he replied in a tone of real pleasure, and at once started leading me across the fields to the house of another negro. Here I was given something to eat, both the man and woman treating me with the

Passing the guard.

greatest kindness; and after a short rest I set out again, this time with my host as a guide, for the main road. Parting with my black friend, I pushed on. The road was thick with pickets and scouts, and I was obliged at almost every turn to dodge aside to avoid discovery.

"My adventures the day following were numerous, many perilous in the extreme, but by eleven o'clock that night I reached the goal of my wanderings."

After all his suffering, Bray worried he might be caught almost at the gates of the "promised land." Exploring with extreme caution, Bray tried to determine the best way to cross the lines and get into Williamsburg. One time, pickets challenged him from a distance but Bray could not figure out who they were, so he ran away into the darkness, always slipping closer to town. Finally, starving and shaking with cold, he decided he had to take his chances and approached the nearest home:

"Seeing a light in the windows, I cautiously crept up. I was raising my head to look in, when, suddenly a hand was laid heavily on my shoulder, and a loud voice exclaimed, 'Hello here!—who is this? A spy?'

"I started as if a ball had struck me. Was I again a prisoner? I answered at once, 'I'm a Union soldier escaped from Richmond.'

"That was enough. Before I knew it I was within the lighted room, which proved to be the head quarters of the post commandant; an armchair was placed before the fire; my shoes were drawn off, and I was as cozy as kindly hands could make me. Of course, the moment my story was told I became a hero."

Bray was aware he could have never made it without help from slaves. In his account "My Escape from Richmond," which was published while the war still raged, he concluded with this hope that he would soon be entering the Rebel capital again—this time as a liberator: *"When we march into Richmond I trust that there will be with us men of darker hue than ours, who, having fought their way from a prison-house worse than the Libby, will have won the right to rejoice in the triumph of the Stars and Stripes."*

Elizabeth Van Lew's secret group was also dependent on African American Virginians. Some were free but most were slaves. Many worked for Unionist owners who were also part of the Underground.

Spymaster Van Lew was experienced at exploiting the cracks in Southern society and security. Upper-class women lived on a social pedestal that placed them above common society and its profane problems. Women, for instance, were not required to take the loyalty oaths forced on any male who remained in Richmond. For any man who did not declare his fealty to the Confederacy, the consequences were severe; but women were never even asked. And though some officials might have suspected Miss Van Lew of not being totally loyal, they were bound by social convention to make no direct challenge to members of the upper class, much less enter their homes, without hard evidence.

The most important "crack on the Confederate system" that Van Lew found was the one concerning passes and personal movement. In Richmond, a capital city at war, all men had to carry passes but women did not. Since everything was in short supply, it was considered women's duty to scour the town in search of scarce food and household items, so they were seldom obstructed. Van Lew and her female compatriots were able to walk about town with almost complete freedom—while any man trying to do the same could expect to be stopped by authorities and asked to show a military pass or proof of employment. Since a strict military draft was in force, any white male who could not explain himself might be sent directly into the army, and any Black male could be forced to join a Confederate labor battalion.

But a Black man who had a pass from his owner could go almost anywhere. Since slavery was a revered institution, any slave with a pass was left alone. Van Lew and her cohorts made sure the slaves working with them always had the right papers. In many ways, this made the slaves more secure from police than free white men. Van Lew could only protect her servants if they were still, officially, her slaves.

Hundreds of teamster slaves moved the food and supplies that were essential to the Confederacy, and Richmond authorities paid them little notice. They were considered too dumb and lazy to cause any trouble, much less be part of an extensive spy network. And the slaves certainly encouraged this delusion, as slaves have done throughout history, by acting overly obsequious.

No one suspected the wagons they were driving might be hiding escaped Blacks or Yankee prisoners. Or that the reason Van Lew's slaves wore heavy brogans was that they were hiding messages inside them. Each teamster had two pairs of these boots, so they could wear one pair when they left the city and another when they returned.

Two of Van Lew's Black operatives crossed in and out of Richmond every day, ostensibly to collect produce from a farm she owned outside the city limits. The Rebel guards would see the same old men repeatedly pass—probably shuffling and mumbling in slave dialect, eyes toward the ground. Or maybe the Black men took the smiling approach and acted friendly—all while transporting valuable information, gleaned from inside the Confederate capital.

History does not record the exact arrangement Van Lew made with her slaves. Perhaps she had secretly freed them at the start of the war, but such freedom would have only been symbolic in the Confederate States of America. In Virginia, any manumitted slave had to leave the state immediately. It is likely Van Lew's slaves didn't want to abandon every person they'd ever known for an uncertain future as "contraband." It is not hard to imagine that Van Lew's "servants," as she called them, decided to stay on and fight the fight.

What we do know is that, after the war, most of them decided to live out their lives in Richmond with Van Lew; and we may assume she continued to run a progressive and supportive household. It can't be a coincidence that her cook's daughter, Maggie Lena Walker, who grew up underfoot, later became the first African American, and the first woman of any race, to form and run a successful bank.

Elizabeth reflected on her legacy in her diary: *"If I am entitled to the name of 'Spy' because I was in the secret service, I accept it willingly. For my loyalty to my country I have two beautiful names—here I am called, 'Traitor,' farther North a 'spy'—instead of the honored name of 'Faithful.'"*

She had a personal, visceral hatred of the South's "peculiar institution," describing herself as *"this heavy heart pulsing and looking upon slavery as it really is . . . No pen, no book, no time can do justice to the wrongs it honors."*

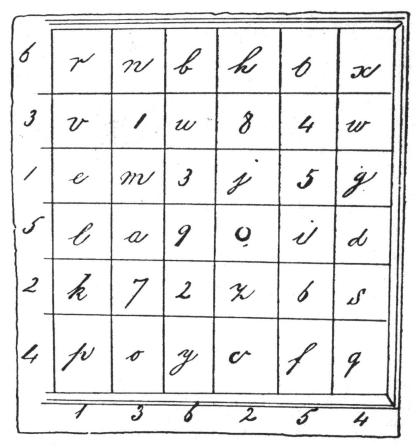

Copy of cipher code that was found among Elizabeth Van Lew's papers.

After Lincoln's Emancipation Proclamation, which went into effect on January 1, 1863, it was clear that a Union victory meant freedom for every slave in the Confederacy. Van Lew considered slavery to be the *"sole cause"* of the war: *"In this belief my head and heart agree. Slave power is arrogant—is cruel—is despotic—not only over the slave but over the community, the State."*

Now these diverse members of the Union Underground, white and Black, were risking their lives together. One betrayal and they'd all be swinging from the nearest tree. *"We consult with our negroes, we mingle our hopes, our fears, our prayers. When I open my eyes in the morning, I say to the servant, 'What news, Mary?' and my caterer never fails! Most generally our reliable news is gathered from negroes, and they certainly show wisdom, discretion, and prudence which is wonderful."*

Miss Van Lew folded into her network many of the brave people who had run the Underground Railroad before the war. The loose organization that called itself the "Railroad" continued to help slaves, their job made easier by the fact that after 1862 they only had to smuggle escapees as far north as Maryland, no longer all the way to Canada. The experience of these Southern abolitionists and slaves would have been invaluable to the Union Underground.

The parallels with Yankee prisoners were obvious. Van Lew wrote about how the South treated POWs just as it treated slaves; it hunted them down using the techniques perfected by slave catchers. Bloodhounds were the most feared because they could be so precise and inexhaustible. Southerners had been training them for three hundred years to find and attack runaway humans.

"The guards were always ready to mount their horses and scrub the country to recapture fugitives. They kept bloodhounds to hunt us," remembered Chaplain McCabe. One day he asked an old slave working in the prison how best to deal with these relentless dogs, and the man had advice based on hard experience: *"I'll fotch you a little cayenne peppah, and when you gits out a ways put a little pile of peppah in yo' tracks. Along comes dat dog, sniff! sniff! and when he sniffs dat peppah, for a few weeks he's gwine to fergit all about dis war."*

Four escapees from a Richmond prison reported to the *New York Herald* in August 1862 that they *"visited a house occupied by a lady of the most thoroughgoing Union sentiments, who furnished us with food and clothing. We also met other Union friends here, who did everything in their power to aid our escape."*

Throughout the war, Van Lew continued to hide fugitives in her own home. Her young niece once saw Elizabeth going upstairs with a plate of food and decided to follow. She observed her aunt moving a box that covered the door to an attic room where a man was hiding. Later the niece went back and talked to the man in the secret room. He warned her: *"If your aunt had caught you what a spanking you would have got."*

Due to Van Lew's postwar destruction of her own legacy, the full truth will never be known. But at least one more extraordinary tale remains to be told about the extent and effectiveness of her spy network. As related by Col. D. B. Parker, who served under Gen. Grant, it is one of those stories that is hard to improve upon.

After the war, Col. Parker met former Libby inmate Capt. William Lounsbury who spoke to him about Little Ross. According to Parker: *"Lounsbury said that one afternoon Ross came into the prison as usual to call the roll, cursing the d——— Yankees, and as he passed him said in a low tone, 'Be in my office at 9:30 tonight.' To his surprise he had no difficulty in getting to the office past several guards. Once there he found Ross, who gruffly said, 'See here, I have concluded to try see if you can do cooking. Go in there and look around see what you can find.'*

"Lounsbury went into a back room where he found a complete Confederate uniform hanging over a chair. He took in the situation instantly, donned the uniform speedily and walked back into the office, which he found vacant, and stepped out into the street. The guard did not stop him, and he had walked only a few steps from the door when a black man accosted him and asked if he desired to find a way to Miss Van Lew's house. He was guided to her residence on church hill, where he was secreted until an opportunity was found to get him out of Richmond. He got off safely and came into our lines.

"Miss Van Lew kept two or three bright, sharp colored men on the watch near Libby prison, who were always ready to conduct an escaped prisoner to a place of safety."

Erasmus "Little" Ross had been part of Elizabeth Van Lew's spy network from the very beginning. He played his character so well that the *Libby Chronicle* called him *"the hateful prison clerk."* The prisoners did not realize he was often permitting them to mess up the count. Little Ross clearly knew that the best way he could secretly help an escapee was to tie up the count for hours—since the authorities couldn't start searching for a man they didn't know was missing. Giving the uniform to Lounsbury, then instantly sending him on his way, insured the man could not betray Ross to the Libby inmates. It's probable he helped others escape in this manner. Since Bray's lively account of "trading" clothes with Ross was published during the war, it's possible that Bray was making up a cover story. Maybe Ross just handed him the uniform and a way out, as he did with Lounsbury.

Ross was in a position, through his job of visiting every prison in the city, to gather many types of valuable information. The upper windows offered good views of the city in all four directions, and Confederate troops regularly passed through the Rebel capital on railroad and foot. Plenty could be learned about conditions in the Confederacy and its capital from seemingly innocent conversations with the guards.

At the end of the war, when Richmond fell and the city was filled with men who had spent time in Libby, Little Ross took refuge in Van Lew's house because he was afraid of retaliation. Like Van Lew, he stayed on in Richmond after the end of the war and did his best to conceal his past as a secret Unionist.

Ross is one of many subjects on which history comes up short. He died just five years after the war, in Richmond's Spotswood Hotel fire. We'll never know the extent of his legacy—how many Lounsbury-type escapes he produced or the extent to which he cooperated in derailing the prisoner counts.

By New Year's Day 1864, Elizabeth Van Lew had done what she could to prepare for the escape of Streight and the other tunnelers. Then she awaited developments. It was all up to Rose and his men now.

Chapter Thirteen

Exertions Almost Superhuman

Les Misérables was a particularly popular book in Libby Prison. The massive novel was published in English in 1862 and instantly became a sensation on both sides of the Atlantic. POWs wrote home to their families about sending them a copy. Of course all books in Libby were valued, but this novel was especially prized:

"The owner of a book in Libby was the object of immeasurable envy, and I remember on one occasion seeing an officer with Hugo's <u>Les Miserables</u>,*"* wrote Lt. Glazier after the war. *"I sought out the owner, who put my name down on his list of applicants to borrow it, and my turn to read it came six months afterwards."*

Apparently six months was not long to wait for the chance to dive into a 1,400-page novel of crime, revolution, war, love, death, and, above all, escape. The hero of the book, Jean Valjean, escapes from various schools and prisons at least six times. This often plunges him into the worst environments, such as the extensive sewers of Paris, but Valjean is always ready for another attempt: *"His old science of escape rose to his brain like a flash."* Rose's men couldn't miss the parallels to their own failed attempts to enter the sewer system of Richmond.

At the very least, the famous book delivered hope for success. The hero ultimately survives and begins a new life, but of course the men in Libby were dealing with a reality at least as harsh as anything Jean Valjean ever encounters.

They were putting all their hopes on a tunnel so tiny they would have to slither through it—without even the room to crawl. The passage was so narrow a man could not turn around but must instead back out inch by inch. Most accounts claimed that the tunnel entrance was only two feet wide by eighteen inches tall, a mind-boggling dimension that takes one beyond claustrophobia. The shoulders of most men would barely leave one inch to spare on either side. To get out of Libby, each POW would have to insert himself into this tight-fitting hole and squirm through 60 feet of it—in total darkness.

The digging went on slowly but surely during January and early February 1864. Maj. Tower described the conditions for diggers: *"One would lie on his back, draw the spittoon to his chest by means of a string, loosen the dirt behind his head with an old chisel, fill the box with his hands and pull the string, when the spittoon full of dirt would be drawn out by a comrade and replaced with an empty one. As we had no means of propping the tunnel, the sensation of being buried alive was fearful and men could only work for periods of time."*

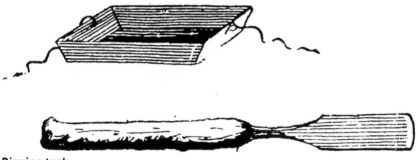

Digging tools.

Rose was the type of commander who led by example. *"We made fairly rapid progress,"* he recorded. *"One night I dug six feet with my own hands. My whole party was divided into reliefs of five men each, so that the same men went down to work every third night."*

The work was so grueling, each crew needed two days to recover after a night in Rat Hell. Col. Rose continued to be the indefatigable cheerleader, assuring the men that the sand through which they were digging was compacted enough to ensure *"no danger of caving in,"* even if the diggers themselves weren't fully convinced.

Lt. Moran wrote a number of articles about his experiences in Libby, and he was a natural admirer of Rose. *"An inexorable rule of the leader was that when not actually on duty himself, every incident, however trifling, should be fully reported to him, a command never known to be violated by his faithful comrades, who recognized in this silent man the commander for the hour and ordeal."*

Every evening for two months the crews slipped away around 10 p.m., after the nightly "catechism" chaos, and worked until they heard the sentinels call out the time at 4 a.m. If Rose felt it was safe, *"sometimes the whole four would remain down and work all day, in which case the guard in the cooking room would draw up the ladder, rebuild the wall, and go to bed, but as soon as light he would go to the window and watch all day. This was considered extremely hazardous, however, and was not often done."*

Capt. Johnston wrote about his feelings during these long periods of dreary and dangerous digging. *"This labor was not only extremely difficult in itself, but in addition was the constant anxiety lest the attempt we were making should be discovered. Moreover, the fact that all previous attempts had failed was calculated to fill our mind with fears.*

Tunnel entrance.

"On the other hand, the hard fare and confinement of our prison, the monotony of which had become unendurable, and the possibility of escape at last roused us up to exertions almost superhuman. Under any other circumstances the work would have been deemed impossible."

They were also trying to do their work as winter overtook the Rebel capital. Richmond was the northernmost city in the Confederacy and winters were inclement. Freezing breezes whipped through the prison's open windows as the men hunkered down inside. Everything in the space was hard and cold. Clothing was falling apart. Pairs of men often had to share a single blanket.

"Such hard frost, we are told, has not been experienced in Virginia for many years past. The face of the James [River] is nearly covered with ice, and deeply do we feel the cold wind whistling through the windows," wrote Hungarian colonel Szabad in his diary. Maj. Tower was from New England, but he had never suffered from the weather as he did in Libby: *"Winter was cold and cheerless without fires and with scanty clothing. Life was dreary indeed; we had long given up hope of exchange, but all willingly submitted to the decision made by our government, that no arrangement for a just and equable exchange of prisoners could be made."*

Maj. Byers's diary recorded the lonely worries shared by most of the POWs: *"No mail and not a word from home. Have they forgotten us?"*

A universal sentiment was expressed by Col. Roach. *"Many nights when suffering with hunger and cold, I have laid down in my place on the floor and devoutly prayed that I might remain in the unconsciousness of sleep until the day of deliverance from my wretched condition."*

The Rebels' only plan for the winter was to tell the Libby prisoners to write home and request warm clothing and blankets. Though suspicious of Confederate intentions, POWs were cheered when the first shipments to arrive were distributed in the prison. The men then collected their worn and threadbare old uniforms so that by sewing they could be *"manufactured into curtains and hung in the windows; they keep out all of the light and some of the cold air, but the darkness even of a dungeon was preferable to the suffering we would otherwise have to endure from the cold."*

A little of the holiday spirit had seemed to infect their captors, who suddenly allowed the POWs to receive their food boxes. This made quite a big, if only temporary, difference in their physical condition and attitude. *"Christmas came and we had a grand ball in one of the lower rooms, were allowed to burn candles until midnight; we sang and danced until then. Soon after lying down some one started singing 'Home, Sweet Home,' and soon, I do not think, there was a man but that joined in singing the grand old tune, and grand sad it must have sounded."*

Most men focused on the Christmases of their memories, their minds obsessed with thoughts of home and hearth. *"I am thinking of happy firesides today in the far-off North,"* recorded Maj. Byers, who always wrote in the present tense. *"In my imagination I see the over-joyed faces; the parties; the balls; the laughing girls and boys who wish that 'Christmas might last all the year.'"*

But the Yuletide cheer in Libby was short-lived. The very next day, men were witnesses to a wretched drama that played out in full view of the prison windows, one block away. *"A company of little boys were at play on the ice which covered the canal. All at once they broke through, and cried for help. Several of our officers gave their word of honor not to attempt to escape if they might be permitted to rescue the little fellows, but they were not allowed to do so, and before help could arrive from outside one or two had been drowned."*

"It was a very sad affair," Capt. Lodge wrote in his diary.

Just a few days later came New Year's Eve. Capt. Glazier was an eyewitness to the exuberant stag dancing: *"Evening advances, and the dance ensues. For a time they seem to forget that they are enclosed within these inhospitable prison walls. The merriment and hilarity continue till the old year passes away. With significant beating of feet, it seems as if the very roof must give way before the accumulated volume of sound. All make a 'watch-night' out of it, for sleep is entirely out of the question."*

"Such a welcome to the New-Year never went up from a prison-house before. 'On with the dance; let joy be unconfined!' and again the old floor quakes with the tramping troopers, as they dash up and down the room, in waltz, polka, or quadrille."

When they woke the next day it was back to repellent reality—to long hours sitting in silent stupefaction, trying to forget the hunger and cold. Lt. Cavada wrote about contemplating the candle he had purchased for a dollar. *"To sit there staring at your one yellow Confederate candle, stuck*

Corn bread. Drawing by Lt. Col. Cavada.

in a cake of corn bread for a candle-stick, staring at it as though you were spec-
ulating on the frightful probability of having to devour it for your breakfast
to-morrow, tallow-drippings and all. Finally, you arrive at one conclusion,
which is, that if there be any one thing in this world more utterly unsatisfac-
tory than any other, it is to be a prisoner of war."

It was January 1864. Lt. Col. Cavada, Maj. Szabad, and most others
did not know the crews were already digging in the east cellar. Very few
beyond Rose's small circle did know—and it was quite an accomplishment to keep it hidden for so long in such a public place. Some others
might have suspected, but if so they kept it to themselves.

"The opening of the year 1864 was, in truth, not very bright. One week passed, two weeks passed, and no prisoners for exchange, no flag of truce boat, no mail, nothing from the North!—not even a rumor," recorded Szabad. A shipment of boxes finally arrived by truce boat, *"but the authorities, in consideration of something we did not know, again put an embargo on the boxes, and the much-coveted articles of food remained guarded in the storehouse."*

At the same time, the rations fed to Libby inmates were actually cut back. For ten days in January only rice and corn bread were issued, and *"the dry crusts of wheat bread, which lay scattered in the rooms, the remains of half rotten potatoes and cabbage, the dregs of coffee and tea, all had long since been consumed.*

"Our boxes lying in the storehouse near us would have banished hunger in a few minutes. Not willing, or as they said, 'not able' to give us necessary food, they at the same time stubbornly refused to permit us to eat our own!"

The Rebels argued that they had no more food to give. The Confederacy was dealing with any number of shortages. In the middle of the month they passed a new military draft law, extending it to cover all males from ages 18 to 45. The only exception was for those wealthy enough to own 20 slaves or more. Soon the draft would be further expanded to include those as young as 17 and as old as 50.

"An occasional prisoner gives up to grim despair; he grows melancholy, weak, and careless; finally, sickens and dies. His remains are taken out and buried, we know not how or where—we never being allowed to assist at the funeral of any one."

The prison did have a one-way station on the route to death and a shallow grave. It was the room the Rebels called the hospital—a room in which precious little aid, medicine, or even comfort was to be had.

CHAPTER FOURTEEN

The Hospital

"'FALL IN, SICK, AND GO DOWN,' WAS THE FAMILIAR CRY, EVERY MORNING, OF THE rebel sergeant when he came in to gather up the sick and escort them to the hospital below." This daily ritual was more about getting the sick separated from the general prison population than it was about therapy or treatment.

To many POWs it was a "hospital" in name only. *"This is nothing but an immense charnel-house! We are constantly in the midst of the dead and dying. Nearly every day some of our comrades are borne away, coffinless and unshrouded, to their unmarked graves."*

The room that served as the hospital was on the first floor, directly above the Rat Hell basement where the tunnelers were working away. At least cots were there for the men to lie on; but little medicine or food, and the doctors were not exactly the best the Confederacy had to offer. As Lt. Glazier remembered: *"I appeared before the prison surgeon. With something like the air of a grocery-clerk came the rapid questions, 'Where are you sick? How long have you been so? Have you taken any medicine?' And without waiting for answers, he turned to the sergeant with, 'Take this man to the hospital,' and thus ended the examination."*

The hospital was one long room with 50 cots arranged in rows. Some men, such as Lt. Harvey Reid, felt that at least it was an improvement over the main part of Libby Prison. He was allowed to wash and was *"then given a clean shirt and put into cot no. 15, on the west side of the room. The bed was clean, but consisted of a straw mattress only, the straw in which was like the butter on our toast here—thinly laid on. There were four rows of these cots across the room, and each row had its nurse. If a patient wanted anything he would call out his number, which would bring the nurse belonging to that row to him."*

The so-called nurses were not trained medical assistants; they were Yankee soldiers who had deserted to the Confederacy. Suspicious of their motives and intentions, the Rebels didn't want these "traitors" in their own army, so most were assigned to support duties. These men had little motivation to be healers for the Yankees they had abandoned; according to Lt. Reid, with few exceptions they *"were perfect brutes: would do nothing except what they were absolutely compelled to do."*

Like everything else at Libby, the hospital was subject to constant changes. Doctors came and went; sometimes help was available and sometimes not. Lt. Roach observed, *"Rebel hospitals for prisoners were more suitable for horse stables than places for sick human beings. In the hospital connected to Libby Prison, there were some rudely constructed 'bunks,' not enough to accommodate more than half of the patients brought there for treatment. The others were placed in rows on the hard and dirty floor, sometimes without blankets, and frequently without any clothing except their shirts and drawers."*

Willard Glazier wrote evocatively about what he experienced as a patient. *"There was the ominous stillness, broken only by a choking-cough or labored groan; the chilling dread, as though one were in the immediate presence of death; and the almost frantic yearning—which one feels in the contemplation of suffering which he is powerless to alleviate. And worse than all, soon came that hardened feeling which a familiarity with such scenes produces.*

"Pneumonia is making serious work among the sick. Many, reduced to extreme weakness, are attacked with it, and cough their lives away. Scurvy, pneumonia, chronic diarrhea, and fever are the most prevalent diseases. The former of these, it is well known, originates from an exclusive diet of salt rations and cornbread. The hospital-surgeons appear to be gentlemen, and treat us with some consideration. They seem to make the best possible use of the means at their disposal, and even remonstrated with their authorities for with-holding those medicines and comforts without which a hospital is not a hospital."

Some of the doctors might have tried their best, but they could do little for men whose *"rations consist of one small slice of bread for breakfast, a table-spoonful of rice and a small piece of meat for dinner, and the breakfast repeated for supper."*

The city had numerous "hospitals" for the 12,000 Yankee prisoners in Richmond; all were inadequate. The one in Libby, since it was for officers, might well have been the best of them.

When imprisoned Union doctors were exchanged and sent home in 1863, they made an official report to Washington about conditions they had observed. They concluded that an average of 50 prisoners died every day in the Rebel capital—1,500 per month—due to *"insufficient food, clothing, and shelter, combined with that depression of spirits brought on by long confinement."*

In some months of the year, more soldiers would die in prisons than on battlefields. The miserable deaths of so many young men had become routine. *"The burial of the dead is a very business-like affair. As fast as men die they are carried out to the 'dead house' and piled up, much as bags of corn, until there are enough for a load, when the keeper calls out to the prison carter, 'A load of dead Yankees! Drive up your mule.' The carter then drives up, and takes in his load with as much unconcern as though he was drawing wood."*

Indeed, the hospital's death rate was so high that some POWs decided they'd take their chances upstairs. No matter how sick they became, many men were convinced that going down to the hospital would be the end of them. Junius Brown: *"The malignant, tenacious fever brought me to my rough boards and blanket, which served in lieu of a bed. I determined not to take any medicine and not to go to the hospital, preferring to remain in quarters of the Union officers. If I had had my wits about me, I should have known that they regarded my case as nearly hopeless."* Brown survived to record his memories three decades later.

Chaplain C. C. McCabe thought he could avoid the hospital by being positive about his situation. He struggled to be cheerful at all times. According to a fellow POW, *"After supper Chaplain McCabe will sing 'Rally Round the Flag' and Scottish ballads. He contributes, probably, more rays of hope and comfort to the despondent soul than any other man in Libby Prison."*

Knowing his family would have read the fearful exposés on conditions at Libby, McCabe sent upbeat letters. *"There is not a calmer, happier man in Virginia than I all the time. God is with me."* To his wife back in Ohio, he wrote: *"Don't believe anything you read in the papers about 'fearful diseases in Richmond.' From all I learn the city was never more healthful."*

But Chaplain McCabe had acquired a fever, and it was getting worse. In his letters home, he worked hard to disguise the facts. On September 6, 1863, he wrote: *"I am well, my health is wonderfully preserved."* On September 14, he admitted, *"I caught cold from going without a shirt while my only one should be washed. I shall be well soon, to-morrow. Be patient. I have told you the truth."*

He was lying. On September 20 McCabe further explained, *"My cold turned into a fever, which weakened me very much. I am entirely free from fever now, however."*

By October 3, the chaplain's declining condition had him fighting for his life. Too weak to write anything, he dictated a letter that was as positive as ever. *"I am still very weak but my fever is almost entirely departed. Whatever you do, don't try to come here. I have every attention paid to me that is necessary to my comfort. I think myself that I am getting better."* It is not known whether his wife was able to read between the lines.

Chaplain McCabe was developing typhoid fever and the Rebel authorities had ordered him down to the hospital, where he would remain for six weeks.

"I went down to the gates of death," wrote Chaplain McCabe. *"One day I awakened to consciousness and they* [the doctors] *were holding a consultation about me. I knew by their faces they thought I could not get well."*

But C. C. McCabe was in luck. A good friend, Col. William Powell, was permitted to sit up with the chaplain and nurse him personally—a luxury available to few others. Powell found the reverend raging with fever and infested with biting greybacks. *"He took out his little pocket scissors and cut off my long beard and unkempt hair. He told my wife that the condition in which he found me as he turned back the soiled blanket and saw me lying covered with vermin was a sight he could not endure."* Col. Powell carefully picked the greybacks from his body and obtained some insecticide from the doctors. Then he lived beside the chaplain for weeks, staying with him, sleeping in the hospital, helping in any way he could.

Chaplain McCabe began to improve slowly, and claimed he was finally cured upon hearing from a Methodist conference. *"Two hundred and fifty preachers got down on their knees and asked for my release. I was used to suffering but that tender letter broke me down. The tears rolled down my cheeks. I began to sing. I broke out in perspiration and the tide was turned."*

Soon afterward, one of the rare prisoner exchanges sent all chaplains back to the North and South. McCabe was determined not to be left behind; he had himself carried in a litter to the truce boat. *"They laid me down on the deck of the vessel under the flag that was floating above me. A Union soldier called out, 'Hello, don't you want something to eat?' Then he put a tin plate down on my breast and on it was a piece of beefsteak and a baked potato. Friends, I have seen Niagara, I have walked Yosemite Valley, but I never saw anything that moved my soul like that beefsteak and baked potato!"*

Chaplain C. C. McCabe had survived with his faith and positive nature intact. He would spend the rest of his life traveling America and delivering his upbeat lecture, "The Bright Side of Life in Libby." He is credited with raising hundreds of thousands of dollars for Methodist and other charitable causes. Libby had tried to kill him; instead it made him famous.

CHAPTER FIFTEEN

Trapped in Rat Hell

JANUARY 1864 BROUGHT A FAMOUS VISITOR TO LIBBY PRISON, IN A social call that would be both odd and ironic. Confederate general John Hunt Morgan had just escaped from a Yankee prison in spectacular fashion and was being feted throughout the South. Dinners were held in his honor. Confederate women lined up to kiss his hand. When he got to Richmond, the ex-POW added Libby Prison to his travel agenda.

Gen. Neal Dow, the Maine politician and prohibitionist imprisoned at Libby, wrote in his diary for January 10: *"Yesterday afternoon had a call from General Morgan and his staff. He is a fine looking man, was gentleman-like every way, and very kind and courteous."*

Gen. Morgan was flamboyant, a beau sabreur, the hard-riding embodiment of the Rebel hero. He was handsome and dashing; his cavalry raids were lionized and legendary. When he married his Southern belle in 1862, the ceremony was attended by Confederate President Jefferson Davis and officiated by Leonidas Polk, a leading Southern personality who had relinquished his bishop's chair to become a major general in the Rebel army.

But on a cavalry dash across Ohio, Morgan reached too far. He was forced to surrender after superior Union forces ran him down near Steubenville. The Yankees were so angry about the destruction he had caused that Morgan and his top officers were treated as common criminals. They were separated from their men, their heads shaven and their uniforms replaced with striped prison garb. Finally they were marched into the formidable Ohio State Penitentiary, an ancient stone structure designed to foil any escape. But Morgan and five others dug their way out and successfully made it back to the South.

"I witnessed his introduction to General Neal Dow," wrote young Lt. Earle about Morgan's short talk with the Maine officer, *"and as the conversation between these two gentlemen was sarcastic, I note two sentences. 'General Dow,' said General Morgan, 'I am very happy to see you here; or rather, as you are here, I am happy to see you looking so well.' General Dow immediately replied, 'General Morgan, I congratulate you on your escape, although I can not say I am glad you did escape, but since you did, I am happy to see you here.'"*

Morgan was accompanied by an entourage that included his brother-in-law, Gen. A. P. Hill—one of Lee's principal commanders—and the mayor of Richmond. Amidst the boredom of Libby life, this was a big event and many wrote down their impressions of the famous raider. *"Morgan is a fine looking man, large, with dark moustache and imperial florid complexion. His eyes are small and red from the effect of recent drink, but sharp and searching,"* recorded Capt. Lodge.

Libby POW Lt. Wells had been part of Morgan's capture the year before. *"I was a little apprehensive he might, on discovering me as one of his captors, be pleased to see me placed in like embarrassing circumstances."* Wells decided to observe the visit from a safe distance.

Morgan was brought before the infamous Col. Streight as part of his tour, but we have no record of the conversation between them. That's unfortunate, because the two were living military careers that were strangely parallel.

Both Morgan and Streight had led an invading cavalry column deep into enemy territory. Both raiders were overextended, run down, and captured along with most of their command.

Because they had burned so much valuable property, both Morgan and Streight were separated from their men and threatened with punitive measures. The Rebels said they were going to put Streight on trial for recruiting slaves, while Northern authorities decided to send Morgan and his top officers to the penitentiary.

That wasn't the end of their synchronicity. In the Ohio pen, Morgan's top aide, Tom Hines, read *Les Misérables* in the original French—and determined that he and his superior officer should make an epic escape

General John Hunt Morgan.

like those depicted in Hugo's novel. They tunneled out of their cells, climbed an outside wall with the help of a rope, and caught night trains out of the area before their absence was noticed.

Now, less than six weeks after his escape, Morgan was visiting the prison that held Col. Streight. The Rebel general probably wanted to compare the penal systems for himself, and conditions at Libby did improve slightly after the visit. But the ironic thing was that Morgan did not know he was standing just two stories above the tunnel that would soon become Streight's conduit to freedom. Morgan's escape had been the most spectacular of the war. The Libby breakout would soon upstage it.

On the very day Gen. Morgan and his entourage toured Libby, down in the east cellar the POWs were digging away. Rose and his crews drew inspiration from Morgan, in view of what the Rebel cavalryman had accomplished. Rose's men, for their part, were in serious need of encouragement; the work was becoming much harder as the tunnel neared its goal.

By the end of January 1864, the Libby escape tunnel was halfway complete.

"If you would know what it is like to be in hell, just try, even for a short time, working in a tunnel, where you are forty or fifty feet in the ground, lying flat, the hole just barely large enough to admit the body, and with treacherous sand pockets behind and above you and foul air to breathe. Oh, horror of horrors! If a cave-in should occur you would be buried alive and no help for it."

Even though he knew it was hazardous, Rose continued to experiment with leaving diggers in the east cellar during daytime. The men were stuck there until the end of their shift, since the fireplace entrance had to be bricked up during daylight. It was only open for passage late at night, when a full crew of five would be working.

This daytime labor was making the tunneling go faster, but it also brought more risk. In his usual self-effacing manner, Rose noted: *"We proceeded in this manner for some time, when an event occurred which effectually put a stop to our work in the daytime, and which greatly embarrassed all our operations."*

The problem began with Little Ross and his incessant prisoner counts. None of the POWs realized Ross was working with the Union Underground, so they felt they were "tricking" an enemy officer, for entertainment as well as diversion. *"Other prisoners used to see us doing this thing, and thought we were doing it for fun—devilment they called it; and they got to doing the same thing—for devilment sure enough,"* as Rose recalled.

"Confined as we were, no wonder that we should seek to break the dull monotony of this irksome prison by what we chose to call Yankee fun; we determined to have some fun by confounding the prison clerk in his roll count," wrote Capt. Caldwell.

Lt. Lodge recorded one of these pranks in his prison diary: *"Sunday, January 31, 1864. The day is damp and gloomy outside, but full of fun in Libby. The clerk Ross, after all his labor yesterday, called the roll in the usual way just at dark and found 28 more men in the building than should be. In the height of vexation he exclaimed, 'what can one head do against a thousand, and they all Yankees.' The poor little soul was in great tribulation."*

The prisoners had carefully cut small, hidden doors into the big doors that separated the rooms. Once the count was underway, it was a simple matter to slip a few men from one room into another. Occasionally a guard would discover one of these little trap doors and seal it shut, but as tunnel conspirator Capt. Johnston explained: *"The door had not been nailed up half an hour before some quick-witted fellow sawed the door completely in two, extracted the nails, placed some benches near to conceal the crack, and we were thus able to pass in and out at pleasure."*

Quite often, Little Ross would give up and merely average a total count. His justification was that things were fine as long as his counts showed extra prisoners instead of fewer. *"Two days have now been spent in vain endeavors to find out how many prisoners they have here; they seem to have given up in despair. It is great sport for us to outwit them."*

With the counts never seeming to match, Col. Rose and his crews began to relax. *"The consequence was that Ross could not make the same count two days alike, and towards the last we did not take the trouble to account for our men at all, Ross seemed so careless about it."*

The POWs took all credit for confounding Ross, not realizing he was secretly complicit. And like any gang of young, bored, boisterous officers, they began to push their luck. The German captain Domschcke reported what happened next to Little Ross.

"One day, after failing again and again of an accurate total, he shouted in futility: 'More are here than are here!' Again he complained, 'I am too few for so many Yankees.' Then he counted 143 more than were there. Discovering the absurd sum, he slammed his book shut and marched away double-quick."

The prisoners had finally gone too far. Little Ross couldn't keep his counting troubles hidden anymore and a serious crackdown was ordered. The next day, Ross surprised the POWs by entering the prison with twice the usual number of guards. They forced all the prisoners into rooms at the eastern end of Libby and laboriously named and counted them out one by one. The extra guards insured no one could sneak off and be recounted.

Two men were working in Rat Hell and the other prisoners had no way to cover for them. *"On the day that the rebels adopted this plan, Johnston and McDonald were down below at the tunnel. Dick Turner was calling the roll. Everything went well until he called out I. N. Johnston, I. N. Johnston, I. N. Johnston; but nobody answered.*

"The next name was then called, answered, and the man passed out, and so on, until the name of B. B. McDonald was called, when the same result followed as in the case of I. N. Johnston. Turner then went through the rooms calling the names of the missing prisoners for some time, but of course he could not find the absentees."

Both guards and prisoners were startled by the sudden disappearance of these two officers. *"A thousand tongues were now busy with the names of the men and their singular disappearance. The garrulous busybodies"*—other Union prisoners not aware of the escape plot—*"told Confederate officials that they had certainly slept near Johnston the night before. Lt. Fislar"*—one of the working party—*"boldly declared this a case of mistaken identity, and confidently expressed his belief that Johnston had escaped. To this he added that Johnston had not been in his sleeping place for a good many nights. The busybodies, who had indeed told the truth, looked at the speaker in speechless amazement. But other conspirators took Fislar's bold cue and stoutly corroborated him."*

That night, when the bricks were removed to open the fireplace passageway, the two men below were told the bad news by Col. Rose. *"They asked my advice as to what they had better do. There were only two plans. One was to face the music and tell the prison officials the most ingenious story they could invent. The other was to remain concealed every day down below."*

McDonald, on contemplating the consequences, chose to return to the prison and try to talk his way out of it. But Johnston opted to remain below in Rat Hell, knowing this meant he'd be confined there until the tunnel was completed. *"To remain in this cold, dark, and loathsome place was most revolting, but the fear of being put in the dungeon if I returned induced me to stay."*

McDonald went upstairs and rejoined the prison population, knowing he would soon be called to account by Turner. He had a firm explanation ready when the interrogation came.

"'Major Turner, believing that honesty is the best of policy, Sir, I have made up my mind to tell you the whole truth of the matter, and whatever you choose to put upon me I will endeavor to bear with the fortitude of a good soldier.'

"'Very well,' said Turner, 'let me hear the whole thing just as it is,'" recorded Capt. Caldwell.

Maj. McDonald then proceeded to deliver his carefully prepared lie. He revealed to Turner that the prisoners had cut small doors in the dividing partitions between rooms, then claimed he had used them to pass through in hopes of visiting a friend. When roll call had been announced, he was in the wrong room and therefore decided to hide.

"'But,' says Turner, 'Sir, we hunted for you yesterday in every room and you were not to be found.'

"'True,'" replied Maj. McDonald, who then explained that he had climbed up on a joist in the ceiling and hidden there. It wasn't much of an excuse, but to everyone's surprise Turner accepted it, handing down his judgment that *"An open confession is good for the soul. And as you have been so honest as to confess, although I had premeditated a punishment for you, I now heartily cancel the whole thing, and you can return to your quarters."*

As simple as that, the whole affair was over for McDonald. Not so for Johnston, who now was trapped by choice. One night some of Rose's men allowed him to sneak upstairs and sleep with the other POWs, but he was almost spotted. It was decided Johnston could not leave Rat Hell again. Because of his disfigurement from being shot through the face at

Fighting the rats.

Shiloh, Johnston knew he could not successfully hide among the anonymous mass of POWs.

A rumor was allowed to circulate that Johnston had bribed a guard and was long gone from Libby. According to his own memoir, *"This story was taken up and stoutly confirmed by all who knew where I was, though a few still contended that I must be in the prison still. I then resolved to make my appearance at my quarters no more. I never saw my room again."*

"The cellar was now my home. I was fed by my companions, who nightly brought me down a portion of their own scanty fare. I had plenty of company—little of it, however, agreeable, as it consisted of rebels, rats, and other vermin. With the former I had no communication; whenever they appeared I leaped quickly into a hole I had prepared in the straw, and pulled the hole in after me, by drawing the straw so thickly that I could scarcely breathe."

Johnston said that the rats left him alone; and that their screeching always helped alert him to guards entering their domain. But the greybacks continued to be an extreme nuisance, biting him constantly during the days he waited for the tunnel to be completed.

It was early February, and the diggers were close to their goal. Or so they believed.

CHAPTER SIXTEEN

Big Mistake

ON FEBRUARY 6, A LARGE PARTY OF LIBBY GUARDS ENTERED THE CEL-
lar room known as Rat Hell. Only Capt. Johnston was there, and he
hurriedly hid among the straw. From his place of concealment, he noticed
that the Rebels seemed to be searching for something. They poked
around the straw and even passed directly in front of the tunnel entrance.

This news was excitedly sent on to Col. Rose. As usual he made a
sober assessment. The Rebels must be investigating suspicions, not facts.
If they knew about the tunnel, they had only to stake out the room and
collar anyone who entered.

Still, the heightened activity of the Rebels made everyone nervous.
Col. Rose and his men knew the tunnel was close to completion, but the
key question was: How close? Where were they in relation to their goal
of reaching the small, fenced-in area across the street from Libby?

It was easy to guess at the distance, but hard to calculate with real
precision. Their tunnel was eight feet deep; they needed to know exactly
when to stop digging forward and start up to the surface. The whole
escape depended on getting this right.

Discussion was intense. The POWs decided that they needed to have
one of their men pace the distance above the tunnel. Capt. Johnston, the
man trapped down in Rat Hell, described how the plan played out: *"Captain Gallagher had obtained permission to go to a building across the street,
where the boxes sent from the North were stored, to obtain some perishable
items. He measured the distance by stepping it both ways and came to the conclusion that fifty-two or three feet would bring us to the shed. On measuring*

the tunnel it was found to be fifty-three feet long, and we fondly hoped that our labors were ended."

Col. Rose disagreed with their calculations. "*Some of the workmen got it into their heads that we had reached the desired point. I tried to convince them of the absurdity of the notion. They, however, insisted upon it.*"

The inexactness of the methods they had to use left plenty of room for disagreement. As Rose noted: "*To ascertain the space we had to pass under was not an easy matter. We could only see this vacant lot from the windows of the third and fourth stories, and as these windows were closed with iron bars, we could not see the whole width of the street. It therefore looked much narrower than it really was. Yet, I could trace the beats of the sentinels from the corners of the yard opposite to near the corners of the prison building. I counted his paces as far as I could see him approach the prison building.*"

Col. Rose couldn't see the guard once he got close to the prison; but by pressing up close to the barred window he could hear the man's steps and use them to try extrapolating the whole distance.

"*By sitting in the window and making a great many careful observations, I came to the conclusion that one walked about ten feet more than I could see. I had no other instrument than the carpenter's square, but by measuring the height of the stories I soon determined the distance from the window to each of the sentinel's beats, and finally arrived at a pretty accurate estimate of the distance we had to dig, and I knew very well we had not dug far enough yet.*"

What happened next is a matter of sharp dispute. Rose claimed he told the diggers they were short and therefore should not start digging upward. Lt. Moran and others confirmed Rose's story. But diggers Randall and Johnston wrote later that Rose had directly ordered them to break through.

"*It began to be whispered that the tunnel was ready, except a small crust that was left purposely on the surface to prevent discovery. I began to prepare myself as well as I could with a map of the country through which we would pass, also with a little hard tack, etc.,*" remembered Capt. Caldwell, one of the original crew members.

In the middle of his preparations, Caldwell was abruptly needed to officiate at an evening candlelight service for two fellow officers who had recently died. "*At this I felt a little embarrassed, my mind being wholly absorbed in my contemplated escape, and after faltering for a time; not telling them why I did so, I complied with their request. You will naturally suppose that my mind was not the most clear and active, under the circumstances. The funeral services ended, I repaired to the place of egress, to hold myself in readiness to escape upon the opening of the crust that now concealed the tunnel."*

Johnston remembered: *"So confident were we that the work would be completed in an hour or two, that we had our rations already prepared in our haversacks, fully expecting to begin going out at nine o'clock."*

On the night of February 7, Capt. Randall, with Maj. McDonald fanning air to him, needed only a few hours to dig to the surface. As soon as he broke through, a flood of cool, fresh night air washed over him and through the whole tunnel. He had only made a tiny hole when a small rock fell with a thud. Randall finally could see out and realized they were a full five feet short of the fence!

Instead of being shielded by the fence, they had come up in front of it. They had put a hole in the edge of 21st Street, directly in view of the guards pacing their endless rounds.

"The guard heard me burst through the surface, and he left his beat and came and stood right astride my face, leaned on the fence and looked over into the inclosed yard. He thought the noise was over the fence. He stood there, I suppose, for about half a minute. It seemed like half a century to me. Great drops of cold sweat stood out on my forehead; I couldn't breathe; the events of my life seemed to flit before me, and I lived ages in a moment's time. But he did not see me, and went away."

Apparently, all the sentinels thought they were just seeing another rat hole—hardly an event worth noting, even in the middle of the guards' normally boring night.

Meanwhile, sitting in the pitch darkness of Rat Hell, Capt. Johnston and others waited for word from Randall that the escape route was finally open. *"There are times when minutes seem lengthened into hours—this was one of them. The suspense began to be painful; it seemed as if we could hear the beatings of each other's hearts. At length he emerged from the tunnel, and, in answer to the question 'What success?' in an excited tone he replied 'All is lost! I could see both guards; I have no doubt they discovered the tunnel, and perhaps will soon be here to arrest us.'*

"Imagine if you can, our feelings; our bright hopes so suddenly crushed. Great excitement prevailed, yet no one was able to suggest how to act in this unexpected emergency."

The men left the cellar as quickly as they could, leaving only Johnston, McDonald, and Hamilton. These men had decided they would all share the same fate, whatever happened.

They strained their ears but could hear nothing. Maj. McDonald then determined to go to an upstairs room from which he could see the guards and the hole. From all he could tell, it seemed that things were normal. Certainly the sentinels hadn't yet noticed the hole—or if they did, had decided it was the work of the ubiquitous rodents.

Rose was sleeping upstairs when, at about *"one o'clock A.M., McDonald came to me in great consternation, and told me the whole thing was discovered. He said if it was not already discovered that it would be without fail when daylight came. I asked him if they had closed the hole in the fireplace; he said 'No, that is played out,' using his own phrase. I told him to come along with me and we would go down and give the place a little examination.*

"We went below and into the tunnel, and quickly discovered that the opening was not within ten feet of the sentinel's path. The air in the tunnel, as I had expected, was now pure and delightful, so that one could stay in any length of time. The orifice at the surface was very little larger than a rat-hole. It was therefore the most unlikely thing in the world for the sentinel to discover it; but in order to prevent this effectually, I took one of my working garments and shoved it into the hole, so as not only to prevent it from getting larger, but to keep any one from the outside discovering it. We then went upstairs to bed."

Observations the next day confirmed Rose's theory—the guards suspected nothing and, now that the small hole was plugged with dirt and a shirt, they were unlikely to see it at all. So, what was to be done? *"At this critical moment a question arose as to whether the whole plot had not better be abandoned; some arguing that we had been heard, the chances were against us, and that ten to one we should fail. Major McDonald now resolved, that if the thing failed, the failure should not be until every possible effort had been made to succeed."*

Rose agreed with McDonald that it was time for a final push. The two of them would go down together, join with Johnston in Rat Hell, and

An extraordinary photo of Libby Prison, with guards in the foreground and prisoners in the windows on the upper two floors. This is the west side of the building. The tunnel was dug from the east side.

not stop digging until the breakthrough had been achieved. Everyone else would stay above and keep watch at the windows. They had ten horizontal feet to go, and the two of them were considered the best diggers.

They would make no more crew changes. The pair determined to dig until they broke through again, this time on the other side of the fence.

Chapter Seventeen

Breakthrough

AFTER TWO MONTHS OF WRETCHED LABOR IN RAT HELL, THE TUNNEL-ers were only a few yards from their objective. Col. Rose made the decision that he and Maj. McDonald would do the rest of the digging. The others, except for Johnston—the man trapped in Rat Hell—would stay upstairs and watch for trouble.

At that extreme end of the tunnel, almost 60 feet in, oxygen became more of a problem than ever. A little leaked in from the plugged-up hole on the wrong side of the fence, but once Rose had tunneled beyond that point, almost no fresh air could reach him. McDonald struggled mightily to fan the entrance, but he was a long way from Rose.

Seventeen days had been spent digging the tunnel. Rose decided that this day, February 8, 1864, would be the last. Experience had demonstrated that he was still the strongest of the diggers, and certainly the most monomaniacal. On that morning, he entered the tunnel and was determined to not stop until he had finally broken through to the outside.

According to Lt. Moran, once Rose took up the chisel he didn't turn it over again. *"As midnight approached, Rose was nearly a physical wreck; perspiration dripped from every pore of his exhausted body; his staggering senses warned him that to faint where he was meant at once his death and burial. He could scarcely inflate his lungs with the poisonous air; his head swam like that of a drowning person."*

The small candle he had with him for illumination sputtered from lack of oxygen. His limbs began to weaken, then spasm from the physical strain and from the terrible, stench-filled air.

Still Rose dug onward until he felt he had gone inside the fenced courtyard above. There he stopped digging forward and turned upward. Clods of dirt fell down around him as he worked on. Retreat was now out of the question. He knew he had to break through or be asphyxiated in the attempt.

Lt. Thomas Moran interviewed Col. Rose after the war and penned this dramatic conclusion. *"His strength nearly gone: the feeble stream of air which his comrade was trying, with all his might, to send could no longer reach him. His senses reeled: he had not breath or strength enough to retreat backward through his narrow grave.*

"In the agony of suffocation he dropped the dull chisel and beat his fists against the roof of his grave with the might of despair—when, blessed boon! The crust gave way and the loosened earth showered upon his dripping face; his famished eye caught sight of a radiant star in the blue vault above him; a flood of light and a volume of cool, delicious air poured over him. At that very instant the sentinel's cry rang out like a prophecy—'Half-past one, all's well!'"

Breakthrough! After a short rest, he dragged his body out of the hole and carefully surveyed his location. Sure enough, the board fence of the courtyard shielded him from the eyes of the Rebel sentinels.

Moving silently, the newly freed Rose started exploring the immediate area. It appeared to be abandoned at night—just as they had hoped. He found a shed where the POWs boxes from home were stored, but not much else.

He looked through the cracks in the fence and saw the guards on their appointed rounds. When the closest sentinel turned his back, Rose opened the gate and slipped out into the clear Richmond night. It was already after midnight, so if he was careful he had little chance of being noticed. As for the guards, they were watching the prison itself, not the area around it.

Rose carefully walked down to the canal and inspected Libby from different directions. He had not been outside the building since the day of his arrival many months before; he wanted to survey the possible escape routes. Moving cautiously, he was ultimately able to see all four sides of the prison and take mental notes.

Col. Rose was free. He could have left the prison right then and made his escape. But the colonel was an American officer, a gentleman, and most of all a leader who knew his responsibilities. He returned to the courtyard, closed the gate, and dropped back into the narrow hole. He pulled a large plank over his head to conceal the tunnel opening, then slowly squirmed back through the tunnel into Rat Hell.

"McDonald was overjoyed," wrote Moran, *"and poor Johnston almost wept with delight as Rose handed them his victorious old chisel and some other trifle he had picked up in the outer world as a token that the Underground Railroad to God's Country was open."*

Johnston stayed below while McDonald and Rose left Rat Hell, rolled up the ladder, and sealed the fireplace entrance. Whispers spread the word that the crew members were to assemble in the empty kitchen.

All were terribly anxious for news. Sitting in the dark kitchen, they finally heard from Rose—*"Boys, the tunnel is finished"*—and could barely repress a cheer. Instead they silently shook hands and danced around with childlike glee.

By now it was 3 a.m. Hamilton and Rose argued for everyone to escape immediately. But the other crew members were extremely anxious about the chances of being discovered. They argued for an additional day to prepare themselves.

The lateness of the hour was a good reason to wait. The dawn would soon break, and all the POWs knew they had to be beyond Richmond when that happened. If they began early the next evening, as soon as it got dark, they would have the entire night to get ahead of their pursuers. Therefore they chose to wait.

The group decided that each of them could invite one other to go along, making 30 men for the first shift of the escape. The hole would then be sealed, the next night 30 more would go out, and so on until the Rebels caught on.

"I had been a prisoner in Libby for over six months and had mingled freely among my fellow captives," remembered Lt. Moran, *"yet so well had 'Rose' and his party kept their secret, that it was not until I had lain down on the night of February 8, 1864, that I learned of the existence of the tunnel. The startling information was given me by my friend, Col. Aaron K. Dunkel, who slept beside me. It was after 'taps'; and the floor of each of the rooms were covered by prostrate forms of hundreds of prisoners. I could see no evidence of an intended escape and half suspected my friend Dunkel of one of his practical jokes, for which he had a deserved reputation in Libby."*

Lt. Wells was one of the original 15 diggers, and he'd been working for weeks to get himself as fit as possible. *"Those who had been let into the secret of the tunnel began to put themselves in readiness for the exodus. To harden our limbs and muscles, persistent walking and other physical exercises were resorted to. My comrade and myself once walked a distance of 22 miles around the room in a single day."*

The men had tried to gather anything they thought would help them on their journey, particularly food. Small scraps, having been hoarded, were now jammed into pockets and into the few haversacks available. But mostly the men prepped mentally, imagining what might be before them and steeling themselves for the extreme trials that were sure to follow. At least one of the crew members, Lt. Mitchell, decided to back out, and another man quickly took his place.

On February 9, 1864, the inmates of Libby woke to another freezing day of boredom and semi-starvation. To the majority of inmates, this morning was the same as any other. But to the Rose crew of 30 it was to be a day of intense, silent apprehension as they waited for dark and worried that their scheme might be detected or betrayed.

"Never was my anxiety so great as for the setting of that day's sun," wrote Capt. Johnston about sitting alone in Rat Hell. It didn't help his nerves

to see more Rebel guard activity in his cellar room than was normal. *"One party brought a dog with them, and hissed him after the rats, and in his search for them he passed over and around me; but I was too large game for him and I escaped. Soon after a rebel sergeant came in, with some negroes, after some empty barrels that were stowed in the cellar. In one of the barrels they found a haversack full of provisions, left there by one of our party the preceding night. This I thought would certainly awaken suspicion; the negroes, however, took the food and ate it, without question being raised how it came there."*

The sergeant's crew carried some barrels out of the cellar, almost stepping on Johnston as they went. But no suspicions were aroused.

Capt. Hamilton: *"Freedom was within our grasp and thoughts of home and loved ones came thick and fast. At 8 o'clock that night the kitchen fire-place was opened for the last time."*

Darkness came early in winter, so that by 7 p.m. the thirty men began to gather in the kitchen. It was all they could do to keep their apprehensions in check, yet all agreed they must not turn back. It was escape or die.

Breakout

"The grandest thing that ever took place in Libby"
—Lt. Frederick Bartleson

It was finally time. After dinner, the thirty conspirators surreptitiously made their way down to the dark kitchen. Despite living cheek by jowl with over a thousand other POWs, their secret was apparently safe. Some of their fellow prisoners might have imagined something was up, but they did not know any details. The unsuspecting Gen. Dow simply noted in his diary: *"Bright, clear, cool. Slept well."*

The escape unfolded according to a strict plan, as explained by Capt. Caldwell: *"A countersign was instituted, and each one entitled to pass out was entrusted with the same, which he gave to the man guarding the entrance, and which served as his passport to the cellar from whence proceeded to the tunnel."*

Rebel guards walked their beats right past the barred kitchen window, so the preparations included collecting the kitchen kettles, pans, and pots: *"These were all carefully set around one of the counterposts of the building, out of the way, so as not to be stumbled over in the dark."*

For Capt. Johnston, trapped in Rat Hell, the escape couldn't come soon enough. But even he had mixed feelings: *"The working party was assembled in the cellar for the last time. There was a shade of sadness on many a brow; for we were about to separate to meet again—when? Perhaps never!"*

Capt. Randall: *"Our last meeting and parting in that old cellar that night will never be forgotten until the last one of that little party is laid away in the grave."*

Lt. Wells, one of the original diggers, was not happy about taking on winter weather without a hat or a decent pair of boots. Negotiating for those items had failed, so once the owners were asleep he decided to help himself. First he slipped on a fine pair of boots that belonged to the man who lay next to him each night. *"[The] head needed protection as well as the feet, and in passing out among my sleeping comrades I stumbled upon a hat. Without compunction or unnecessary ceremony, I placed the hat where it would do the most good and proceeded on my way."*

Capt. Hamilton removed the bricks, dropped the ladder into Rat Hell, and climbed down. One by one the members of the original crews followed. Lt. Hobart stayed behind to seal up the fireplace until the proposed second escape the next night. *"As the guards were under orders to fire upon a prisoner escaping, without even calling him to halt, the first men who descended into the tunnel wore that quiet gloom so often seen in the army before going into battle."*

In the meantime, some prisoners began a dance to distract the guards and cover up any noise. *"It was a living drama; dancing in one part of the room, dark shadows disappearing through the chimney in another part, and the sentinel at his post announcing 'eight o'clock and all is well!' and at the same time a line of Yankee soldiers were crawling under his feet."*

Col. Rose organized the thirty men in the pitch darkness of Rat Hell, lining them up at the tunnel entrance. He was the first one out, followed

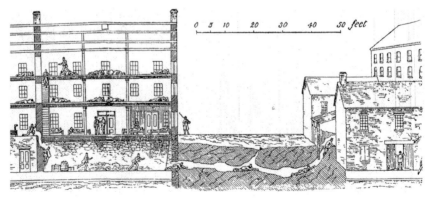

From the pamphlet "Colonel Rose's Story." The escape runs from the kitchen on the far left to the wooden gates on the far right.

by his loyal companion Hamilton. The rest of the original digging party followed close behind.

The tunnel was narrow, cold, and completely dark, yet each man wriggled through it quickly. One by one they climbed out at the other end where they could see the guards through the cracks in the fence.

One guard's beat was to walk toward the fenced-in area where the POWs were hiding, then turn about-face and walk back to the prison. Each time he turned, a few of the escapees would step onto the Richmond streets.

The astounded prisoners on the top floor could see all this clearly. While the guards were screened by the fence and shed, the POWs had a perfect overall view. *"From the upper floor you could see the fugitives pop out of the tunnel, cross the yard, clear the gateway to the street, and disappear into the dark."*

"It was a glorious sight to see them pass out so cleverly from this hated prison. One felt impelled to throw up his cap and shout, 'Huzzah!'"

At first they watched in awe, quietly cheering each inmate as he set out on his journey. But this led to another realization: If they hurried, maybe they could go through the tunnel themselves. Silently, dozens of men crept down into the kitchen. The dozens quickly became hundreds.

Lt. Moran had heard of the finished tunnel just the day previously and was supposed to be one of the original men out, but he had been delayed. Now he hurried to join the second wave.

"Picking our way among sleeping comrades stretched in hundreds upon the floor, we descended the crazy stairway into the kitchen, which was dark and dismal as the grave. Reaching the bottom, we heard no sound save the familiar drip, drip, of the damaged water faucet. I groped along the East wall, and, we ran suddenly against a silent and densely packed crowd of men around the fireplace."

Order had broken down. It was every prisoner for himself. Only one man could get through the fireplace at a time, so soon men were jammed around the entrance as tight as sardines. Lt. Moran thought he might faint from the pressure. *"In my anxiety, I was magnifying minutes into hours; there seemed no reduction of the crowd in front, while the crowd behind had increased by hundreds and were pressing us to suffocation. The measured tread of the guard echoed on the sidewalk, within ten feet of where we were. Fainting and weak men were begging for room and air."*

"At the mouth of the tunnel were hundreds eagerly awaiting their turn. No respect was shown to rank or name. Mere physical force was the test of championship. I had not at that time much muscle to back my claims, they were not recognized, and I spent the whole night without avail in this bootless struggle for freedom," wrote Lt. Glazier, who tried but never made it into the cellar.

Lt. Hobart now realized that it would be impossible to close up the fireplace and continue the escape for a second night. Too many desperate men were fighting for a place in line. *"A wild excitement and enthusiasm was created, and they rushed down clamoring for the privilege of going out. The thought of liberty and pure air, and the death-damp of the loathsome prison, would not allow them to listen to any denial."*

All the original party having gone through, Hobart decided to leave the entrance open for any who dared follow.

Word had crackled through the prison like lightning: *"Knowledge of the hole then became general. The scene that followed was truly amusing—officers running hither and thither, begging, borrowing, stealing, buying a few crusts of corn bread or other edibles, anything to stay the cravings of nature for a day or two, or until they could find a friendly negro."*

Lt. Earle was one of the first ones through after the original thirty had departed. *"Only one man was allowed in the tunnel at the same time, on account, I suppose, of the bad air. The exit of the man preceding could be easily determined by the cessation of the terrible noise made in forcing one's body through a long, narrow shaft, which the tunnel really was. The noise and racket produced by one man kicking and floundering against the walls of this cavern were simply indescribable, comparable to a steam engine, or cyclone, or an army reunion."*

However loud the noise was to the prisoners waiting at the tunnel entrance, the guards didn't hear it. Lt. Earle entered the tunnel wearing an army overcoat stuffed with bread, and immediately became stuck. *"I pulled myself back, took off my overcoat, and pulling it behind me proceeded to worm myself through the tunnel."*

When he finally reached the exit he heard someone whisper, *"Don't breathe so loud, stop blowing',* and I felt a hand and was pulled out of the opening. We could now breathe the pure air of heaven, but our dangers were by no means passed."

At once everything stopped. A man described as "fat" had become stuck in the tunnel. Of course the term "fat" was relative among the starved of Libby, but nevertheless a man had become wedged because of his girth, and *"the news sent a chill of unutterable disgust through the crowd; muttered curses were rained upon the unlucky victim's stomach."*

The men couldn't guess who had blocked the tunnel, but they learned soon enough. *"Here Col. Streight, who is inclined to corpulence, stuck fast, and was compelled to back out, divest himself of his coat, vest, and shirt, when he was able to squeeze through, pulling the garments with a string after him."*

Up in the kitchen, Lt. Moran patiently worked his way toward the hole in the fireplace, while even more men crowded in behind him. *"When I neared the stove I was nearly suffocated, but I took heart when I saw but three men between me and the hole. At this moment some idiot on the edge of the mob startled us with the cry, 'The guards, the guards!'*

"A fearful panic ensued, and the entire crowd bounded towards the stairway leading up to the sleeping quarters. The stairway was unbanistered, and some of the men were forced off the edge and fell on those beneath. I was taken off my feet, dashed to the floor senseless, my head and one of my hands bruised and cut, and my shoulder painfully injured by the boots of the men who rushed over me."

Capt. Calder was another eyewitness to the chaos: *"They rushed forward, falling over kettles, skillits, pots, and stovepipes, making such a tremendous noise that one might have mistaken it for an earthquake."*

When Lt. Moran finally gathered his senses, he realized he was lying in a pool of water along with a few others who had also been trampled. *"All noise had ceased upstairs and I concluded it was a false alarm. I crept cautiously to the front door and looked out. A sentinel at that moment was looking toward the door through which I was watching him. He was less than 8 feet away and appeared to be looking straight into my eyes. I did not move, fearing to betray my presence by the slightest motion."*

Frozen in place, Moran listened to the guards discussing the racket. They stood just outside the kitchen windows; one was heard to joke that the Yanks must have had a ration of apple-jack that night, for they had been *"fighting and raising hell"* inside. Lt. Glazier heard another guard joke: *"Hallo Bill,—there's somebody's coffee-pot upset, sure!"*

Lt. Moran saw the corporal of the guard react. *"He made no response whatever, but lazily turning on his heel, slowly crossed the street and disappeared. My belief was confirmed that, not withstanding the unearthly racket the Confederates had no suspicion of our dangerous game."*

All this time, men were continuing to slip through the tunnel and walk into the February night. Capt. Caldwell remembered: *"When passing I touched on four sides, and at some points there was considerable friction."*

The POWs on the upper floors, having stampeded away from the tunnel, now realized that the guards had not come inside. They began filtering back downstairs, to the fireplace hole and Rat Hell.

Lt. Moran was determined to get out before the mob could form again. He squeezed through the narrow aperture of the fireplace and *"let my feet down, hoping to touch bottom, but found none, whither or to what depth I knew not, for it was a pit of rayless darkness. With a sort of faith in fortune I shut my eyes and let go. I fell into a pile of straw and found myself among hundreds of squealing rats. Before I could recover a score of the repulsive creatures ran over me. The place seemed alive with rats that thumped against my ankle at every step. At last I reached the wall and ran my hand along the cold damp surface, in search of the tunnel."*

Lost in the darkness, Moran paused to listen for his comrades but could only hear the vermin. He began to panic at the thought of being trapped there all night, only to be captured by the guards come morning. *"I thought I had surveyed an acre of wall and was on the border of despair when, to my boundless joy, my hand fell upon a pair of heels. I knew they were live heels, for I had no sooner touched them than they vanished like magic in the wall.*

"The hole had an average diameter of two feet; at times descending and then rising. The hole grew narrower as I advanced. The earth was clammy cold and the air suffocating. The length of the hole seemed interminable.

"At last, fainting with suffocation, pain, and fatigue, a ray of light glad-dened my eyes and I felt the most delicious air I have ever breathed in my life."

One hundred nine Yankee prisoners made it through the tunnel that night. Lt. A. B. White was one of the last men to get out. After so many men had tunneled through, *"it was but the work of a moment to propel our-selves through the hole, as the bottom was as smooth as glass."*

With dawn approaching, the POWs closed up the fireplace and returned to their sleeping quarters. They hoped to be lucky and fool the Rebels during the day's count, so they could open the tunnel for a second night.

But so many men leaving the area were unlikely to go unnoticed. Some of the guards must have seen men stepping out into the street, as the escape had gone on for more than eight hours.

But another fact worked in the prisoners' favor. Right next to the end of the tunnel was a building which housed the many boxes that had been sent from North to the POWs. Rebel authorities were no longer deliver-ing those boxes to the inmates. Richmond citizens and soldiers regularly broke into the warehouse to steal the food and clothing. The guards knew of this. They figured the escaping prisoners were actually looters; they did nothing to stop or question them.

Lt. Bartleson saw it as *"righteous retribution for their mean pillaging of our boxes, and that the hand of God was in it. It was a glorious sight to see them pass out so cleverly from this hated prison. I myself saw the guard stop and watch them as they came forth on the street, but his guilty soul approved of the meanness which he supposed was taking place."*

"We had to pass through a gate which opened on Canal Street. Along this street, to within ten steps of the gate, a sentinel walked who, on reaching the end of his beat, would face about and go forty paces the other way. Taking advantage of the time when his back was turned the prisoner would open the gate and, stepping out to Canal Street, pass out of sight."

The prisoners went out by themselves, in pairs or threes. Lt. Moran waited as two men left ahead of him: *"As they moved away, I watched the two nearest guards, who gazed at the retreating forms of my friends. I resolved should they show a sign of firing, to shout to my comrades. The guards appeared to have no suspicions and resumed pacing their posts. Feeling this to be my opportunity, I leisurely followed in the wake of my friends.*

"It would be difficult to convey an idea of the peculiar sensation I felt when, after an imprisonment of six months, I first found myself in the open air; and yet I felt a pang of regret as I turned to look at the grim walls of Libby, where I was leaving, perhaps forever, many of the most valued friends of my life. My feet stumbled over the uneven walk, as if I had just landed after a long sea voyage, and the cool February air had an intoxicating effect."

Lt. Wells also reported having trouble walking, but he was keen to be on his way. *"After standing so long on the hard floor the soft ground under my feet was noticeable at once, and I looked about me, as if to assure myself it was not all a dream.*

"Every nerve was strung to the highest tension, all fear had vanished and my senses were alert as those of a wild animal."

CHAPTER NINETEEN

First Night

ROSE AND HAMILTON, AS INSTIGATORS OF THE ESCAPE, WERE FIRST through the tunnel. The hope was for pairs and trios of POWs to stick together and help each other along the way.

However, as Hamilton recorded, *"We walked two squares and then turned. Here we passed a hospital guard who insisted upon knowing where Rose was from. Not receiving satisfactory replies, Colonel [Rose] was taken to the chief officer of the guard, where he must have made some clever explanations, for he was away again in half an hour. In the meantime I came to the conclusion that the quarters were too close for me, and I trudged on alone."*

Just minutes into their journey the two were already broken up and on their own. Rose remembered, *"Hamilton turned back and we became separated. I did not see him again for several months.*

"No plan had been arranged to be pursued after we left prison. It was expected of each man to take care of himself and be governed by circumstances."

It might seem like an unlikely recipe for success, but not making specific escape plans actually worked in the prisoners' favor. The more than 100 men who passed through Richmond that night would have caused suspicion if they had gathered together or followed the same route. As it happened, every escaping man had to rely entirely on his own wits to get him through whatever he faced. The anarchy of their situation favored the POWs.

Lt. Wells, for example, knew little more than the direction he wanted to go. *"I slipped out and walked eastward on Canal Street. I had no fixed plan for getting out of the city, but was guided wholly by impulse and by circumstances.*

"The Federal uniform and overcoat I wore was rather an advantage than otherwise, for the Confederate soldiers had appropriated clothing sent by our government and were then commonly wearing our overcoats on the streets."

Many of the POWs did not have Union uniforms, but instead wore civilian clothes they had received in their boxes shipped from home. Richmond was a crowded boomtown full of strangers, which also worked to the prisoners' advantage. In a close-knit city the POWs might have stood out and been spotted, but the Rebel capital was already full of scrawny young men wearing all manner of ragged uniforms in every state of disrepair.

It was a crisp, clear night. Any escaping officer could orient himself by the North Star. Everyone knew that 50 miles to the east were the front lines of the Union Army.

Young Lt. Earle was one of the first out, at around eight o'clock. It was still early evening. He strode boldly down one of the busiest thoroughfares in the city. *"We passed out and walked slowly and deliberately—in full view of the guards, remember—but, assuming the manners of those walking in the streets who had a right to do so. This was one of the most dangerous points we passed during the escape, and in many respects the most wonderful. For the first time were out of the range of the guards' muskets. Of course we took a long breath.*

"We came to Cary Street, which was brilliantly lighted, and many of the shops were still open. We observed a group of soldiers walking in front of us, talking and laughing. We mingled freely with them, talking to ourselves on subjects similar to those they were discussing. We avoided coming into direct contact with them, however, and gradually as we approached the outskirts of the city, allowed them to pass us, until at last we found ourselves about one mile to the east of Richmond."

Cols. Hobart and West also decided the safest course was to go straight down the main streets of the city, all the while working their own special ruse. *"My face being very pale and my beard long, clinging to the arm of Col. West, I assumed the part of a decrepit old man who seemed to be badly affected with a consumptive cough. In this manner we passed through the glar-*

ing gas lights and the crowded streets without creating a suspicion. We met the police, squads of soldiers, and many others who gave me a sympathizing look and stepped aside. Approaching the suburbs we retreated into a ravine which allowed us to leave the city."

Obviously, pretending to have a dreaded, communicable disease was an effective disguise.

Capt. Johnston was ecstatic just to be out of Rat Hell for the first time in days. Despite his worries, fortune was with him and he made quick progress. *"As my comrade and myself were passing through the city, two ladies who were standing at the gate of a house, observed us; one of them remarked to the other that we looked like Yankees. We did not stop to undeceive them, and met with no further trouble until the city limits were passed."*

Men continued to flow out of the prison all night long. Lt. Moran, who had fought so hard to get down into Rat Hell and through the tunnel, had to walk the city after midnight when few others were about.

"We moved quickly, but with great caution, for we knew that the provost guard compelled every one on the streets to exhibit the proper pass. In spite of care we found ourselves almost in the hands of the patrol several times. After repeated narrow escapes we turned a corner, and before we had a chance to exchange a word, a dozen Confederates, without arms, passed us without a suspicion that we were escaping Yankees. Grateful for our good fortune we moved rapidly forward. Dogs rushed at us from every house and set up a hideous howl."

Col. McCreery remembered how he and his partner *"locked arms and marched out into the street under the archway near which was burning a bright gaslight. At first we took to the center of the street, but gaining confidence we ventured upon the sidewalk. We had not proceeded far when we were ordered by a sentinel to halt, and in reply to his interrogatory, 'Who goes there?' I answered, 'We are citizens going home,' to which he replied, 'Take the middle of the street! You know no one can walk on this yer' sidewalk in front of this yer' hospital after dark.' We were in hearty accord with the sentinel, and taking the middle of the street passed the hospital without further annoyance."*

Col. Abel Streight and three companions almost came to disaster that first night. The plan was for them to shelter at Elizabeth Van Lew's mansion, then move to a safe house until things calmed down. But communications had failed and Van Lew did not receive information about the actual time of the escape. On the night of the 9th she had donned a disguise of rough clothing and left home to spend the night with her brother, a Rebel deserter who was also trying to get out of Richmond.

The next morning her servant arrived to bring her back to the mansion. *"As soon as he called, he said that there was great trouble and excitement; that many prisoners had escaped during the night, and that some had come to his door & begged to come in, but he was afraid they were not prisoners, only people in disguise to betray us & would not let them in.*

"We knew there was to be an exit, had been told to prepare & had one of our parlors—had dark blankets nailed up at the windows and the gas had been kept burning in it very low. We were so ready for them, beds prepared in there. I returned home, after going as quickly as I could, in despair."

Luckily the POWs found a spot to hide through the night. Next day they were connected with a Mrs. Green, who led them to the humble home of fellow Unionist Mrs. Rice. Though Mrs. Rice was in poor health she treated her guests royally; they stayed a week, waiting for the Rebels to stop searching for POWs.

The rest of the escapees hoped to get well out of Richmond before dawn. They knew it would be extremely difficult to travel in daylight and not be noticed. Lt. Fales and his two companions had just reached the edge of the city when they had a risky encounter. *"We heard the jingling of sabers, indicating that a small force of cavalry was coming towards us, and jumping over the fence, we suddenly came face to face upon a man who was out with a lantern getting a pail of water. This peaceful citizen was frightened, and in tremulous tones said: 'What is the matter; what are you running for?' We replied that we were going to our regiments out at the forts, and passed on without stopping to explain further."*

"The cavalry having passed by towards the city, we returned to the road, and just as I jumped over the fence, four more cavalrymen came riding round the corner, and my comrades started back on the run. The enemy were too near for me to think of running, so I stood still, and on coming up, one of the soldiers asked: 'Where are you going?' I replied: 'Out to my regiment.' Then he said: 'What are those other fellows running for?' I gave some reply, exactly what,

I do not now recollect, but the idea was, that they were absent from their regiments without permission. This satisfied the cavalrymen and they passed on without further conversation, greatly to my relief, for if they had asked me what regiment I belonged to, where the regiment was stationed, and other details, I should have been in a very dangerous situation."

It was logical for the Confederates to believe that these ragtag men were their own soldiers hustling back after a harmless sojourn in the big city. The cavalrymen probably did the same thing on occasion.

Lt. Wallber came out of the tunnel at 2 a.m. The city had quieted considerably and the gaslights had been turned off. He and his companion decided, because it was so late, to avoid the main streets.

"A few steps away, a sentry called 'Post number six—all well.' He turned his back on me and I ducked around the corner to freedom.

"Free, rid of the shackles that had held us so long, we breathed deep drafts of night air and shouted: 'Thank God, Free at last!' From the bottom of our hearts we resolved to die rather than return to that dungeon. 'Out of this hellhole as fast as possible to the land of freedom!'—and away we went double quick. We jumped fences, crashed across gardens, raced down boulevards, hustled through alleys, and startled dogs that barked at us."

Evading Rebel patrols, the pair got to the edge of the city without incident and found a railroad track that led east. *"Briskly we followed it in single file. We had not gone far when a nearby hiss stopped us. We called out. A pair of comrades appeared beside us. They too had just escaped. We exchanged greetings and resumed the march along the railroad. At daybreak we took shelter in a piney woods."*

The next barrier to get through was the elaborate system of defensive earthworks that surrounded Richmond. These interlocking fortifications were a formidable maze of ditches, ramparts, mines, trenches, bombproofs, and large siege guns. They had been constructed, on and off, throughout the war and formed an in-depth system so impressive that the Union never dared attack it.

However, with the Confederacy suffering a serious manpower shortage, and with no sizeable Yankee forces anywhere near Richmond, only a thin line of pickets was posted to watch over the trenches. These men were meant to form the first warning line against any attack from outside the Rebel capital; they were not on the lookout for individual Union prisoners escaping from inside the city.

"*We made our way over numberless rifle pits, huge earthworks, tangled brush and fallen trees that would have proved a bloody path to an assault column,*" wrote Lt. Moran about his delicate passage through the trenches. "*A dozen times we came within an ace of walking into the hands of guards. Having passed the city limits and the line of works successfully, our spirits rose in spite of empty stomachs and shivering limbs. The first gray streaks of day appearing in the East as we saw ahead a number of small fires, and as they seemed to be at a uniform distance we concluded we had reached the outer line of pickets.*

"*We saw no advantage in going to the right or left, hence we voted to attempt a passage in our immediate front. We went forward to within a hundred yards of the nearest post, and saw five armed Confederates. Their faces were to the fire and their backs were to us.*

"*We dropped upon our hands and knees, and crept in single file, toward the center of the intervening space. Most of the ground was nearly bare, and, as we crept along the frozen earth, the brittle brush cracked treacherously, while the blazing logs illuminated our perilous way. At every snapping branch we looked anxiously on both sides, resolved, if challenged, to take to our heels and run the gantlet. The Confederates were laughing and talking, their faces turned towards the genial fire.*

"*Having passed* the *danger point, and well out of hearing, we rose to our feet, and giving three cheers (in pantomime), broke into a lively trot, with increasing hopes of success; for fortune thus far had singularly favored us.*

"*We entered a swamp, thickly grown with a low underbrush that afforded the best available concealment. Selecting a spot at the base of a large oak tree well carpeted with leaves, we stretched our exhausted limbs and soon shivered ourselves to sleep.*"

After he had successfully talked his way out of a tight spot with Rebel cavalrymen, Lt. Fales was rejoined by the two comrades who had run away. Together the trio quietly passed by the forts and made their way into the open country beyond, which brought them to their next barrier—the swampy Chickahominy River.

"We came to the Chickahominy, and started to go in search of a bridge or ford, but after going a short distance I saw a rebel picket lying beside a few glowing coals, only twenty feet away. The sentinel had apparently been asleep and was just commencing to rise when we started on the run back to the spot where we first struck the river. The sentinel did not challenge us or shoot, but threw some fresh fuel on his fire and made it burn brightly, as if trying to discover by the light what had disturbed him."

Terrified of being recaptured, the men quickly stripped off their clothing, held it over their heads, and waded into the icy river. It was only about thirty yards wide at that point but deep enough that they had to swim.

"Our teeth were chattering with cold when we reached the opposite shore, though when we plunged in we were wet with perspiration. We dressed rapidly and were about to move on, when I found I had left my haversack with all my rations on the opposite bank. I did not think it prudent to abandon my supplies, and stripping again, I went back across the river and recovered my rations, but paid dearly for them, finding myself thoroughly chilled through on my return."

After three trips across the river, Fales found he could not warm his body up, and this would cause troubles later. The trio of men found a dry spot at the roots of a large pine tree and tried to rest until daylight passed.

Lt. Johnston and his companion made it out of Richmond with little trouble, but then found themselves disoriented by the dark defenses surrounding the city. The city had been all bustle and gaslight, but now they were out where it was silent—and they felt the presence of Confederate troops in every direction.

"We soon came to the Rebel camps, which stretched round a great portion of the city. We were excited, of course, and bewildered for this first hour, not knowing whether we were in the path of safety or danger. All at once I became perfectly composed and told my comrade to follow me and I would conduct him safe through."

The pair carefully passed between the picket posts, aided by a briskly blowing wind that loudly rustled the leaves. Moving rapidly, they crossed over four different lines of unmanned defenses. Once they passed the last line, they found open land on which the timber had been felled to provide clear fields of fire for Rebel artillery.

"Among this timber was our hiding place the first day—all the safer, no doubt, for being within a few hundred yards of the Rebel guns. The weather was excessively cold and our pantaloons were frozen stiff up to our knees. We did not dare to make a fire so near to the Rebel camp."

The escape had started out almost perfectly. Only one of the 109 escapees was captured inside the city limits. The other 108 successfully made it out of Richmond, crossed the earthworks that surrounded the Rebel capital, and reached a hiding place in time for dawn.

The Rebel Confederates were still unaware that anything major had happened. The guards at Libby awoke to what they saw as another boring day.

A Day of Amused Excitement

NEXT MORNING IN LIBBY THE REMAINING ELEVEN HUNDRED POWs were tense with anticipation, but the authorities knew nothing and sensed nothing. The daily counting of the men started later than normal after breakfast, probably because Little Ross knew what had happened and wanted to give the escapees every possible minute to get ahead.

The prisoners hoped they could disguise the fact that so many men were missing, and that another escape would happen each night until the Rebels stopped them. But when it came time to cover for the missing men, they did not know for sure how many were gone.

"On 10 February, a day of amused excitement among us, we began asking at the crack of dawn; 'How many got away?'" remembered the German Domschcke. *"Intending to tricks to confound the clerks during roll call, we looked forward to the customary count at 8:00."*

But Little Ross, the Confederate in charge of the count, did not arrive at the regular time. Lt. Glazier didn't know that Ross was secretly part of Elizabeth Van Lew's Union Underground when he wrote, *"For some reason, the authorities were late that morning and did not make their appearance until about ten o'clock. In calling the role, the men attempted to cross the room but were discovered, so the count came one hundred and fifteen men short."*

Lt. Prutsman was one of the men trying to fabricate the count. *"I did this by falling in on the right, and being counted, slipped down to the rear of the line, when I was counted again. The count being complete the adjutant announced 'over a hundred men had answered roll call who were not on the floor.'*

"*We began to smell trouble.*

"*The adjutant returned with Dick Turner and a guard who drove all of the prisoners out of the room and then passed them back one by one, counting as they filed through the door.*"

"*Turner counted us two or three times, but with equally unsatisfactory results. He asked where they had gone and how they got out, but not a man knew*"—by which Lt. Glazier meant no one was willing to say.

All the confusion and repeated counting took more than four hours. The Rebels just couldn't believe what was happening, couldn't believe their own figures. If more than a hundred were missing, how had they gotten out of Libby? How had they gotten out of Richmond? Where were they all now? At least the counters finally got the number right: 109 Union officers were gone.

'At first they suspicioned that the guards had been bribed; this suspicion we tried to strengthen, hoping that the true manner of their departure might remain secret until another night, which would give a hundred more an opportunity of bidding our Rebel hosts farewell.'

Rebel General John Winder walked down to Libby from his office in the center of the city. Winder was in charge of all Union prisoners in the Confederacy, and when he heard of the escape he was furious, according to Lt. Moran. *'After a careful examination of the building and a talk, not of the politest kind, with Turner, he reached the conclusion that such an escape had but one explanation—the guards had been bribed. Accordingly, the sentinels on duty were marched off under arrest to Castle Thunder* [another Richmond warehouse prison] *where they were locked up and searched for 'greenbacks.'"*

Meanwhile, Rebel officers continued their meticulous search of Libby, but they were unable to find any clues. "*Turner appeared in the rooms. Nothing to be discovered there, they went into the street, ramrods in hand. They poked into each handful of loose earth, delving for the crack by which the birds had flown. Watching from the windows, how we rejoiced at those futile probes!*"

A few Libby prisoners hung a rope made of blankets from one of the barred windows, but it failed to fool the authorities for long.

Finally, a small hole was uncovered under a plank across the street. Then the tunnel entrance was located in the east cellar. According to the *Richmond Examiner*, the entrance *"was hidden by a large rock, which fitted the aperture exactly. A small negro boy was sent into the tunnel, and a shout announced his arrival at the terminus of the subterranean route."*

Even the highly partisan Rebel newspapers were impressed. For the previous month they had been applauding the ingenious escape of their own Gen. Morgan, and here was a mass exit that was bigger in every way. *"The whole thing was skillfully managed and bears the impress of master minds and indomitable perseverance,"* wrote the *Richmond Daily Dispatch*. The paper also published a full list of the men escaped, which broke down to include 11 colonels, 7 majors, 32 captains, and 59 lieutenants. It formed quite a collection of valuable field officers.

"The excitement in Richmond next morning after the escape was intense. In a twinkling, church bells were ringing, cavalrymen were out with horns blasting, and all hounds obtainable were yelping. The excitement was at white heat.

"A thousand and more prisoners in Libby were compensated, in a measure, for their failure to escape by the panic they saw among the 'Rebs.' Messengers and dispatches were soon flying in all directions, and all the horse, foot, and dragoons of Richmond were in pursuit of the fugitives."

Capt. Domschcke remembered the feeling inside the prison: *"Ecstatic over our comrade's success, we had rejoiced at the Rebels' dismay—but then we grew anxious. We knew too well the Rebel character; we must expect rage to be vented upon recaptured prisoners. We agonized especially over Col. Streight. Fate decreed ill for him, should he be retaken."*

Nothing seemed to bother prison officials more than the realization that their most infamous prisoner was among the missing. The Richmond *Dispatch* singled him out as *"Col. A D Streight, 51st Indiana regiment, a notorious character captured in Tennessee and charged with having raised a negro regiment."*

Lt. Roach remembered: *"Dick Turner and a posse of the prison attaches galloped off, the redoubtable Dick swearing that he would bring Streight back dead or alive."* Arming himself with sword and pistol, Turner rode out in blind pursuit with as many men as he could find.

Once the tunnel had been located, the Libby guards were released from their incarceration in Castle Thunder Prison. Col. Cesnola couldn't help making fun. *"The next morning I conversed with some of the sentinels, and laughed at their great vigilance during the previous night. They said that they had seen men coming out from the yard, and running as fast as they could, but they supposed it was some of their own guard making a raid on our boxes."*

The prisoners enjoyed the chaos they'd induced for at least a day. They could see the activity all around them from the windows of Libby's upper floors. They also followed the escape closely in the Rebel newspapers, which featured a story about a mistaken wild chase for Streight across the rooftops of downtown.

According to the *Richmond Examiner*, city detectives acting on an anonymous tip hustled to the downtown offices of a pair of dentists and demanded to *"See Streight!"* (Everybody loved this pun.) After hearing the dentists deny any knowledge of the escapees, their offices and the basement were thoroughly searched. Nothing was found.

However, the noise of the investigation apparently spooked the patrons of an illegal card game being held on the second floor of the same structure. When the detectives decided to search upstairs, the card players made a quick exit through the roof and attempted to escape to other buildings.

"Meanwhile," according to the *Examiner, "the report spread that Colonel A. D. Streight and several of his officers were in the house. Hundreds of excited citizens rushed to the spot, and in five minutes the house was surrounded."*

Watching the card party flee, as the men leapt from roof to roof, seemed to confirm the rumors. *"The cry arose on all sides, 'there they go, there's Streight! Shoot him, shoot him!'"* Armed citizens began to fire at the running figures, with what the *Examiner* described as their *"plug ugly revolvers."*

Enthusiastic civilians got the range of the man they imagined to be Streight and *"blazed away at him as he dodged between two chimneys, but the excited marksmen did not see straight, or shut both eyes and missed him, wounding a chimney severely.*

"Finally, after a lapse of about an hour, people regained their senses."

"The incident dramatized the eagerness to nab Streight," noted Domschcke.

Lt. Roach obviously enjoyed telling this story in his memoirs. He had served under Col. Streight and was able to conclude: *"At the same time this exciting hunt for Streight was going on, he and his whole party were lying concealed, and had the satisfaction of reading the account the next morning after it transpired."*

Col. Streight and his three companions were still sequestered in their safe house; but all other escapees were on the road, hoping to hit Union lines before the Rebels caught up to them.

In rural areas without telegraph service, news couldn't travel faster than the person carrying it. The escapees had a good twelve hours' head start, but they had to lay low during the day due to constant patrols. It didn't help that the summer leaves were down in this cold, swampy peninsula.

Col. McCreery and Lt. Hobart went looking for a good place to hide for the day. They found it just outside Richmond *"among the trenches where the Confederates had buried the Union soldiers killed at the battle of Fair Oaks, and a strange feeling of security came over us, as if we were among our friends. It was the step and voice of the living that we dreaded."*

CHAPTER TWENTY-ONE

A Bare Chance

THE ESCAPEES ALL WENT TO GROUND THAT FIRST MORNING. THEIR movements would be too easy to spot in the daylight. Exhausted as they were, wrung out and freezing, many were still able to fall asleep. The cold, leafless forests and swamps offered places to lay low, but the prisoners had to stay quiet and could not build fires.

Lt. Moran, who had fought his way into Rat Hell and through the tunnel, rested with two companions in a small stand of trees and thick brush. He was enjoying pleasant dreams of banquets when *"I became suddenly conscious that some one had seized me by the hair with a savage grip. Morgan was butting my head violently against the big oak, exclaiming: 'Damn it! stop snoring or you will have us all captured.' Before I could realize the cause of my comrades' alarm, I heard a rustling and a small dog bounded into our hiding place, gave a quick, sharp bark and disappeared.*

"This naturally gave us alarm, and within a minute we heard voices approaching. We were preparing to run, when a number of armed Confederates appeared. We dropped upon our faces in the thick underbrush, clinging to the desperate hope that we might escape their notice. The party, dog and all, passed within ten feet of where we lay and disappeared. Was it possible that twenty men could pass so close and none of them see us? It seemed incredible."

The three men held a whispered debate about what to do next. Moran's companions decided to stay behind while he trailed the Rebels to see if they were leaving the area. He had not gone very far when *"I heard a dozen whistles, followed by the clear command of the Confederates, 'Close in!' The thought of going back to Libby a captive was like a knell of death, and I resolved to take any chance short of actual suicide rather than be taken. I tore through the low bog, lost my left shoe in the treacherous mire, and to increase my speed took off the other and threw it away. I struck a path running and, without shoes, fairly flew over the ground."*

Moran proceeded to run squarely into a group of four Rebels, one of whom tripped over his own carbine and fell to the ground, while the other three *"leveled their carbines at my head and commanded me to halt. The fallen man, recovering his gun and his wits, came savagely toward me, and amid the laughter of his companions, in a fog-horn voice, shouted, 'Surrender!' I hoped my two comrades might meet a better fate, but they were soon in sight, attended by guards.*

"The Confederates hunted up my shoes and treated us with considerable kindness. They fed us liberally from their haversacks, admitted that our discovery in the swamp was a great surprise to them, and added that we were outside of their lines."

Lt. Moran's luck had come to an end. The three unfortunate POWs were soon on the road back to Richmond.

Capt. Starr was another Libby escapee who had forced his way down to Rat Hell and into the tunnel. He and a companion had dodged a path through Richmond and the outlying defenses. They avoided all roads and bridges, plunging into the thick woods and swamps until they were stopped by the Chickahominy. The river was just too difficult to cross in their exhausted state, so they *"got into a dense thicket of scrub pines where we sought a place for rest and hiding, under a low and wide-spreading tree.*

"Shortly after noon we were aroused from sleep to look into the muzzle of an old-fashioned Colt's revolver held by a Confederate scout, who ordered us out and put us on the march before him. Unarmed, and enfeebled by long imprisonment we could not very well resist, and were thus led to the highway to Richmond. There we came up with a party of about thirty others who had been recaptured, and being put in charge of a band of troopers at about night-fall we again beheld the grimy face of grim old Libby.

"As we stood upon the pavement of Carey Street and gazed up at our late comrades peering out at us through the bars, it was indeed a gloomy, heart-sickening moment."

Back in Libby, the prisoners waited and speculated about how many would get away. Capt. Domschcke didn't get a chance to join the escape but he was anxious for any news. *"Suddenly a cry, 'Yanks! Yanks!' We dashed to the windows and saw the return of the first to be captured, brought back under heavy guard."*

These escapees had barely been gone 48 hours, and now they were back in Libby. It was a depressing sight for everyone; and yet when Capt. Starr looked up at the prison, *"It seems as if the sense of humor would not desert some men, even when in the jaws of death, so to speak. This was illustrated when some of the boys at the barred windows overhead, shouted out at us, 'Fresh fish! Fresh fish! When were you captured?' 'How were you captured?' 'I told you so,' etc."*

One man decidedly not laughing was Dick Turner, the prison jailer. The recaptured POWs were brought before him for interrogation; but Turner learned little, according to Lt. Moran. *"Turner was lashed into fury by the ridicule rained upon him for this escape. Finding us determined to answer none of his questions, he called Sergt. George Stansell, and ordered him to lock us up in the spies' cell.*

"We knew that a slow process of starvation awaited us, for we knew that we must struggle from day to day, to preserve health and life without food or drink sufficiently nourishing to us, and it was a prospect gloomy enough to appall any one!

"As Stansell turned the key and bolted us in we found ourselves in a dark and horrible dungeon occupied by a single prisoner. This proved to be Captain Gates of the 33d Ohio Regt., who apologized for being glad to see us, as he said it was frightfully lonesome. Captain Gates was one of the 109 who got out through the tunnel but he was the only one retaken within the city limits."

Lt. Starr recorded the fate of those, like him, who were returned to Libby: *"Others recaptured were put with us, bringing up the number to about fifty. Each cell was ten feet by twelve and was partitioned off with boards from the cellar proper, and had no light except such as was derived from the dark cellar, through a small hole in the door. Here to the number of about a dozen in a cell, we sat and slept upon the damp ground. Each of us had but one loaf per day of hard corn-bread, and this, with muddy water from the James River, constituted the entire supply of food and drink."*

Capt. Domschcke was an eyewitness to the crackdown. *"Dick Turner's face glowed in those days, radiating hellish delight. He knew how many had been forced to suffer."*

It was the fear of this dungeon that kept the rest of the escapees moving through horrible winter conditions in the flat Virginia countryside. Many of those men had little but luck and prayer going for them.

Some of the Libby escapees were recaptured when they asked the wrong person for help or were spotted by Rebel citizens. Others were overrun by Rebel cavalry using bloodhounds trained to hunt runaway slaves, sarcastically described by Libby inmate Bartleson as *"those instruments employed by the South in humanizing and Christianizing the African race."*

The swampy environment made it much more difficult for the dogs to operate; the escapees put water between themselves and their pursuers whenever possible. Crisscrossing your tracks also helped to confuse the animals. Lt. Randall had heard the stories and came prepared with a gift: *"They trailed us with bloodhounds, but we broke their trail with cayenne pepper that was sent to me in a roll of butter, in a box that I received from home."*

Capt. Caldwell and his companion, Lt. Williams, realized they needed to find a place of concealment during the day. *"We selected for our first head quarters a large pine brush-heap, under which we crept and where we remained during the next twelve hours."* However, soon after they arrived a local farmer came out with a cart and dog, intent on collecting firewood from the grove in which they were hiding. The dog immediately approached their hiding place. Capt. Caldwell proposed that their only salvation lay in an instant, simultaneous prayer for the dog to be distracted.

"The dog came up a few paces from us when lo, and behold, his attention was arrested by something. Off he started at the top of his speed in another direction, and we have not seen that dog since. 'There,' said I, 'didn't I tell you the Lord could direct that dog some other way, and he has done it.'"

The two watched while the farmer spent all day collecting wood, but his dog did not return. They lay on the ground and waited for the cover of night. *"I should like if I were able to describe the thoughts and feelings that possessed us on that thrillingly exciting day. We were compelled to remain in*

Chickahominy swamp in winter.

agony from cold for twelve long hours in that unenviable position. It seemed almost as though the sun did really stand still, and that night, long wished for night, would never come."

When it finally became dark enough they shared some of the hard-tack and dried beef they'd brought along and ventured out from their leafy blind. Only then did they notice a squad of Confederates moving toward them, establishing a picket line with a soldier posted every 100 paces. The escapees could easily calculate that the line would come right to their hiding place, so they prayed with all their might a second time. *"Here again we had a striking interposition of Providence in our favor. The good Lord sent a tremendous gale of wind, which caused such a rustling of leaves that we were permitted to move off unheard and unseen; and thus we soon passed out into a field where we were safe from our enemy."*

Capt. Caldwell became a minister after the war.

During the winter the muddy Chickahominy was wide enough to stop many an escapee. All struggled to find a way across this barrier, but Lt. A. B. White had the fortune to be paired with Capt. Daily. Daily had served in this region for two months in 1862, and had memories of an obscure crossing that he thought he could find.

It was hard work as the pair searched the muddy woods in the darkness of their second night out. But eventually they found it and *"we crossed with hearts beating high, for once across the Chickahominy, final escape became reasonably certain. We were congratulating each other that our strength has lasted so well through two nights and a day, in which we had not closed our eyes and had very little food—when some of the 4th Virginia Cavalry dashed out from behind a clump of bushes and, alas, we had the enemy 'just where he wanted us' again."*

White realized he had just been retaken by the very same Confederate unit that had captured him the first time: *"They remembered that we had met them often in battle, and greeted us as old friends. They escorted us to the home of one of the officers who lived nearby, who made us cordially welcome to a good breakfast and insisted on our enjoying his hospitality.*

"We reached Libby in due time, and were placed in a dungeon 10 by 12 feet in area."

Capt. Johnston had been shot through the face at Shiloh and had been trapped for days in Rat Hell; but once outside of Libby, fortune was with him. His companion was Lt. Fislar. The first night they had crossed the Richmond fortifications and found a good place to hide among a copse of fallen timber. That morning a party of Rebel soldiers came out from a nearby camp and began cutting cord wood all around their hiding place. But the escapees were never noticed, and although it was bitter cold, *"our suffering was greatly lessened by the thought that we were free.*

"This, the first day of our escape, was full of anxiety and fears, lest we should be retaken and subjected to captivity far worse than we had experienced before. About sundown the working party withdrew, and we resumed our journey toward the north star."

The two avoided Rebel cavalry patrols and when they arrived at the Chickahominy conveniently found a fallen tree bridging the banks. Using it to cross over without getting wet, they found concealment for a second day but could do little about the cold. *"That day I thought our feet certainly would freeze; and as necessity will often set the wits to work, I fell upon an expedient which doubtless saved us. Before leaving prison I had taken the precaution to put on two shirts—one of them a woolen one; this I pulled off; and having taken off our shoes and socks we lay down close together, and rolled our feet up in it, and found great relief.*"

Another Libby prisoner with luck on his side was Lt. Wells, whose hiding place for the first day was on a gentle slope above a spring *"where some colored women came to do washing. At times I could understand their conversation, and as the cavalry passed up the road, I heard them say something about 'de Yankee pris'ners.' Chicken and hogs came through the day, all seeming to view me suspiciously, the hogs especially.*"

After escaping Richmond, Col. McCreery and his companion, Maj. Clark, were hiking on the second night, *"avoiding all houses, clearings and roads, and whenever it became necessary to cross a road we always walked backwards.*

"Just at daybreak the next morning we could hear the approach of footsteps, and we fell flat on the ground and awaited developments. We saw two figures stealthily approaching. The Major whispered, 'There are only two of them, and unless they are armed we can and will dispatch them if they discover us.'

"The two men came nearer and nearer, and I soon recognized them as Col. Hobart and Col. West of the Wisconsin infantry. We arose from the ground, they quickly recognized us, and right there we had a love feast. We then and there agreed that no one of the four should be recaptured while any of the others remained alive."

Col. Hobart picks up the story of how the quartet made their way toward Union lines. *"The country was alive with pursuers. We could distinctly hear the reveille of the rebel troops and the hum of their camps. It was arranged that one of the four should precede, searching out the way in the darkness and giving notice of any danger.*

"During all this toilsome way but few words passed between us, and these in low whispers. So untiring was the search, and so thoroughly alarmed and watchful were the population, that we felt our safety depended upon a bare chance."

The escapees were all slowly starving and freezing to death. They were still dozens of Rebel-patrolled miles from Union lines. They needed help desperately—and when they asked the right people, they would get it.

CHAPTER TWENTY-TWO

Saved by Slaves

"*IT WAS MY TURN TO ACT THE PART OF PILOT,*" WROTE COL. HARRISON Hobart, who was the point man for three fellow escapees on their fourth night out. "*While rapidly leading the way through a wood of low pines I suddenly found myself in the presence of a cavalry reserve. The men were warming themselves by a blazing fire and their horses were tied to trees. I was surprised and alarmed; but recovering my self-possession, I remained motionless. Carefully putting one foot behind the other I retreated out of sight, and rapidly returned to my party.*"

After much discussion, the four decided to take the chance of returning to a plantation they had passed. They would try approaching one of the rough slave cabins which, by design, were built well out of sight of the main house. The POWs were so desperate they felt they had no other choice.

Col. Hobart volunteered to do the talking while the others lay in the grass. He rapped at the door. A slave woman replied. Hobart launched into a tale about being a lost traveler who needed information about the roads nearby.

Through the door she directed them to "the massa's house," but Hobart would not budge. He could hear conversation inside, and eventually the door opened.

"*I was surprised to find a large, good-looking negro stand by her side, who had been listening to the interview. He invited me to come in, and as soon as the door was closed said: 'I know who you are; you're one of dem 'scaped officers from Richmond.' Looking him full in the face, I placed my hand firmly upon his shoulder and said: 'I am, and I know you are my friend.' His eyes sparkled as he repeated: 'Yes, sir; yes, sir; but you mustn't stay here; a reg'ment of cavalry is right thar,' pointing to a place near by, 'and they pass this road all times of the night.' The negro proved to be a sharp, shrewd fellow."*

Col. McCreery was listening outside the door and later recorded Hobart's plea: *"We are here because we know that every black man is the friend of the Union solider and of the cause. We know you will not betray us. We are in trouble and seek information in regard to the rebel picket line. Can you and will you aid us?"*

"'Yes I can and will,' he replied, 'but if it should ever be known my life will pay the forfeit. I am a slave and have a wife and two children who look to me for protection. I will do all I can for you, but remember, I am in great danger.'"

After giving the escapees milk and corn bread, the slave led them to a concealed thicket in the woods, *"where we sat down on a log and listened to all he had to say. He was intelligent, thoroughly acquainted with every foot of the country, but he would not consent to act as our pilot, fearing he might be discovered."*

The Yankee officers continued to push their case. According to Hobart, *"After impressing us in his strongest language with the danger both to him and to us of making the least noise, he conducted us through a long cane-brake path, then through several fields."* The slave would ultimately lead them, silently, for three miles until they had passed all the local Confederate cavalry and pickets. He then gave them useful instructions on the way to Yankee lines.

The four prisoners were quite aware that they would have had little chance of getting this far on their own. Wrote McCreery, *"We gave the negro all the money we had and, bidding good-bye, he started for home and we for Union lines. If good deeds are recorded in heaven, this slave's name appeared in the record that night."*

Lt. Earle and his companion had gone through the Libby tunnel with a small stash of saved food. They'd carefully divided it into six equal parts, in anticipation of a week's journey. But by the fourth night all the food had been eaten and they were famished: *"Finding that our strength was becoming exhausted, we planned to approach a farm-house and confiscate a chicken, which we intended to eat raw. While we were reconnoitering the* out-buildings of a farm-house, we were discovered by a negro. He knew at once we were 'Yankee officers, 'scaped from prison,' but he gave us such an assurance of sympathy that we trusted him at once.

"We were taken immediately to his cabin, and were soon before a blazing fire. A guard of colored people were posted to prevent surprise, and the mother of the family began to prepare us something to eat. How the pones of corn bread, shaped in the old granny's hands, disappeared, and how delicious was that meat; I have always thought it was stolen expressly for us, from the slaveholder's pantry.

"We were thoroughly warmed and well fed, and started out with new courage and definite directions regarding our route."

The prisoners were far from Richmond, traveling as fast as they could walk, yet the slaves had already heard about the breakout. This happened in many cases, puzzling escapees such as Lt. Wells, who wondered, "What intuition or knowledge aforethought was it that told this ignorant old man that his visitor was an escaped Yankee prisoner? But such seems to be the case. It is a fact that the negroes of the South were thoroughly alive to the situation and stood ready at all times, even at the risk of their lives, to aid Northern soldiers. Held in bondage though they were for two hundred years, they are religiously devoted to our institutions and the land of their birth. It is hoped that these facts will be taken into account, and thrown into the scale in the negroes' favor when an adjustment of the race problem comes, as it must."

There were many stories like Hobart's. Almost every Libby inmate who successfully escaped did so with the help of local slaves. In each instance the slaves risked their own lives when the ragged Yankees came to them for aid. None were turned in, even though the rewards for doing so would have been substantial.

Southern slave owners believed their "chattel" were isolated and ignorant, yet stories like these demonstrate they had a formidable Underground of their own. It is likely this Underground was connected to Elizabeth Van Lew and her Unionist spy network. The slaves clearly had private paths and channels of communication that their owners knew nothing about. Messages traveled so quickly that they heard about the Libby breakout before the escapees had even arrived on their doorsteps. Yet officially, slaves couldn't travel anywhere without a written pass from their white masters. Southerners patrolled their roads constantly; any white person could challenge any Black person and ask for letters of passage. In response, the slaves had developed their own messaging system.

Capt. Caldwell, the POW who tended to see God's helping hand in his escape, was pausing to rest when his companion remarked, *"'Cap, there is somebody coming,' at which I raised my head and discovered a black man in Federal uniform coming up toward us. He seemed to observe that we displayed a little embarrassment when he spoke, and said: 'Gemmen, don't be scared; I'se your friend.' To which I replied, 'Yes, your face betokens that fact.'"*

The trio engaged in small talk for a while, feeling each other out. Caldwell's account conveys his impression of the man's dialect at the moment of getting down to business: *"Gemmen, I'se so glad I met you heah; I know who you is; you is some ob dese sojers from Libby. Some ob your men went along heah yesterday, and de pickets fired on 'em, and you is gwine in de same road, an' I'se afraid you'd ha got into trouble if I'd not ha' met you jus' now.'*

"'Well, Uncle,' said I, 'I suppose the Lord sent you out here to save us from getting into trouble.'

"'Well,' said the old man, ''tis strange indeed. I'se been sick all the forenoon, and sumpin say to me I mus' walk out. I know not what it was say to me "walk out," but now I b'lieves it was de Laud.'"

They thanked the man for giving them such crucial information, and then told him how hungry they were. He replied that he could get something if they were willing to wait until nightfall; the ex-prisoners agreed because they were ready to do anything for a bit of food.

The slave informed them that his wife lived on another plantation close by, and the trio set off on what was to be a two-mile walk through the woods. After a while the slave told them to lie down in the grass, *"while he would go into a house nearby which he said was the dwelling of a free man of color, and see if he could not get something for us there. In about fifteen minutes the old man returned, but lo and behold, he brought out a white man. At this our suspicions were aroused, and we began to conclude that the old negro had betrayed us."*

An intense interrogation ensued as the prisoners tried to sort out the situation. To their great surprise and relief, they were told this other person really was *"a free man of color"* after all. He told them he had a white woman in his cabin who would surely turn them in and cause him to be punished severely, so they should continue hiking to the home of the slave himself. But first he and the slave entered his home and returned with a corn dodger, butter, and pork.

The friendly slave then led them to his own cabin but insisted they not enter until after dark, so the POWs lay down again and waited. Once dusk had passed, he returned. *"As soon as he observed me he began to beckon with his hand and say in a low tone of voice, 'Come on, come on; all right, all right,' when we followed him, and were soon introduced to his beautiful wife and little ones.*

"Supper being ready, which consisted of fried eggs and ham, and a corn dodger, we sat down while the old uncle went out to stand sentinel. Every few moments the old man would put his head in the door and say: 'Gemmen, help yousef's, no danger, all's right.'

"Supper being over, I now feel called upon to say that I never ate a more palatable meal in my life, or one that seemed to do me so much good as did this humble repast."

After enjoying every bite of their banquet they rested for a short time. When they rose to continue their journey, the slave again offered to help: *"The old uncle volunteered to go with us a mile further, and direct us how to flank the pickets. Of course we were ready to accept any kindness and again, in company with the old man, we resumed our journey onward.*

"Having conducted us past the point of danger, the old patriarch now let fall his parting blessing upon us, and took an affectionate farewell and returned to his home, while we plod our way onward, wondering whether we shall ever in this world be able to reciprocate, and at the same time invoking Heaven's richest blessings to fall on him and his little family for the kindness shown us in our extremity."

Lt. Johnston and his escape companion believed their key to survival was eternal watchfulness and suspicion. They scrupulously avoided any man or woman that they encountered until *"on the fourth night we came to a path along which a negro man was passing; we stopped and asked him a number of questions and were convinced he was a friend. We then asked him if he could get us something to eat."*

The man pointed to the house he was approaching and assured the escapees that friends lived there. *"But we had suffered so much that we did not feel inclined to trust strangers; however, I asked him to go to the house and see if any rebel soldiers were there. This he did readily, and soon returned, telling us that the way was clear, and supper, such as they had, would soon be prepared for us."*

This sounded like the most wonderful offer, but Johnston could not shake his nervousness and asked if the man would stand guard while they went into the house. Hearing that he would, they entered and found friendship, food, and a good fire: *"We happened to have a little coffee with us, the very thing of which they seemed most in need. We added this to their store, and soon had the first good meal we had taken for months before us, and a cheery cup of coffee, which made it seem a feast."*

They rested at the home, which they sorely needed to do, *"and gave our entertainers all that we could—our heart-felt thanks. When we were ready to start, the faithful negro sentinel offered to be our guide and conducted us about four miles on our journey. He added directions which we found to be valuable, and we shall never forget the kindness of the warm heart that beat in that black man's breast."*

Lt. Wallber and his companion had been walking day and night. But without maps or outside help they didn't even know if they were going in the right direction.

"Again and again we lost our way in the forest. At last we could endure no longer exertion, hunger, and pain. We collapsed, stiff with cold and weak, one after the other as if by electric shock. We lay in a grimy heap of misery and distress incarnate: hair long and disheveled in our faces, clothing tattered, feet slashed by thorns and bleeding."

Lt. Wallber fell into an anxious sleep and dreamed of tables laden with glorious delicacies. Instead he was brought back to reality by the pounding of horse's hooves as a Rebel cavalryman passed by and almost saw them. The trio pulled themselves up and continued on their difficult way. Finally they got some luck.

"Toward evening we found a negro at work on a plantation. We called to him. He looked on us with astonished eyes, unable to conceal amazement at

men who could come so far from Richmond and suffer no mishap. 'Stay here in the woods until dark,' the negro said."

The slave returned that night and provided them with bacon and exquisite fresh-baked corn bread. It took no time to devour everything. *"We gave him $6 Confederate. This gratuity, every last cent we could shake out of our pockets, so delighted him that he declared one good turn deserved another."*

They were told to wait, and the slave went out to find a friend. *"The friend suggested we accompany him to his place to discuss what could be done to aid our flight. Kind hearts welcomed us to their humble home. We sat at the hearth and warmed ourselves at the cheery fire.*

"'I'm a free negro,' our host said, 'Name's George Washington.'

"I trusted him even before he said his name. He took keen interest in our stories of suffering in prison. His face confessed determination to help us any way he could and thereby overreach the Rebels." While they discussed plans, the woman of the house served a simple, wonderful meal. Then they waited for dark.

When they were feeling rested, Mr. Washington led them to the nearby Chickahominy River where he rowed them for eight miles, advancing as far as his personal safety allowed. After giving additional advice, he returned to his home while Wallber pressed on, though the comforting hearth had caused him an unexpected problem. *"I had removed my shoes by the fire. The wet shoes had shrunk so that I could not get them back on feet bloody and swollen. But (as the proverb teaches) necessity knows no law. I removed my coat collar with one cut of my knife, halved it, wrapped a half around each foot, and walked the whole night."*

All of these slaves, deprived as they were, gave whatever they could to succor the Libby escapees. They are high on the list of unknown heroes in the Civil War.

Slaves helped the desperate POWs in ways that were crucial, but they couldn't rescue them. That would be the job of the US Cavalry.

CHAPTER TWENTY-THREE

Pluck and Luck

To succeed at escaping from Libby, a man needed pluck and luck and four aces and all his ducks in a row. He needed good fortune, Godspeed, and God on his side. And even then he might be caught.

But the POWs had one advantage over their pursuers: extreme motivation. They pushed on when the Rebels took breaks, built fires, or had their meals. The Yankees didn't have fires or food anyway.

Almost a week into the escape, only the hardiest and most fortunate had survived. Any man with a physical or mental weakness had stumbled and been caught. Dozens of failed escapees were already streaming back to Libby and the dungeons. The others pressed on, driven by the knowledge that they were close to salvation.

No pursuer could anticipate the prisoners' movements because the prisoners themselves didn't know where they were going from one footstep to the next—just east by the North Star. Always east.

Many of the escapees had the misfortune of running into Diascund Creek, an obscure tributary to the Chickahominy known only to locals. It had been flooded by recent rains that had swollen it into a wide barrier.

Cols. Hobart and McCreery, along with their two companions, found themselves stymied by this latest obstacle. At the same time, they knew they were close to their goal of Williamsburg and freedom.

"The water being extremely cold, and we being very wet and weary, we did not dare attempt to swim the stream; and expecting every moment to see the enemy's cavalry, our hearts sank within us.

"*At this juncture a rebel soldier was seen coming up the river in a row boat with a gun. Requesting my companions to lie down in the grass, I concealed myself in the bushes close to the water to get a good view of the man. Finding his countenance to indicate youth and benevolence I accosted him as he approached, 'Good morning; I have been waiting for you; they told me up at the houses that I could get across, but I find the bridge is gone and I am very wet and cold; and if you will take me over I will pay you for your trouble.'*"

Col. Hobart, oldest of the group, had a long, flowing grey beard. The young man in the boat felt compelled to help him.

"*The boat was turned in to the shore, and as I stepped into it I knew that boat was mine. Keeping my eye upon his gun I said to him: 'there are three more of us,' and they immediately stepped into the boat.*"

Before the startled Rebel could react, his boat was occupied by the four men. Col. McCreery recorded the conversation: "'*Where did you all come?' said the boatman. We told him that we were farmers and that we had been down to Richmond with our produce and that the government, being in great need, had confiscated our teams and we were obliged to walk home.*

"'*The officers don't like to have me carry men over this river,' he said, evidently suspecting who we were. 'That is right,' we replied, 'you should not carry suspicious characters. Pass your boat along.'*"

And quickly all four Yankees crossed to the other shore, dry and rested.

"*We gave him one or two greenbacks and he rapidly returned. We knew that we were discovered and that the enemy's cavalry soon would be in hot pursuit. Therefore we determined to go into hiding as near as possible to the river. The wisdom of this course was soon demonstrated. The cavalry crossed the stream, dashed by us, and thoroughly searched the country to the front, not dreaming but we had gone forward.*"

This quartet of POWs had survived now for six days. They were close.

Lt. Fales had come to regret his decision to swim back for the rations he had mistakenly left behind a few days earlier. "*I had thus given myself thrice the exposure of my comrades to the ice-cold water, and had been sick from the very moment of the final landing. This sickness had constantly increased and I had been unable to eat any of the dearly-bought rations. All this day I was hot and feverish, and while my companions were peacefully sleeping I was wide awake and wracked with frequent pain."*

At dark the three men pressed on, but Fales could not keep up. He told his companions to leave him behind, but they would not hear of it. With a man on each side supporting him, Fales was able to move slowly until about ten o'clock, *"when I found I could go no further, and seeing a house with negro huts around it, I told my comrades to leave me. They were reluctant, but I insisted that they should not lose their chance for escape."*

Fales approached one of the huts and boldly told the slave woman who came to the door that he was an escaped prisoner from Libby. Without hesitation she invited him inside, where Fales asked if she had any medicine he might take, but she had none. Then he asked for tea, because he could not eat any food, and she made him two quarts of sage tea. He drank it, she made some simple food and then, *"She brought me a comforter, and rolling up in it I laid down before the blazing fire, and after a while had profuse perspiration and went to sleep, resting until morning, when I felt a new man.*

"Just before daylight the negro woman came down the ladder from the loft where she had slept and said I had better be going, as her master might be out before long and he might shoot me."

The woman set Fales on a path that led to Union lines. He ran into a white man he felt he could not trust, and so after leaving him spent the rest of the day hiding in the forest. *"In the afternoon the clouds gathered, and at night it was very dark, so I could not see my way through the woods, but I started in the direction of Williamsburg and soon struck a road which had evident marks of the passage of troops, there being frequent tracks."*

Since Fales could no longer travel in the darkened forest, he made a calculated decision to follow along this road. He had seen no one and determined that if Rebel pickets were around, they would be on horseback and he'd spot them in enough time to escape into the woods. Then, as Fales remembered it:

"I had not gone far before I was startled by the command, 'Halt!' and discovered a dismounted rebel cavalryman standing behind a tree not five yards away, with his carbine covering me. The following conversation ensued:

CHAPTER TWENTY-THREE

Reb.—'Who comes there?'

Yank.—'A friend.'

Reb.—'Advance and give the countersign.'

Yank.—'I have no countersign.'

Reb.—'It's no use, I know you.'

Yank.—'Who am I?'

Reb.—'You are one of the Yankees that escaped from Libby prison.'

Yank.—'How do you know I am a Yankee?'

Reb.—'I know you by the way you talk.'"

Lt. Fales realized the chase was over. The Rebel picket called for a lieutenant of the guard, and a soldier was detailed to take Fales to their camp. They had a fire; the Rebels gave him some food and a blanket. He lay down by the flames and pretended to sleep. He realized his guard was dozing off. It was only the two of them, and Fales noticed an ax lying near the fire. *"I was just reaching for the axe when I heard the lieutenant and two soldiers coming, so my plan was knocked on the head instead of the guard. I then gave up the idea of trying to escape and went to sleep."*

The next morning, when Fales began the 50-mile return to Libby, he saw Union pickets only half a mile away. That was how close he had come. *"I was marched about 20 miles that day, and about five o'clock arrived at a railroad station where I was put on a car, and before seven o'clock was back in Libby prison.*

"On my return, all the prison officials seemed to be very angry. Dick Turner said to me: 'Take off that overcoat.' I said: 'What for?' He replied: 'Because I tell you, that's enough.' The coat cost me forty dollars and I never saw it again. Dick Turner undoubtedly stole it for his own use. I was then taken down to the cell, where I found five other officers who had also been re-captured."

Lt. Johnston and his companion Lt. Fislar had been considerably revived by the aid the slaves had given them, and they continued their walking by night. But the next morning they were too cold to rest and decided to keep going.

"We had not traveled any in the daytime before, still, we kept a vigilant watch, but met with no interruption, and we gradually became bolder. About sundown we saw a negro chopping wood, and our adventure of the previous night had given us confidence in those having black skins, we walked directly

toward him. Judge our surprise, however, when we came within a few paces of him, to find a white man with him, seated at the foot of a tree!"

It was too late for them to change their course, so they went up to the man and asked how far it was to a small town that they had already passed. A curious conversation ensued as each tried to discern the truth about the other. The white man let them know that he recognized Johnston and his companions to be Union soldiers—but that he personally took no side in the war. *"He had heard of the escape of the Libby prisoners, but did not credit it—but must believe it now as he had the living witnesses before him. He talked freely with us, saying that he was a citizen and had taken no part whatever in the war, and even expressed the wish that we might make our escape.*

"I told him that I expected as soon as we were gone, that he would go to the nearest picket-post and inform his rebel friends what course we had taken. He declared that he had no such intention, and repeated the wish that we might have a safe journey."

They then discussed the nearest Confederates and the latest sightings. The white man gave them some directions, but the prisoners were suspicious. Johnston was always suspicious. *"I could not resist the conviction that he was treacherous. He assured us that no harm should come to us through him, shook hands with us, and wished us again a safe journey.*

"We had not gone over a hundred yards, when I happened to look back, I saw our friend traveling at a pace quite unnecessary for one so friendly. I turned to my comrade and said, 'We are gone up; that scoundrel, I feel near certain, has gone to report us to the nearest picket-guard.'"

Johnston was so convinced of the man's treachery that he and Lt. Fislar changed their route and set off on an entirely new direction. They had not traveled half a mile when they heard men talking and stopped to listen: *"It was even as I had suspected—the professed friend had informed the rebels; and the officer was now placing his men on the road we were expected to cross, and we were now within twenty paces of them.*

"It was a moment of fearful suspense; we were screened from view by the bushes; we started but the rustling of the leaves beneath our feet betrayed us, and we were sternly ordered to come out of the brush. We hesitated, and the order was repeated in fierce, quick tones, which was accompanied by a volley of musketry."

The two men came out at the double-quick, but in the opposite direction from the Rebels, who continued to fire at them. *"We broke away and ran for life. With a shout our enemies joined in the pursuit, and pressed us so closely I lost my overcoat, and Lt. Fislar lost his cap. On came our pursuers, nearer and nearer, till, in order to save ourselves we had to take refuge in a large swamp."*

The Confederates fanned out to cut them off, but the swamp was too big to encircle. The two POWs pushed on as far as they could, then found a place to hide. *"While thus lying concealed in the swamp our reflections were not of the most agreeable character. We had almost reached the reward of much toil and suffering; we had even begun to think of home and the loved ones there. We contrasted the duplicity of the civilized white man who had betrayed us into the power of our enemies, with the fidelity of the African slave who had proved so kind and true, and felt that under the dark skin beat the nobler heart."*

Eventually the pursuers withdrew. Johnston and Fisler had no choice but to head deeper into the swamp. Wet, muddy, and cold, they kept going until *"looking both before and behind us, it really seemed as if we were the first human beings who had ever penetrated to that dismal and solitary place."*

They were safe again, but where were they? They knew Union lines must be close, so they pushed on as best they could.

Capt. Calder and his companion passed their third day by hiding in the forest. They lay on whatever ground cover they could find and listened carefully, all the while praying for the long hours to pass. About three o'clock in the afternoon, after waking from sleep, his companion began to shake Calder, saying, *"'Cap, I hear somebody coming.' I had heard the same but said nothing. He again suggested leaving, but I replied we were safer in our present position than we would if we should attempt to move, for in that case we would be seen.*

"We therefore remained quiet, and as we listened with breathless anxiety, the man seemed to get closer at the sound of every step, finally he came in full view, and just about fifteen steps in front of us, when behold! our man proved to be a huge, long black bearded wild turkey gobbler."

This scare had gotten them wide awake, and since they couldn't rest anymore they decided to resume their journey. They had many close calls while avoiding local citizens and found themselves having to strip nude to cross another freezing stream. Calder began to feel sick and said that he had to rest—but his companion pointed out, *"We can't stop here in the swamp as there is no place to lie down."* They had no choice but to keep walking. Eventually Calder threw up and felt much better. The two finally reached the edge of the mire and found solid ground covered with high, white grass. It was a perfect place to hide, and they were able to take their daylight's rest unmolested.

The pair continued on like this for several days—hiding and always watchful, but advancing. On the morning of the sixth day it began to snow, making it too uncomfortable to sleep on the ground. *"Night at last came, but with it no cessation in the snow; it continued to pour down, and thus having no stars by which to steer our course, it was impossible for us to travel with any degree of certainty. However, we felt that if we remained inactive we should surely perish. The primary object now was not to reach our lines—as we knew nothing of the course we were going—but it was to preserve life."*

Again providence intervened, as it somehow tended to do for the future preacher. The POWs emerged out of dense forest into a clearing that held a farm and a cluster of small buildings that appeared to be slave quarters. But all was abandoned so they decided to spend the night in one of the shacks.

"The house we entered had the window and doors all torn out, but it had a roof, a floor, and a wooden chimney. Now, for the first time, we saw the necessity of having matches with which to make a fire. But we also remembered the matches that had been provided for our journey had been left behind by the man's not coming out who had them in his possession.

"We began to search our pockets, and by some good Providence I found to my surprise that I had one match in my pocket." They could not waste this single chance at a warming fire, so they carefully prepared a pile of fine pine shavings in the fireplace. *"I then gave the match a strike upon the chimney jam, and off it went, to our great delight, and in a few moments we had splendid fire, and soon we were warm and comfortable."*

For the first time in their awful journey, the two men were able to relax. They congratulated themselves on their good fortune and began recounting some of their closest escapes, *"when lo! and behold we heard a tremendous roaring in the chimney, and upon looking up we found to our great chagrin the chimney was all on fire! We ran from the house scarcely knowing what to do, and found the fire was threatening to destroy the house in short time.*

"In this state of confusion we fell to snowballing the fire, and in about fifteen minutes hard work succeeded in putting it out"—but inside the chimney the flames still raged. The two men hauled snowballs into the fireplace but they could not snuff it out completely until Caldwell doffed his overcoat and climbed up in the chimney. *"After some minutes of hard labor in applying the snow to the burning chimney wall, I succeeded in putting the fire out."*

The exhausted men slept the sleep of the dead; they woke thoroughly refreshed after their adventure. Waiting for the morning sun to melt any snow that would show their footprints, they set off again in search of the Union Army.

Young Lt. Earle had also been surprised by the sudden snowstorm. The 19-year-old gave up trying to hide during the day and instead set out walking, though the going was rough, with *"the snow falling rapidly, and thawing quite as fast, making it very difficult to travel. We were deprived of our only safe and constant guide, the North Star, and after proceeding till nearly dark we came to the exact spot whence we had started two hours before. We were exceedingly tired, cold, wet, and hungry."*

At just this time they noticed a covered horse cart approaching, one they assumed was driven by a slave teamster. They halted it but were surprised to find the driver was white. Then they had another surprise, as the white man asserted that he was a Union supporter, and backed this up by giving them valuable information about the roads and directing them to *"a negro family who had the means to furnish us some food, and also assured us that we would come in contact with some of our troops if we eluded the Rebel scouts during the next 24 hours. He informed us, however, that we were on very dangerous ground—the scouting ground between two armies—a place full of guerillas and bushwhackers."*

For days on his own, Lt. Wells had struggled to put distance between himself and Richmond, but *"hunger, fatigue, and loss of sleep were closing in upon me with a deathlike grip. I pushed on, however, and though from sheer exhaustion often stumbled and fell to the ground."*

Hiding during the cold of the next day, as Wells later recalled, he had plenty of time to reflect *"upon the mutability of human affairs and the vicissitudes of a soldier's life,"* and it left him quite discouraged. Then, while waiting for night to come and with it the guiding star, Wells heard footsteps approaching. Frightened, he could distinguish the steps of two men and crouched down as low as possible.

As he watched the men creeping closer, almost on tiptoe, he realized they were fellow escapees Randall and McCain. He hailed them with a whisper; the trio were soon sharing what food they had and planning to stay together.

Next day, out of desperation, they decided to take a chance and continue their journey in daylight. First they came upon a schoolhouse; while they debated whether to approach it, 75 Rebel cavalrymen rode up and halted at the building. Lt. Randall was determined to find a path around. He set off from the other two and quickly disappeared. When they heard distant gunshots, they logically presumed that Randall had been either caught or killed.

McCain and Wells tried to retreat, but local dogs would give them no peace. *"The firing below and barking of the dog had set everybody else on the lookout, and the soldiers discovered us and gave chase down a lane, but we finally eluded them and, for the balance of the day, remained in the swamp."* They resolved never again to try so foolhardy a thing as moving in daylight.

That night they were hiking when they saw a man standing in the doorway of a modest cabin. Assuming him to be a slave, they approached—only to see the man was white. As it was too late to run away, they boldly asked him for some food, confessing who they were and saying they *"were likely to perish for want of something to eat. He said he had been in the Confederate service and knew the life of a soldier, 'But,' said he, 'I never turned a hungry man from my door, and do not propose to do so now.' He gave us half a dozen dry biscuits, stating the biscuits comprised his entire stock of food on hand."*

They followed his advice about where to go next. But the next day was the one in which it snowed, and afraid to proceed in daylight they hid under a thicket of boughs and leaves until nightfall.

"How long we had lain there is uncertain, but presently I was awakened by McCain who said we must get up as we were likely to become stupefied and perish from the cold. I agreed with him, but neither one made an effort to rise. While lying in this state of half-consciousness I found my memory was failing and could not recall my brother's name. But suddenly, as if by a concert of thought and action we sprang to our feet and soon found ourselves in an open field near a road that proved to be the Williamsburg Pike."

This was the main road to Williamsburg; they could tell it was heavily travelled. That night they followed it, careful to stay well back from the road, always ready to run deeper into the nearby woods.

They heard cavalry approaching. Secreting themselves in bushes nearby, the two attempted to figure out the colors of the mounted men but could discern neither blue nor grey.

The pair heard the clattering of scabbards as the cavalry came closer. They agreed that Union troopers were much more likely to carry swords than their Confederate counterparts. But that was far from enough to lead them to expose themselves.

"They came up and passed, but nothing occurred and no word was spoken to give us any clew of their identity. The situation was anything but pleasant. The cold, freezing rain was coming down in sheets and our bones were chilled to the marrow. The main column had passed and the rear guard, about twenty in number, were in front of us.

"We could endure the suspense no longer and resolved to hail them, and if it be proved to be the enemy, trust to the mercy of the darkness to enable us to get away without being shot. Accordingly, both stood up and I cried out, 'What regiment is that?'

"As quick as thought the entire squad drew their pistols, demanding at the same time our immediate surrender. The click of the hammers, which we could hear as they came into position, added to the horror of the moment and I said to McCain, 'We are gone up.' He seemed to agree and replied that we had better surrender, as our lives depended upon it. Accordingly, we threw up our hands and together cried out, 'We will surrender.'"

Troopers and escapees closed toward each other. Anxious eyes strained in the starless darkness. Then the soldiers announced themselves to be the Eleventh Pennsylvania Cavalry, sent out to find any escapees from Libby.

Wells and McCain were safe—rescued—free!

CHAPTER TWENTY-FOUR

Freedom

As soon as he heard the first reports about the Libby escape, the Union commander for Eastern Virginia, Gen. Benjamin Butler, ordered his forces to move forward from Williamsburg and start searching. Butler had two units of cavalry at his disposal, with about 300 men each. Their orders were to drive Confederate pickets out of the no-man's-land that separated the two armies and bring in as many escapees as they could find.

This no-man's-land was the last barrier the POWs had to cross. Escapee Col. McCreery described the destruction both armies had brought to this part of Virginia: *"There were no buildings, no inhabitants, and no sound save our weary footsteps—desolation reigned supreme. Lone bare chimneys stood along our way like sentinels over the dead land.*

"We knew we were near the outposts of the Union troops, and began to feel as if our trials were nearly over, but we were now in danger of being shot as rebels by scouting parties from our own army."

Lt. Wallber and his companion were cautiously walking the road to Williamsburg late at night when they suddenly encountered a force of cavalry. Running into the nearby woods, they did not have time to hide and were overtaken.

"In a moment they surrounded us (so quickly it made our heads spin) and issued an order.

"'Come out with your hands up or we'll shoot.'

"Unable to find a hole, we could only surrender and accept fate.

"A gruff voice demanded, 'Who are you?'

"'We're farmers, we live around here.'

"'You lie,' said the commanding officer. 'The truth now or you'll hang from that tree.'

"'So you want the truth? Well, we're Union officers who escaped from Richmond.'

"'State your corps, regiment, and rank.'

"We complied.

"They shouted, 'You're in good hands. We're the Eleventh Pennsylvania Cavalry!'

"What? Pennsylvania cavalry? Union forces, our men, greeted us with glee. Saved! To witness their happiness, to receive their sympathy, meant more than any money to us.

"I forgot the horrors of prison and the dangers of flight. I relished the moment in bliss. Nor shall I forget the scene when battle-hardened veterans, used to the abominations of war, could find no words to express their feelings.

"Tears rose to their eyes and they wept without shame. The tears, which signified indignation and rage, also proclaimed joy at meeting us here. What a happy circumstance! The storms of time can never erode my memory of that moment, so firmly is it fixed forever!"

Lt. Wells and Lt. McCain were now safely behind Union lines; but they assumed that their companion, from whom they'd become separated, had been captured or even killed. However, Lt. Randall was still a fugitive in the Virginia wilderness. He was alone but had been able to evade his pursuers and was close to Williamsburg.

Finally Randall came in sight of what he supposed were Rebel cavalry dressed in blue uniforms. Afraid to expose himself, Randall watched these cavalrymen for an entire day. "They came so close to me that I could see the U.S. on their belts. They did not see me as I was so well concealed. After satisfying myself that they were our men, I came out of my hiding place, greatly to their surprise and my joy. They were a detachment of the 11th Pennsylvania Cavalry.

"This certainly seemed to be the crowning event of my life."

Supreme emotion overwhelmed everyone who witnessed these men crossing from fear to freedom. For most it was beyond description, as with young Lt. Earle, who had been imprisoned for almost a year. "It is

HARPER'S WEEKLY.
A JOURNAL OF CIVILIZATION

VOL. VIII.—No. 375.]   NEW YORK, SATURDAY, MARCH 5, 1864.   [$2.50 FOR FOUR MONTHS.
$3.00 PER YEAR IN ADVANCE.

Entered according to Act of Congress, in the Year 1864, by Harper & Brothers, in the Clerk's Office of the District Court for the Southern District of New York.

THE ESCAPED REFUGEES FROM THE LIBBY PRISON.—[SEE PAGE 18.]

The escaped refugees from Libby Prison.

impossible to express in words our feelings at that time—indeed, I doubt my ability to do so. The thousand mile trip to a Confederate prison, the joys and sorrows, the hopes and disappointments, the peril and suffering, the swamps and briar thickets, the anticipation of success and the despair at the thought of recapture; all this, and finally freedom and home and friends—what words can express it all?"

Earle and his companion had been found by the First New York Mounted Rifles, a second cavalry detachment working the area along with the Eleventh Pennsylvania. *"No one can describe the kindness shown us by this body of men. Every attention was showered on us. We were banqueted at Company A's head-quarters, and feted at Company B's, and banqueted again at Company C's, and so on."*

Cols. Hobart and McCreery also found themselves cornered in the darkness by a troop of cavalry they could barely see. Hobart prepared for the worst: *"Looking at their coats I concluded they were grey and was nerving my self for recapture. It was a supreme moment of the soul. One of my companions asked 'Are you Union soldiers?'*

"In broad Pennsylvania language the answer came, 'Well, we are.' In a moment their uniforms changed to a glorious blue, and taking off our hats we gave one long, exultant shout. It was like passing from death to life."

Prisoners continued to stagger into Williamsburg at all hours, but many were still wandering the countryside. Capt. Caldwell and his companion had been on the run eight days and knew they needed help, so they approached a slave cabin. Barking dogs appeared from every direction, but Caldwell pushed forward and *"an old black woman came out, leaning on her staff and calling on the dogs to be still, when I spoke saying 'Good evening, aunty.' 'Good evening, suh,' she replied, when I observed, 'Aunty, my comrade and I have been travelling all day and are hungry, can you get us something to eat?' To which the old lady replied, 'You's some ob dese Yankee sogers, aint you? I knows what you is—some of you men done gone by yah yesterday. I knows you, I knows. God lub you honey, come in. I fry you some ham and some eggs and I bake you hoe cake; and bress de Lord, I make you good cup coffee. I know you no get coffee up dar to Richmond.'"*

The old woman was well supplied and willing to share, but Caldwell was still paranoid and wondered if it would be safe to remain very long.

The woman's husband was 90 and blind, so she soothed their fears by asking her brother to come by and serve as lookout.

The two then enjoyed a meal that was better than what she had promised. They even had buttermilk for dessert. Neither man had tasted any dairy since the beginning of their eight months' imprisonment. They drank the whole pitcher. Next she washed and dried their pants by the fire; she not only cleaned their boots but greased them as well—*"and by the time we were ready to start on our journey, the old lady had fixed us up, almost feeling like new men."*

That night they were ready to continue their escape, but the woman was not finished with them, saying: *"'Don't go yit, I'se gwian wid you. You comed safe so far, I don't want you make no mistake now. Wait til I find my cane, an I go wid you.' So off we start, the old aunty leading the way."*

The trio moved slowly for three-quarters of a mile, where they found a road she had mentioned. She told them Williamsburg was close and that they should use this road as a guide. *"And after receiving another 'God lub you, honies' from the old lady we bid her farewell, but concluded as we were within 13 miles of our lines, that there could not be so much danger, and for once we would risk the road."*

They had not gone far when they saw a man cross the highway ahead of them. Thinking him to be a Yankee picket or scout, they approached, but when they reached the site the man had disappeared. Later they would conclude this had been another escapee, who obviously feared they were Confederates.

At four o'clock in the morning they were startled by a sharp command to *"Halt!"'* coming from their front. *"By whom are we halted?' The reply came back, 'By the picket.' 'By what line of pickets?' said I. 'By the outside line,' was the ready response. I repeated the interrogation, when he responded, 'the outside line, the cavalry videttes.'*

"Finding our picket a little dull of comprehension, I simplified my question by asking whether we were halted by the Confederate or Federal line. 'O,' said he, 'Is that, is that what you mean; why by the Union line.' 'Very well,' said I, 'I report two prisoners escaped from Libby prison.'

"At this the men seemed elated with joy, and gave us a hearty welcome, telling us they were expecting us all night, and now thanked God that we had come.

"*You may well imagine our feeling when, as by an electric shock, all the perilous and intensely thrilling adventures of the past eight days and nine nights broke in like a thunderclap upon our vision afresh. We were truly thankful to that divine Providence who had conducted us through our numerous perils in the wilderness.*" Capt. Caldwell, the future preacher, was always thankful for his good fortune.

The men immediately enjoyed a big breakfast, took to sleep, then had another breakfast upon awakening, "*until I believe we had eaten about four times that forenoon. The good people were so hospitable that I almost feared being surfeited through their abundant kindness, and we had to say, 'cease, it is enough.'*"

Lt. Johnston, having been wounded at Shiloh and trapped for days in Rat Hell, had spent a week struggling across the countryside, but finally he stumbled into the arms of the men in blue. Along with his companion Lt. Fislar, he was rescued by the Pennsylvania Cavalry, and the two were expected to enjoy a long recovery.

But when Lt. Fislar heard the cavalry was going out again on another patrol, he sprang up, requesting a horse and sabre so he could come along. His wish was granted, and soon he was aiding the search for his companions from Libby.

Lt. Johnston was too exhausted to rejoin the cavalry right then, but the next morning he was up with the rest. "*Having been furnished with sword, horse, and pistol I moved forward with the column. My position was in front with the captain—every man with eager eyes on the look-out for the late inmates of Libby.*"

They had barely traveled two miles when, to their delight, they discovered a pair of escapees who had worked with Johnston in the original digging party: Capt. Gallagher and Maj. Fitzsimmons.

"*Spurring my horse in advance of the rest, and swinging my hat and cheering as I went, I hastened to meet my old companions. We wept, we laughed, we shouted aloud in our joy. Our men came up and welcomed the fugitives warmly—not a man in the band who was not willing to dismount and let the wearied ones ride; and together we rode in search of others. During the day eleven more were added to our number—each one of them increasing our joy.*

"As we rode along we talked of our past trials, and the dangers we had passed since the night we parted in the cellar of Libby Prison, and speculated concerning the fate of others. During the day we had several skirmishes with rebel scouts, captured a few horses, and returned the same evening to Williamsburg."

Lt. Wells also joined the rescuers in looking for Libby POWs. The units now rode out equipped with *"horses already saddled for the prisoners to ride, and in their haversacks carried soft bread and meat in abundance, including a ration or two of whiskey for all hands."*

Wells was happy to be back in the saddle, helping soldiers traverse the sandy roads that spread out from Williamsburg. It was monotonous work, but Wells felt that *"one never knows, when scouting on neutral ground between two armies, what he may run into or what an hour will bring forth."*

He quickly got more than he'd bargained for when the entire squad suddenly spurred their horses and took off at full gallop. The young lieutenant had no idea who they could be pursuing. *"The whole squad was soon on the run, those in the rear having to 'take sand' from the more fortunate ones in the lead. Soon the Sergeant was seen in full chase, firing at a mounted man about 150 yards ahead, who was lying close to his horse, and with a six-shooter deliberately returning the Sergeant's fire.*

"Here was a race and shooting match in one, free to all comers, with 'nothing barred.' I was riding a good horse and already ahead of the main squad and the object of our chase did not seem to be more than fifty yards distant. I was becoming a little uneasy, fearing I might have to be the first to overtake this desperate man, whoever he might be."

Luckily for Wells, the chase ended when the fugitive suddenly leapt from his horse and took off into the woods and *"was soon out of sight and beyond the reach of our shots."*

It turned out they were pursuing a notorious guerrilla, or bushwhacker, named Hume, who was known for ambushing Yankee patrols in the area. He got away, but the Union men got his horse and his hat.

The cavalry squad went back to searching for POWs. Wells writes of finding a group of prisoners that included his friend, the white-bearded Col. Hobart. The two had been close in Libby, where Wells learned to admire the experience and intelligence of the older man: *"Colonel Hobart was a man of more than ordinary accomplishments and intellectual power. I had learned to look upon him with an admiration almost amounting to reverence.*

"Recognizing him here bedraggled, worn and travel-stained as he was, I dismounted and with my arms about him supported him for a minute or more, while his arms lay around my neck. Not a word was spoken.

"Officers and soldiers gathered around and stood respectfully awaiting the outcome of this affecting scene, and the silence was only broken when Colonel Hobart, his eyes cast upward and with tears streaming down his face exclaimed, 'This is the happiest moment I ever expect to see on earth.'"

In a few days all realized it was unlikely more prisoners would be found. Some had made the journey in as little as four days, but into the second week it was clear almost every escapee had been accounted for.

Eager journalists were keeping score on the biggest story of the day—complete with lists in the Union papers of those who had been rescued, and in the Confederate papers of those who had been recaptured. *"Every paper was full of the escape from Libby,"* wrote Lt. Earle.

But an important mystery was still unsolved: Where were Col. Rose and Col. Streight—the mastermind of the greatest escape, plus the most famous and most wanted of the escapees?

CHAPTER TWENTY-FIVE

Rose and Streight

COL. ROSE, THE INSTIGATOR OF THE TUNNEL PROJECT AND ITS LEADER through thick and thin, had intended to escape with his co-digger, Capt. Hamilton. But the two became separated in Richmond almost as soon as they got through the tunnel, when Rose was challenged by guards, while Hamilton was allowed to proceed. By the time Rose had successfully talked his way out of the situation, Hamilton was gone.

That first night Rose easily made his way out of Richmond but was stopped by the slow-moving Chickahominy River. Just as the sun began to rise he stumbled upon a camp of Rebel cavalry that was sounding reveille. He was lucky to find a large sycamore tree that was hollow, and he climbed inside.

It was cold and uncomfortable, but a safe place to hide for the day. Heading out in the evening, Rose had to wade across the Chickahominy and all his clothes were soaked. After walking a while, he spotted some Rebel cavalrymen and decided to lie down until they went away.

"When I attempted to rise I found myself perfectly stiff and my clothes completely frozen. I pushed right ahead, however, and I found several deep places filled with water."

Rose was not a man easily deterred. He did not try to maneuver his way around the ponds but plunged into them, forging through the swampy water until he reached higher ground.

"I was still very lame from the effects of a broken foot [from a previous escape attempt]. *This wound now became very troublesome, as the nights were dark and I could not see the inequalities of the ground.*

"I was in great danger of freezing to death. I had with me a haversack which I had held at arms' length while crossing the Chickahominy in order to keep it dry. I had a box of matches, and upon coming to a large thicket of cedars I resolved to build a fire."

Lt. Moran later interviewed Rose and recorded that the colonel felt building a fire *"was hazardous, but the necessity was desperate, since with his stiffened limbs he could no longer move fast enough to keep the warmth of life in his body."*

The cedars screened the flames, and he was finally able to relax his aching frame. Rose fell quickly into a sleep so deep that when he awoke he realized he was on fire, *"My coat was burned through in several places, as well and my pants and boots."* Rose put out the flames and resumed his journey, remarking: *"I had been nearly in as much danger of burning to death as I was before of freezing."*

Col. Rose traveled by night and avoided the occasional Confederate pickets that he spotted along the way. *"But in crossing a small open space I was seen by one of them, and the man rode up to me. He was a stupid fellow, and asked me if I belonged to the New Kent cavalry. I had on a grey cap. Of course I answered him in the affirmative. He turned and rode back, and I slipped into a thicket of laurels."*

Rose moved as fast as his lame foot would allow. He suspected the Rebel would report the encounter to his superiors, and he soon saw *"that the others had taken the alarm and were in full pursuit. Some of them evidently had seen me enter the laurel thicket, and in a minute it was surrounded."*

Rose ran to the edge of the forest and found it bordered by a large, open field. Frantically searching for a way out, he spotted a gully that ran across the field. *"It was neither wide nor deep, but it afforded my only chance of escape, so I threw myself into it and commenced crawling. It must have been more than a half a mile in length, but I crawled the entire distance without raising my head."*

Added Lt. Moran: *"In this cramped position his progress was extremely painful, and his hands were torn by briars and stones, but forward he dashed, fully expecting a shower of bullets any minute."*

The gully ended at a road, the Williamsburg Pike, which Rose crossed to enter a pine grove on the other side. *"I quickly looked back. I could see the rebel pickets very plainly, but they had not seen me while crawling, though I had passed immediately before them."* Rose hid in the pines by the Pike for several hours until the Confederates gave up the search.

Since he knew this road would eventually lead to Williamsburg and the Union cavalry, Rose began shadowing it, his senses keen for any sign or sound of white people. *"Frequently I had to take to the bushes on account of rebel cavalry, or armed citizens travelling through the country."* Sometimes the soldiers passed so closely that Rose could hear them talking.

He pressed on through the night, and once across Diascund Creek he knew he was near his goal. Despite the bitter cold, Rose lay down and slept again until daylight.

Awakening at dawn, Col. Rose was close to safety but his body felt thoroughly battered. *"I found myself this morning almost unable to move, but crawled along in the direction of Williamsburg, and after travelling for some time, suddenly came upon a spot where a picket had been posted the night before."* Realizing it was a Confederate picket position, Rose resumed his slow and cautious approach to the town. At last he reached an open field.

"Here, to my great joy, I saw a body of United States troops moving on the road to my left. I sat down very much exhausted and awaited their approach."

Only then did Rose notice three men standing between him and the distant Union troops. *"These men were all fully dressed in United States uniforms. The circumstance that I had not seen them before excited a suspicion that all was not right and I watched them closely."* These men seemed to take no notice of the main body of soldiers nearby, and Rose assumed they were functioning as a scouting force.

"They did not appear to pay any attention to the advancing troops. From this I thought they were all right, and that they merely had been sent forward from the advancing column. I now rose and walked towards the troops I had first seen. When I had walked about seventy-five yards I came in sight of the three men in the road, who now challenged me.

"I hesitated a moment and then obeyed their summons to approach. As soon as I came close to them, I saw that I was entrapped, even before they spoke. Their manner indicated they were in great fear of the troops that had halted below."

Rose now saw that he had been tricked. These three in their blue uniforms were clearly Confederates, so Rose tried to convince them he was one too. They didn't believe him. He considered running away, but knew his broken foot and enfeebled condition would make it easy for them to shoot him down.

"*I therefore waited for a better chance. One of these men appeared to be an officer, and he directed one of the men to take me in charge and go across the field that lay to the left of the road.*

"*I started off with him, limping fearfully, but when he got about half-way across the field, I sprang suddenly upon him, disarmed and prostrated him, fired off his piece, and started to run towards the troops.*"

Other Confederates emerged from of the woods and began chasing Rose. "*Two or three of them outran me and struck me with their muskets. This prostrated me, and they all rushed around. I heard one of them say, 'Be quick, the Yanks are right here.'*"

At this point another group of Rebels appeared and ran toward the ongoing struggle. Among this group was Private T. P. Sanders of South Carolina, who many decades later would set down his own eyewitness account. First Sanders saw two men running about an eighth of a mile off: "*The man in the rear had clubbed his rifle and was striking the other as he fled. Two or three times the fellow was knocked down and would scramble on all fours before rising and running on. We started a swift pursuit, not knowing if our man was the pursued or the pursuer.*"

When they came upon the struggling men they found a fellow Rebel named Richardson "*standing over a tall red-haired, red-bearded man, dressed in citizen's clothes lying stretched on his back on the ground, while Richardson belabored him with the butt of his rifle. The man certainly would have been killed had he received the full force of the blows, but Richardson in his fury, was striking the ground beyond the man's head—the broken gun stock making a deep impression in the earth. As Richardson saw us he called out, 'Give me a gun, let me kill this scoundrel—he tried to shoot me after he surrendered!'*"

One man handed over his gun, but then Lt. Hume, the ranking officer, stopped anyone from harming the prisoner. This Lt. Hume was the same guerrilla who had recently escaped a close chase by Lt. Wells and the Union cavalry.

"*In answer, Richardson, who was infuriated, held open his coat and showed where the ball had passed between his body and the coat.*" But Lt. Hume repeated his order that no one could harm their prisoner.

Rose remembered: "*Several of them now seized me and dragged me over a fence into a thickly timbered ravine. The man I had disarmed seemed to be badly hurt. He wanted to kill me at once. Lieutenant Hughes—I think they called him—spoke roughly to this man and ordered him to keep quiet. Just then one of the men called out, 'Be off quick,' when the whole party started and ran. They forced me along with them a short distance, when, finding I was unable to travel, they halted.*"

Confederate private Sanders recorded the conversation that he witnessed:

"'*Get up, you'll have to come with us,' said Hume.*

"'*I can't,' answered Rose. 'That fellow has about killed me. I can't move.'*

"'*You'll have to,' we rejoined.*

"'*I can't take a step,' answered the fellow from the ground, making no motion to rise.*

"'*The Yankees!' cried someone.*

"*The man sprang from the ground as if electrified.*

"'*Saved!' he shouted, 'I am saved.'*

"*We each made a grab for him and began pulling him in the direction of the nearby woods.*

"'*If you don't come with us, we'll have to kill you,' said Hume, and four rifles were leveled at him.*

"*Getting to his feet, he squared himself and faced us. 'Shoot me,' he said simply. 'I am Colonel Rose of the 77th Pennsylvania Regiment. I have tunneled out of Libby Prison and have been without food for the past two days, and I won't be taken back there alive.'*

"*He was as game a man as I ever saw, as he stood there completely at our mercy and looking us fearlessly in the eye. My heart went out to him.*"

Rose's misery might have touched them emotionally, but they were still soldiers and he was their prisoner. While the exhausted Rose tried to struggle, the Rebels dragged him along. The Yankees in the distance apparently concluded these blue-clad men were their fellow soldiers, and did not interfere.

"*Rose finally gave up and said he would go with us. We managed to get him to the woods, and there he told us his story—of his long imprisonment, his nights spent in tunneling out of Libby; his lack of food for the past few days; his getting within sight of his own men, only to be captured.*

"*He told us of his wife and child he had not seen for so long, and begged us for God's sake to let him go.*

"*There were those among us who felt the eloquence of his appeal more than he ever knew, but war is war—and to have the bravery, pluck, and endurance which he had displayed set at large to be used against us once more was more than could be expected. So we took him back to Richmond from where he was returned to the very prison made famous by him.*"

Rose had been on the road for almost a week, but his valiant journey only led back to the dungeons of Libby.

On the first day of the escape, according to Lt. Roach's memoir, *The Prisoner of War, and How Treated*, a member of Elizabeth Van Lew's Union Underground went to Libby to gather the latest information. What he learned was that the commanders of the prison, up to the highest ranks, were furious about the escape of Streight, their most valuable prisoner; they "*talked as though they would be content for all the other prisoners to get through safely, if only they could have the Colonel again in their clutches, either alive or dead. It would appear, however, from the instructions given the parties sent out, that they preferred having him in the later condition, as the order was to kill him if found.*"

But the Rebels failed to locate Streight. One week later, on February 15, 1864, Yankee general Benjamin Butler issued an official dispatch that read in part: "*Col. Streight, along with one hundred and ten other Union officers, escaped from prison in Richmond by digging a tunnel. Col. Streight, with seventeen others, are safe.*" This dispatch was reprinted in newspapers North and South, from the *Richmond Examiner* to the *New York Times*.

But actually Col. Streight had not even left Richmond; he was still hiding in a safe house set up by Elizabeth Van Lew and her cohorts. Gen. Butler's dispatch was just a piece of her spy craft, intended to get the Confederates to believe all prisoners had been accounted for, and to encourage them to stop looking.

The Rebels began to assume that all the escapees had either been recaptured or were safely behind Union lines. They cut back on their active search for the Libby fugitives, and soon called it off altogether.

Only then did Streight and his three companions set out for Union lines. While all the other Libby escapees had headed east toward Williamsburg, Streight's small group would head north. This northerly route would be longer, but it was therefore not what the Rebels expected.

Even so, the entire journey would be through a war zone filled with all manner of Southern soldiers and their supporters, all intensely on the lookout for Yankees, spies, deserters, and runaway slaves.

Before they set out, and at great risk to herself, Elizabeth Van Lew paid a visit, probably wearing one of her disguises—she often went out in simple clothes, with a basket under her arm.

"I followed Mrs. Rice in to the house and found myself in the presence of the four fugitives. I was overcome with terror for them that I quite lost my voice for some time. Two of these men were quite sick and looked very feeble. Colonel Streight seemed to be in good condition. I mentioned that there was particular enmity towards him because he had commanded, it was said, a negro regiment. He replied, 'I did not, but would have had no objection.'

"He asked me my opinion of the cause of this war. I tried to say, Democracy, though in my heart I thought it was slavery. I had a very pleasant visit. How my heart ached all the while for their peril!

"We had a little laughing and talking and then I said goodbye, with the most fervent, 'God help you,' in my heart towards all of them. It was not safe for me to go again to see these gentlemen, though I heard from them through Mrs. Rice."

On the evening of February 17, the eighth day after they had come through the tunnel, Streight's group set out from Richmond. Streight, the senior officer, was accompanied by three other Libby POWs, two Rebel deserters, and a guide from Van Lew's network. Unlike all the previous escapees, this small group was carrying food for the trip and was well armed with pistols. They even had a small pocket compass to keep them on the shortest route north.

The little band stayed off the roads. A few times they felt they were spotted by Rebel pickets, but the pickets did not respond. Nevertheless, the escapees gave them a wide berth. Everyone suffered severely from the weather, which was as cold as it had been the week before, *"and they thinly clad and without blankets, and dare not build fires, which might attract attention."*

When one of the Rebel deserters traveling with them suddenly disappeared, they feared the worst—that he might turn them in to authorities. It led to some anxious hours, but ultimately nothing happened.

In order to reach Union territory, the small band had to cross no less than four major rivers that ran from northwest to southeast across Virginia. On the third day they came upon the first of them, the Pamunkey River, *"which they found flowing with great huge cakes of ice that jammed and crushed each other, producing a roar like a dozen Niagaras. Even if they had a boat it seemed like madness to attempt pushing it through the surging waters. They were brave and determined men, and the situation made them desperate; they, therefore, resolved to build a raft and trust their fate to the angry elements in preference to the ferocious dogs and savage men in pursuit."*

The historical record does not describe the raft they built, but the men somehow put together a river-worthy craft of rails, poles, and bark. They were able to guide it through the cracks in the moving ice and *"after an hour of peril and incessant labor, the north bank was safely reached, and with a shout of triumph the whole party stepped on shore."*

Just before they reached the woods on top of the river bank, the group was seen by some Confederate scouts. The Rebels gave chase, but the prisoners were able to hide in the dense forest and wait until nightfall. When their pursuers gave up and moved on, they set out again.

Once more they were stopped by a large river, the Mattaponi. Luckily, this time they found a boat tied up along the bank. At dark they easily crossed the river and looked for a place to hide at dawn. Almost dead from the cold, they decided to chance a fire and used it to heat the sand. When daylight arrived, the fire was considered too risky and was put out, but the men could still warm their feet in the sand and keep from freezing.

On the fifth night out, they came up against the third and most formidable river yet, the Rappahannock. It was miles wide in this region, and effectively formed a border between Yankee and Confederate America. This river was also full of crashing and cracking ice that could be heard for miles.

They hid during the day, their stock of food now almost exhausted, when, as told by Streight's friend Lt. Roach: *"A negro fortunately discovered them in their hiding place and conducted them to his hut, and gave them an abundant supply of corn bread and bacon. The next morning they were pursued by soldiers, citizens, and hounds; they pushed on and when the dogs came up they fed and urged them on, as though they were not the party whose trail they were scenting.*

"During the day two of the party gave out from over exertion and had to be supported by the others. They were surrounded by the rebels three times, but by concealing themselves in the laurel thickets they were able to hold out until night."

The POWs needed help, so they went to a plantation. One of the slaves hid them in his hut, while the others went with their "masters" to help search for the escaped prisoners. The next day more slaves came to the aid of the fugitives, finding a boat and then rowing them over the Rappahannock. Once across, these slaves also directed them to the home of a German man who was a Union sympathizer.

With the German's help, they were able to find another boat and cross the largest barrier of them all—the Potomac River. In this part of Virginia, where the river empties into the Atlantic Ocean, it is eight miles wide or more. But once they rowed across that great river they would be truly free.

The group finally reached Union territory late at night on February 28. They had been on the road for eleven days and nights of misery and hairbreadth escapes. *"But it was liberty they sought, and they gained it. Bravery, energy, perseverance, the kindly moon and polar star, and the negro guide, brought them safe within our lines. Freedom, friends, and the protecting folds of the stars and stripes, was their reward."*

Streight's group was the last of the POWs to reach Union lines. Their success brought to a close the greatest escape in American history.

According to Lt. Moran, who was one of those recaptured, 59 prisoners escaped to Union lines, 48 were caught and returned to Libby, and two drowned. Some other accounts dispute that anyone died; and no definitive information has come to light about how the two men drowned or if they did, who they were.

The entire affair was a blow to Southern prestige, just as it was a shot in the arm to Yankee morale. The general public couldn't get enough of stories about the escapees' adventures; dozens of accounts would be published in newspapers, magazines, and books. Indeed, the publishing and speechifying would go on for decades.

It was a grand achievement, with few parallels in human history, and it made the participants famous until their dying days.

CHAPTER TWENTY-SIX

Make All the Damn Noise You Please

THE ESCAPEES WHO HAD MADE IT BACK TO THE UNION ARMY WERE exhausted, filthy, scratched, famished—and now they were being treated like kings amidst the security provided by their fellow soldiers. Maj. Tower remembered:

"We were received with open arms by everyone, were furnished with a tent, plenty of blankets and eatables. We slept well that night and were up when reveille was sounded. Never did a flag look as handsome to us as 'Old Glory' did that morning. One who has not passed through the hardships experienced in the last eight months could not imagine the joy we felt in knowing we were wholly free."

When Lt. Wallber was rescued by the Eleventh Pennsylvania Cavalry—and two more men from Libby were picked up on the way back to Williamsburg—the cavalrymen gave up their own horses, allowing the escapees to ride while the troopers walked alongside.

"We rolled into Williamsburg in triumph," wrote Wallber. *"Without delay, Colonel West, commandant of the garrison, made a place in his barracks, laid an excellent dinner, provided footwear, served port wine (a treat!), and in a fatherly way did everything else. As a result, I got tight for the first time in a long while. Questions and stories seemed unending. Then to bed in lodgings prepared expressly for us."*

Their next destination was Washington, D.C., to be followed by a few wonderful weeks at home. Every escapee was promised 30 days' leave, and with the back pay they had accumulated while imprisoned, each man had a chance to really enjoy himself.

The ex-POWs began their long journeys north and home as soon as they could. First they enjoyed the luxury of being transported in ambulances to Yorktown, Virginia, a dozen miles from Williamsburg. There they boarded steamers for a 20-mile trip to Fort Monroe in Hampton, Virginia.

On the ship, Lt. Wallber witnessed a somber group, *"Every face registered emotion, but nobody said anything and no one put an arm around anyone. Neither word nor gesture could have expressed what the long, firm handshake meant.*

"We told our story to a few civilian passengers. They listened in suspenseful excitement."

Maj. Tower must have taken another ship north, because he was with a very different group from the serious men Wallber met. Tower's fellow escapees were not somber; they were wound-up and raucous. *"The officers on board the boat that conveyed us from Yorktown to Fortress Monroe did not apparently know who we were. As we left we occupied the cabin, and of course were jubilant and very noisy. Soon the captain of the boat came into the cabin and said, 'This noise muse be stopped.'*

"He then left, but soon reappeared and asked, 'are you the men who escaped from Libby'? We replied, 'Yes.' He then said 'Make all the damn noise you please.'"

Union general Butler had his headquarters at Fort Monroe; he wanted to meet the men who had liberated themselves from the famous prison. Johnston wrote that Butler *"expressed the greatest pleasure at our escape, and only regretted that some had again fallen into the hands of the enemy. We had, of course, to go over the story of our treatment while in the hands of the rebels, and our perils on the way to the Union lines; and were made to feel the contrast by the attention bestowed upon us."*

Capt. Caldwell remembered: *"We found the General well and were very courteously received by him. After complimenting us very highly for our success, he observed that one of our number was clad in a rebel suit, when he remarked, 'Friend, I can't see how you escape being taken for a Reb.'*

"'Sir, I wanted them to mistake me for a Reb.'

"'Well', said the General, 'if your Rebel suit did you good service, I am glad of it, but I want you to go over to the Quarter Master's department and get you a more Christian looking suit before going to Washington.'

"*Immediately the General ordered a telegram announcing our safe arrival to be sent to the principal newspapers, and soon the news of our escape was heralded, as on the wings of the wind, to our friends at home.*"

Gen. Butler wanted the escapees to cut a good figure when they got to the capital, so everyone was promised a new uniform befitting his rank. Then, after a short speech, Butler "*sent us to a hotel, where each could avail himself of its services to his heart's content. The barber cut hair and beards. Thus groomed, looking a little more human, we marched in formation through the streets. Of course the inevitable reporters set upon us. Details of our hegira appeared in the next day's newspapers. Then a train conveyed us to Washington, and we lodged at the National Hotel. Heroes of the hour and lionized, we brought profit to the owner as people crowded in to see us.*"

The young men continued celebrating their good fortune. Capt. Caldwell offers no details, but he ends his account by explaining: "*If you imagine a jubilee, you will be none too sanguine in your conjectures, for to use a phrase proverbial among soldiers, perhaps I will best express it, and say, 'We had a good time.'*" (emphasis in original)

From Fort Monroe the steamers continued north to Washington. On one of them, 26 ex-POWs gathered to pass a series of resolutions of thankfulness dedicated to God, Gen. Butler, the Union, and the flag. The resolutions were signed by all and given to the Associated Press.

Upon arriving in Washington, Lt. Randall and some of the men "*met the Hon. E. M. Stanton, Secretary of War. I shall never forget his looks when we came into his presence; it was a mingled look of pity, grief, and hatred.*"

Many of the escapees also "*marched to the White House, where we were received by President Lincoln. The news of our escape had preceded us and all along our route we were constantly receiving ovations from the crowds of people that thronged our way,*" remembered Maj. Tower. The meetings with the president must have been short, because the escapees provide few details. The exception is Lt. Wells, who left this interesting, if brief, recollection:

"*President Lincoln took my hand and, while warmly pressing it, asked a number of questions about the escape. A few of the words that fell from his lips I have always remembered. Still holding my hand, he said, 'You are one of the party that went through the tunnel?' Receiving an affirmative answer, he* said: "'I congratulate you on your escape,' and at once put the following: 'What did you do with the dirt?'"

Unfortunately, Wells doesn't tell any more about his encounter. In his memoir, it's clear he was most anxious to leave the capital city and get to his home in Michigan. When he reached there, he was startled to find that the entire town had been waiting for days to celebrate his arrival.

Capt. Johnston was also in a hurry to get home because he had a sweetheart there ready to marry him. They had a whirlwind marriage and honeymoon, and soon Johnston was back with his unit, marching with Gen. Sherman on Atlanta.

"We parted," wrote Lt. Wallber at the conclusion of his escape memoir, *"each hurrying home. I separated from, perhaps never to see again, men who had shared amid hardship. All who endured shall never forget. But stories will shorten the hours at the fireside. And renewed by the salutary peace that now prevails, we can indulge the gentler side of our natures.*

"The beacon of the future beckons with brilliant light! Let us weigh anchor and sail bravely into new and better times!"

As Lt. Randall recorded: *"We felt that our sufferings had not been in vain. We felt as though we had been tried as by fire, and our love for our country was a thousand times stronger than before our capture. I entered the prison weighing 160 pounds and came out weighing less than 90 pounds, and have never reached 140 pounds since."*

It would take a long time for men like Lt. Forsythe to forget Libby. *"For years after the war I dreamed of being in Libby Prison, and witnessed the enactment of the same horrible scenes. On awakening, and looking around my room, and discovering it was only a dream, I would say, 'Thank God, it is not true!'"*

Maj. Tower was unable to get out of Washington because he had fallen into a bureaucratic snare. His thirty days of leave were passing all too quickly; he ends his memoir with this unique story of help arriving just when he needed it.

"At the capital there was the usual amount of 'red tape.' For two days I had vainly tried to get my pay, visiting the Treasury department each morning. On the third morning I again presented myself there, and was met with the usual answer 'that I would have to wait.'

"*I remarked 'that it was mighty hard for a man who had just spent eight months in Libby prison and with a 30 day leave of absence in his pocket, could not get the where-with-all to get home.' As I said this a kindly looking gentleman who stood beside me, asked me my name, rank and regiment, saying to me, 'Wait a moment.' He left, but soon returned, handing me a check for my pay. He then handed me his card, and on it I found inscribed the name of Walt Whitman, known as the poet and the soldier's friend.*

"*Thus ended my experience as a Union prisoner of war.*"

Meanwhile, the situation of the forty-eight recaptured made a painful contrast to the celebrations being enjoyed by those who had successfully escaped. While the lucky ones headed home amid accolades and comestibles, those who had been clapped into Libby's dungeons awaited their fate in shared frustration and misery.

Chapter Twenty-Seven

Aftermath

WHILE 61 OF THE ESCAPEES WERE ENJOYING THEIR FREEDOM IN THE North, 48 others were back in Libby Prison, where conditions were worse than ever. Those recaptured were forced down into the basement dungeons, while the other inmates experienced an overall crackdown.

The Rebels were not only angry about how many had escaped; they were embarrassed by the crowds who flocked to the prison to see "The Great Yankee Wonder," as the tunnel was called. Guards had to be posted at the entrances. As Lt. Prutsman recalled, *"This escape was hard on the rest of us, our liberties being greatly curtailed and our dangers increased."*

Inmate Lt. Col. Cavada, one of the best writers inside Libby, added: *"The great escapade through the tunnel seems to have completely destroyed the mental equilibrium of our young Commandant, Major Turner. The iron bars in the windows have been strengthened, and rendered impregnable. A corporal's guard patrols the building every two hours during the night, (to the tune of the 'Rogue's March,' whistled by the unterrified captives as they lie in their blankets); this patrol examines carefully every fire-place, window, nook, and corner, of every room. Major Turner seems to have been seized with the frantic idea that we might tunnel ourselves out of a third-story window, or that we might be constructing a huge balloon.*

"We now have roll-calls without number. Even in the middle of the night we have been waked to be counted. Anyone late at roll call is compelled to stand under guard, in the kitchen, for four hours."

Prison authorities obsessively searched for any device that could conceivably be used for digging; they confiscated every edged or pointed

241

object they could find, from pens to kitchen utensils. This was an inconvenience, but the main interest of the prisoners was the fate of those in the dungeons. Lt. Glazier recorded in his hidden diary: *February 12.—Twelve of the escaped prisoners were brought in today, and thrown into the cells. Poor fellows! They look crest-fallen enough.*

"February 13.—Sixteen more of the escaped prisoners were brought in this morning and placed in close confinement. Their rations have been greatly reduced, and many of them have been put in irons."

Lt. Moran was one of those escapees who had been run down and brought back to Libby: *"The recaptured officers refused to answer questions, and at last the brutal Turner had thirty of us packed in a twelve foot square dungeon. The recapture of Col. Rose, the brave engineer of the tunnel, caused the deepest regret, for all felt that he had bravely deserved his liberty."*

Aware how sick Lt. Moran was from exposure, his fellow officers pleaded for him to be allowed out for treatment. They told Commandant Turner that Moran would probably die one night, to which Turner *"replied with perfect candor: 'Well, d———n him, let him die; that's what he's here for.'"*

Of course Moran did not die. He later went on to interview the main participants and write the best short account of the Libby escape, for *Century Magazine*. His story was so popular it was turned into a pamphlet titled "A Thrilling History of the Famous Underground Tunnel by Capt. Thomas A Moran." At the turn of the century Libby History Museum sold it for ten cents a copy, complete with illustrations.

"The cell was about twelve feet long by eight wide," wrote Lt. Fales of life in the dungeons. *"We had no fire; every night the water froze in our pail, and one small loaf of corn-bread was all that was given each day for six men. It was not half-food enough, and we were suffering constantly with hunger and cold."*

Prison jailer Dick Turner also took out his anger on Robert Ford, the Black Union prisoner who was put to work in the Libby stables and whom Turner accused of having helped in the escape. White Yankee officers could be tortured by imprisonment in the dungeons or by starvation, but direct physical punishment was reserved for Blacks. According to the postwar testimony of Abby Green, a member of the Union Underground, when Ford protested his innocence, Turner sadistically beat him with 500 lashes. Still, the man *"bore without ever betraying other persons who had aided in concealing said prisoners after their escape."* This torture nearly killed him, but he never gave up the name of Elizabeth Van Lew or any of her fellow spies.

Robert Ford never fully recovered from the beating and lacerations. After the war, the Union government awarded him $800 and a job for his service and suffering. He died suddenly just a few years later.

His anger finally spent, Turner allowed the men out of the dungeons after two weeks of torment. They slowly staggered up the stairs to rejoin the rest of the prison population, *"which seemed like going to heaven, after our fearful life in the cell,"* according to Lt. Fales.

But just when things seemed to be returning to routine, another war drama came to Richmond and Libby. In late February 1864, just three weeks after the escape, units of Yankee cavalry launched a daring raid on Richmond, one of the main objectives being to free all prisoners in the city. The prisoners organized themselves into military units in anticipation, but the force was too small to penetrate the city's defenses and Col. Dahlgren, the leader of the expedition, was killed.

As Lt. Cavada remembered: *"The excitement was tremendous. We had suspected that something unusual was occurring from the fact that we could not obtain the daily papers, and from the hurried movement of troops over the James River within sight of the prison.*

"But when we learned, through some of the negroes who swept the prison, that a brigade of cavalry was within a few miles of Richmond, the true cause of these measures was at once apparent.

"We could distinctly hear the cannonading which was going on near the Chickahominy. This would have been exciting enough, but our anxiety was not a little heightened by the well-authenticated information that the cellars of the prison had been mined, and that it was the desperate determination of Major Turner to blow us up sooner than allow us to be liberated."

This is another unsolved mystery of the Civil War—did Dick and Maj. Turner really place a giant mine under 1,200 men? Stories were told of hundreds of pounds of black powder, in barrels, stacked in the center of Libby's basement, all fused and ready to detonate. After the war the Rebels claimed it had just been a ruse to unnerve the POWs. But the prisoners certainly believed it and they had the corroboration of the slaves who worked on the building. Inmate Glazier had no doubts: *"Such a plan for wholesale murder evinces a state of depravity on the part of the authorities at Richmond, to which we challenge the historian to find a parallel in the records of any civilized nation. None but the blackest of traitors could resort to such an expedient."*

Lt. Moran quotes Turner as telling the men: *"The minute Dahlgren got into this y'her town, I would have blown every one of you Yankees to h———l."*

The prisoners' indignities went on and on. Libby authorities used the escape as a reason to break open all the boxes sent from home in their search for contraband. But mainly this was just an excuse to rob the contents for their own use. Very few of the items ever made it to the POWs, especially the food. *"A package of salt and three candlesticks,"* was all one man reported receiving out of his precious box.

"To-day the rebels capped the climax of their inhumanity by reading the following order, 'Hereafter all clothing hung near the windows will be confiscated; and officers standing near the windows will be liable to be shot!'

"A prisoner enquired of Maj. Turner, 'what he meant by "near the windows"'; what distance.'

"Turner replied: 'Damn you, keep away from the windows entirely!'"

Apparently this vague new command, like many military proclamations, had unintended consequences. As recorded by Sam Byers: *"To-day, [March 23] the rebels killed one of their own officers, through mistake. He was in the lower prison on duty, and put his head out at the window to speak to a sentinel; the sentinel, thinking he was a yankee prisoner, obeyed the above order—shooting him dead."*

At least the warring powers staged some more prisoner exchanges. And finally making the list was the man Libby inmates considered to be most deserving of all: Col. Rose. *"On the 30th of April his exchange was effected for a Confederate Colonel. He rejoined his regiment, in which he served with conspicuous gallantry to the close of the war."*

Rose went on to have the stable career of a life-long military officer. Quiet and unassuming, he was always reluctant to talk about the Libby escape because his own part in it had been such a miserable failure. But that didn't stop veterans and reporters from asking for his perspective until, years later, he finally relented and recorded his essential memories.

It appears that almost all 61 of the successful escapees, from Col. Streight to Lt. Johnston, eventually returned to their military units and continued the fight. And the contribution made by so many officers with combat experience was a great help to the Union in the last year of the war. Escaped officers from Libby fought in battles from Nashville to Atlanta, as the Union slowly pushed Confederate forces toward surrender.

The role of Libby Prison soon changed, as the Confederates did an overhaul of their entire POW system. The Union cavalry raid and the Libby escape had so rattled Richmonders that authorities decided to move most of the prisoners out into the countryside. They began to build and expand facilities that would later become infamous hell-holes, such as Danville and Andersonville, where conditions were even worse. At Andersonville alone 13,000 POWs would die slowly from exposure and starvation.

Libby itself became more of a holding center where prisoners were processed. POWs would arrive to be registered, then they would be redirected to other prisons outside the city. It is estimated that, in the course of the war, more than 50,000 men passed through Libby and spent some time there.

Other prisons, both North and South, would experience dramatic and sometimes successful escapes. But the escapees were always numbered in the single digits. No other breakout ever rivaled Libby, either in size or in accomplishment, nor has any in the century and a half that has passed since. For the men involved, it was the supreme adventure of their lives.

Two Buildings

Col. Hobart, the elderly POW with the white, flowing beard, wrote after his escape: *"I prayed in my heart that I might have strength to return to my command. I was afterwards in Sherman's advance on Atlanta, the march to the sea and through the Carolinas, entered Richmond with the Western Army, and had the extreme satisfaction of marching my brigade by Libby Prison."*

Rebel prisoners held outside and in Libby Prison. Eyewitness drawing by Alfred Waud.

Extreme satisfaction indeed; and if that wasn't enough, a number of former Confederates were soon confined in Libby.

On April 3, 1865, some fourteen months after the escape, Richmond fell to Union forces. Retreating Confederates set the city's warehouses and military sites on fire, and these fires quickly spread indiscriminately through residential areas. The first act performed by Union soldiers was to put the fires out, thereby saving what was left of the former Rebel capital.

Libby Prison and Elizabeth Van Lew's home survived the flames untouched, but both would end up being destroyed, for very different reasons, decades later.

In the first year after the war, Libby became a prison again—this time for Rebels the Union hoped to put on trial. One of the most prominent was Dick Turner himself, and all former Libby inmates loved the idea that he was incarcerated there.

During his time in Libby, Turner was constantly threatened with execution. Henry Wirz, the commandant of Andersonville Prison, was hanged for "war crimes" on November 10, 1865. Further trials were expected, including one for former Confederate President Jefferson Davis. However, these did not take place and eventually Dick Turner was quietly released.

Yankee authorities searched for Maj. Turner too, but he managed to elude them and eventually fled to Cuba. Thousands of Rebels went there and also to Brazil; the economies of both countries were still based on slavery and would be for more than a decade.

After the war the Libby building went back to its old function as a warehouse. Two decades later, in 1889, it was purchased and moved to Chicago. There it became the successful Libby Prison War Museum, visited by hundreds of thousands during the next few years. In 1895 attendance began to fail and the building was dismantled, its various bricks and beams sold off for local construction projects. The Chicago Historical Society still owns a few remnants of the building and some literature on the museum.

The original Libby site in Richmond now holds a river flood barrier, a parking lot, and a few plaques commemorating its role in the Civil War. Behind it stands the Virginia Holocaust Museum, which opened in 2003.

When the Union Army entered Richmond, Elizabeth Van Lew waved from her mansion the first American flag the city had seen in five years. Later, Supreme Commander Ulysses S. Grant brought his wife to visit Miss Van Lew; they shared tea on her porch.

Made destitute by the war, Elizabeth and her family became truly desperate. Then in 1869 Gen. Grant became President Grant, and he did not forget his valuable former spy. Grant gave to Ms. Van Lew one of the finest federal jobs he could offer: postmistress of Richmond.

Denizens of the late Rebel capital were outraged that such a prime post had been given to a Unionist and to a woman, but Grant didn't care. By all accounts Van Lew performed her job well. She further angered white Virginians by hiring former slaves to work for her in the Post Office.

She held the job for eight years until Grant was no longer president. The next administration replaced her and money grew tight, remaining so for the rest of her life. But she was still involved in issues and politics, writing letters to the editor protesting her own "taxation without representation," as women could not vote.

Elizabeth Van Lew lived on in her decaying mansion until she passed away in 1900. By then she was so poor and alone that she was buried in an unmarked grave. Whites refused to attend the funeral.

The Richmond newspapers insulted her nonstop for her support of Black rights, and regularly called her a traitor comparable to Judas or Benedict Arnold. They would add the spin that she was actually a lonely old maid who had acted completely on her own. They didn't want to acknowledge that a network of Richmond citizens, widespread and racially mixed, had risked their lives for the Union. They called her "Crazy Bet."

Children were encouraged to call her a witch. A local Richmond play, supposedly about her life, was titled *The Lone Vixen*. For decades after her death, people claimed to see her ghost.

In light of what she risked, accomplished, and willingly sacrificed, Elizabeth Van Lew is clearly one of the unsung heroes of American history. Maybe someday she will get a statue in Richmond—but when she was buried there her family couldn't even afford a headstone. Two years later, in 1902, a group of women in Boston erected a monument inscribed with a moving tribute: *"She risked everything that is dear to man—friends, fortune, comfort, health, even life itself—all for the one absorbing desire of her heart—that slavery might be abolished and the Union preserved."*

Some argued that the Van Lew mansion should be preserved, as it was one of the finest homes in the city. But as a symbol of anti-slavery Unionism and of Elizabeth herself, it became a target of angry white Richmonders who had it torn down in 1912. An elementary school stands on the site today. A large percentage of the students are African Americans.

NOTES

PROLOGUE

v "Interesting news cannot grow stale": *Autobiography of Mark Twain*, vol. 2, February 25, 1907, p. 436.

vi "Attention, no stranger": Libby Museum pamphlet.

x "We'll tear it down": Porter, p. 295.

CHAPTER 1. CAPTURED

1 "I was about to give him my canteen": MacCauley, p. 18.

3 "Never was the transition": Tobie, p. 7.

3 "I had no choice": Szabad, p. 5.

3 It was so dark": Fales, p. 2.

4 "None are captured at the rear": Ferguson, p. 22.

5 "Within two minutes I saw": White, p. 1.

5 "I was now between two lines": Byers, p. 4.

6 "I addressed him thus": McCabe, p. 125.

CHAPTER 2. ON TO RICHMOND

7 "Here we witnessed an amusing exhibition": Glazier, p. 37.

8 "Yank, hand me that ar hat": Ibid., p. 38.

8 "The sense of gone-ness": Tobie, p. 19.

9 "This filled my captor": Szabad, p. 3.

9 "I made bold to approach him": Tobie, p. 9.

9 "It is pretty severe on a cavalryman": Wells, p. 132.

10 "All through our march": Tower, p. 2.

10 "I had scarcely slept for a week": Byers, p. 7.

10 "The engine was like an old wind-broken horse": Drake, p. 47.

11 "We were put on board": Boggs, p. 9.

11 "Our column must have seemed": MacCauley, p. 27.

12 "We arrived in Staunton": Caldwell, pp. 4-5.

12 "We were paraded through the streets": Ferguson, p. 49.

13 "Afterwards, when I had escaped": Byers, p. 8.

13 "A large crowd was at the depot": Tower, p. 2.

CHAPTER 3. FRESH FISH

15   "As we passed along": Glazier, p. 41.

16   "potatoes, $18 a bushel": Byers, p. 113.

17   "I know there was a riot": *New South*, newspaper, April 25, 1863.

18   "had devoted themselves": Wilson, p. 250.

19   "Slavery has brutalized these men": Byers, "What I Saw in Dixie," January 2, 1864.

20   "So, calling up my companion": Higginson, p. 117.

20   "I was ill": Drake, p. 48.

21   "A concourse of darkies followed us": Ferguson, p. 48.

21   "Our column halted": Wells, p. 135.

22   "Built of brick": Tower, p. 3.

22   "Had we known that": Cavada, p. 20.

23   "He not only deprives us": Glazier, p. 47.

23   "Dick Turner demanded our pocketbooks": Prutsman, p. 14.

24   "Yankee ingenuity": Glazier, p. 43; Beaudry, p. 35.

25   "A Rebel sergeant searched me": Cesnola, p. 2.

25   "The gloomy and forbidding": Cavada, p. 20.

25   "We were escorted up": Wells, p. 136.

25   "What army are you from?": Shrady, p. 93; Prutsman, p. 14; Roach, p. 77.

26   "Our guard tried to reason": White, p. 2.

26   "But in an hour's time": Byers, p. 10.

26   "The prison veterans": Roach, p. 76.

26   "Lighted lathe sticks added": Shrady, p. 93.

27   "It was with a feeling of relief": Drake, p. 48.

CHAPTER 4. THE PRISON AND THE CITY

29   "one Southern man": Elizabeth Van Lew diary, p. 31.

32   "splendid dinner": *Richmond Enquirer*, December 7, 1863.

33   "History hardly records": Fisher, p. 2.

33   "The Johnnies say that": Byers, "What I Saw in Dixie," December 30, 1863.

34   "There was but one honorable": Fisher, p. 2.

CHAPTER 5. CHICKAMAUGA AND COLONEL ROSE

38   "A plain, blunt man": Johnston, p. 9.

38   "the very life of the nation": Ibid., p. 18.

39   "I felt that in such a cause": Ibid., p. 16.

39   "The men guarding us": Ibid., p. 37.

39   "Recovering consciousness": McCreery, pp. 4, 5.

40   "had already built a fire": Ibid., p. 5.

40   "faster and faster, lying here": Ibid., p. 6.

41   "threw himself down upon the ground": Earle, p. 3.

41   "Our orders were imperative": Ibid., p. 2.

42   "I shall never forget the kindness": McCreery, p. 7.

42 "On my way thither": Rose, p. 1.

44, "Almost a quarter century has passed": Earle, p. 4.

44 "We found men here": Ibid., p. 5.

44 "I soon set about": Rose, p. 1.

CHAPTER 6. LIBBY LIFE

46 "Perhaps the most repulsive": Starr, p. 7.

46 "The prison is crowded": Cavada, p.160.

48 "The thirst caused": Drake, p. 49.

48 "As a rule the men": Ibid., p. 49.

49 "Going diving for a bean": Ibid., p. 49.

49 "Dancing was taught": Moran, Philadelphia, December 10, 1881, p. 4.

50 "Oh! How often in Christian fellowship": Caldwell, p. 28.

50 "Resolved, that the Fear of Punishment": Beaudry, p. 5.

50 "issued weekly": Ibid., p. 1.

51 "if old poets wrote of battles": Ibid., p. 2.

51 "Why is our soup in Libby": Ibid., pp. 4, 37, 35.

51 "All will desire": Ibid., p. 21.

51 "Nothing is more revolting": Ibid., p. 12.

52 "were required to raise their left foot": Ibid., p. 18.

52 "Some Americans' venom": Domschcke, p. 43.

52 "There were attached to the prison": Roach, p. 9.

52 "Captured, they now suffered": Domschcke, p. 41.

52 "You are glad to leap to your feet": Beaudry, p. 1.

53 "Great tallygraphic news": Glazier, p. 57.

53 "filled with the most exaggerated": Roach, p. 72.

53 "Whenever they are full": Glazier, p. 57.

53 "The 'General' was quite an original": Roach, p. 99.

53 "How long he had been": Drake, pp. 50–52.

53 "For the most trifling offenses": Roach, p. 98.

54 "those of us on the 2nd floor": Chamberlain, p. 8.

55 "several officers": Lodge, p. 322.

55 "Today I saw the man": Ibid., p. 324.

55 "They hung him for a traitor": Beaudry, p. 38.

56, "Foremost among the races": Samuel Wells, p. 405.

57 "take prisoners Jefferson Davis": Roach, p. 88.

57 "From a Union lady": Ibid., p. 89.

57 "for manufacturing a variety": Breidenthal diary, p. 343; Willett, p. 152.

59 "They call Streight": Byers, "What I Saw in Dixie," December 19, 1863.

CHAPTER 7. ELIZABETH VAN LEW

62 "The most productive espionage operation": Fishel, p. 551.

62 "Some were in favor of trying": Mann, p. 28.

63 "proceed to the arsenal": Roach, p. 88.
64 "the most solemn oath": Ibid., p. 89.
64 "The project was at once": Ibid., p. 89.
64 "We have to be watchful": Van Lew diary, June 21, 1862.
64 "That is Miss Van Lew": Varon, p. 91.
64 Ford could pass information: *Hartford Courant*, May 15, 1869.
65 "machinists, blacksmiths": Varon, pp. 188, 292.
65 "When the cold wind would blow": Van Lew diary, September 27, 1864.
66 "[I] have turned to speak": Van Lew diary, September 27, 1864.
66 "always went to bed at night": Ryan p. 25.
67 "we were fools for remaining": Roach, pp. 90–92.
67 "where their situation": Roach, p. 90.
69 "declared that she had never": Varon, p. 165.
69 "in consummation of Miss Van Lew's": *Harper's Monthly*, June 1911, p. 90.
70 "We were seized and ironed": Roach, p. 92.

CHAPTER 8. COLONEL ROSE TAKES OVER

73 "In the great gloomy rooms": Hamilton, p. 4.
73 "Scheme after scheme": Earle, p. 14.
74 "the doors were made more secure": Rose, p. 1
74 "During all this time": Earle, p. 16.
75 "it was common to see": Moran, "A Thrilling History," n.p.
75 "The impenetrable darkness": Ibid., n.p.
77 "Once while down there": Rose, p. 1.
77 "My only chance to escape": Ibid., p. 2.
78 "To gain the carpenter shop": Ibid., p. 2.
78 "when nearly all the prisoners": Hamilton, p. 5.
78 "We were obliged to make no noise": Rose, p. 2.
78 "Rose guarded his comrade": Moran, "A Thrilling History," n.p.
80 "As the morning hour approached": Rose, p. 2.
81 "So ingeniously were the bricks": Earle, p. 17.
81 "I will never forget": Hamilton, p. 5.

CHAPTER 9. TIGHT FIT

83 "I entered it feet foremost": Rose, p. 3.
84 "each effort only wedged him": Moran, "A Thrilling History," n.p.
84 "He was a powerful man": Rose, p. 3.
84 "as they gave another": Ibid., p. 3.
85 "The darkness therein was perfect": Ibid., p. 4.
86 "I found more difficulties": Rose, "Libby Tunnel," p. 3.
87 "What a stench!": Russell, p. 34.
87 "To the unreflecting": Rose, "Libby Tunnel," p. 3.
87 "got away from there": Rose, p. 5.
88 "It was at this time": Ibid., p. 6.

Chapter 10. From Skirmishing to Catechism

91   "Cavalrymen are used to skirmishing": White, p. 4.
91   "The first scene on opening": Szabad, p. 6.
92   "A soldier must be a soldier": *Libby Chronicle*, p. 2.
92   "They were the most prolific bugs": Drake, p. 49.
92   "The abundance of vermin": Harrold, p. 34.
92   "These little fellows": Starr, p. 6.
93   "This man was said to be a deserter": Earle, p. 7.
93   "comical little fellow": Domschcke, p. 39.
94   "now I am suah": Starr, p. 10.
94   "The meddlers' sole purpose": Moran, "A Thrilling History," n.p.
96   "The prison clerk Ross": Earle, p. 8.
96   "This seemed to be satisfactory": Caldwell, p. 27.
96   "When practical jokes": Wells, p. 138.
97   "With the Yankee tendency": Glazier, p. 44.
97   "You find the cook room crowded": Cavada, p. 164.
97   "The meat and soup": Drake, p. 48.
98   "the avidity with which they": Roach, p. 74.
98   "Our mothers were our ideal": Drake, p. 49.
98   "There is no sound": *Libby Chronicle*, p. 12.
98   "I was so fortunate": Glazier, p. 59.
99   "The bustle of distribution over": *Libby Chronicle*, p. 12.
99   "the so-called United States": *Wheeling Daily Intelligencer*, November 13, 1963.
99   "This correspondence was ended": Fales, p. 4.
100   "There has been great rejoicing": Cavada, p. 76.
100   "Send me as soon as possible": Jones, November 7, 1863, p. 325.
100   "You can place money": Fisher, November 13, 1863, p. 5.
100   "I cannot express in words": Jones, November 12, 1863, p. 326.
101   "A new flag of truce boat:" Szabad, p. 19.
101   "Major Turner allowed:" Glazier, p. 58
101   "The Rebels, sly foxes": Domschcke, p. 40.
101   "My plan of operation": Chamberlain, p. 8.
102   "Notwithstanding all this": McElroy, p. 16.
102   "To the Rebel officers": Domschcke, p. 41.
104   "Different minds are no doubt": Cavada, pp. 155, 156.
104   "I am repeatedly struck": Ibid., p. 156.
104   "It was the law of Libby": Szabad, p. 9.
104   "The sentinels": Fales, p. 3.
104   "the writer vividly recalls": Moran, *Bastiles*, p. 107.
105   "to return to the hot human": Ibid., p. 99.
105   "casualties were not greater": Ibid., p. 110.
106   "A motley mixture of men": Moran, Philadelphia article, 1881, p. 2.
106   "Such an uncouth mixture": Szabad, p. 14.
106   "all silly pride": Cavada, p. 156.
107   "On that very day": Szabad, p. 13.

108   "The ennui of prison life": Ibid., p. 9.
108   "Some of the most ludicrous": Roach, p. 79.
108   "Now McFadden was voted": Shrady, p. 96.
108   "Who hid behind the big gun": *Libby Chronicle*, p. 37.
109   "Against such hilarities": Szabad, p. 9.
109   "Who has exchange": *Libby Chronicle*, p. 37.
109   "Who surrendered": Tower, p. 4.
109   "If any of the comrades": Starr, p. 4.
109   "All enjoyed them except": Glazier, Libby's Bright Side, p. 4.
109   "Who plays the spy?": Starr, p. 4.
109   "The braying of the ass": Szabad, p. 14.
109   "Who washed his clothes": Cavada, p. 63.
109   "Who is the meanest": Shrady, p. 96.
109   "These questions are endless": *Libby Chronicle*, p. 37.
109   "These highly valued entertainments": Cavada, p. 63.

CHAPTER 11. THE FINAL TUNNEL

111   "It did seem to be": Rose, p. 6.
112   "we would have plenty of earth": Ibid., p. 5.
112   "this plan therefore was the best": Ibid., p .6.
113   "This was accompanied": Johnston, p. 67.
113   "It was just 38 days": Hamilton, p. 5.
113   "I then went down": Rose, p. 7.
113   "Having nothing but a small penknife": Johnston, p. 67.
113   "I have been frequently asked": Ibid., p. 72.
114   "To a person coming in": Rose, p. 6.
114   "The tunnel was dry": Ibid., p. 7.
116   "As the whole process was novel": Johnston, p. 68.

CHAPTER 12. ACTS OF COOL DARING

117   "I was not long": McCreery, p. 17.
118   "There was no mistaking": Ibid., p. 17.
118   "considerable amusement": Earle, p. 15.
118   "Before the war he was": McCreery, p. 10.
118   "He coolly walked out": Cavada, p. 78.
119   "The next morning at roll call": McCreery, p. 10.
119   "Hello! What the devil": Sclater, p. 28.
119   "They were ready": Cavada, p. 139.
120   Lt. Kupp: Boaz/Cornwell, p. 101.
120   "A prisoner, if he": Cavada, p. 138.
120   "My resolution was fixed": Bray, p. 4.
122   "My heart throbbed": Ibid., p. 5..
122   "I saw in a moment": Ibid., pp. 4–7.

124   "Seeing a light in the windows": Ibid., p. 8..
126   "If I am entitled": Ryan, p.22
126   "this heavy heart": Ibid., p. 33.
127   "In this belief": Ibid., p. 63.
127   "We consult with": Ibid., May 14, 1863.
128   "I'll fotch you a little": McCabe, p. 130.
128   "visited a house occupied": *New York Herald*, August 14, 1862.
128   "If your aunt": Reynolds, p. 3.
129   "Lounsbury said that": Parker in *New York Herald*, August 1, 1883.
129   "the hateful prison clerk": *Libby Chronicle*, p 14.

CHAPTER 13. EXERTIONS ALMOST SUPERHUMAN
131   "The owner of a book": Moran, *Philadelphia Times*, December 10, 1881, p. 3.
131   "His old science of escape:" Hugo, p. 1251..
132   "One would lie on his back": Tower, p. 6
132   "We made fairly rapid progress": Rose, p. 7..
133   "An inexorable rule": Moran, "Libby Prison," March 17, 1892, p. 35
133   "sometimes the whole four": Ibid., p. 8.
133   "This labor was not only": Johnston, p. 70.
134   "Such hard frost": Szabad, p. 18.
134   "Winter was cold": Tower, p. 4..
134   "No mail and not a word": Byers, p. 16
134   "Many nights when suffering": Roach, p. 71.
134   "manufactured into curtains": Ibid., p.70.
135   "Christmas came": Tower, p. 4.
135   "I am thinking": Byers, p. 16.
135   "A company of little boys": Earle, p. 13.
135   "It was a very sad affair": Lodge, January 25, 1863.
135   "Evening advances": Glazier, p. 74.
135   "Such a welcome": Byers, p. 19.
135   "To sit there staring": Cavada, p. 150.
137   "The opening of the year": Szabad, p. 19.
137   "Our boxes lying in the storehouse": Ibid., p. 20.
137   "An occasional prisoner": Byers, p. 18.

CHAPTER 14. THE HOSPITAL
139   "Fall in, sick": Starr, p. 7.
139   "This is nothing but": Glazier, p. 52..
139   "I appeared before the prison surgeon": Ibid., p. 51
139   "then given a clean shirt": Harvey Reid, *National Tribune*, April 23, 1883.
140   "Rebel hospitals for prisoners": Roach, p. 64.
140   "only the worst cases": Chamberlain, p. 14.
140   "There was the ominous stillness": Glazier, p. 51.

140   "Pneumonia is making": Ibid., p. 53.
140   "rations consist of one small": Ibid., p. 54.
141   "insufficient food": *Green Mountain Freeman*, December 1, 1863.
141   "The burial of the dead": Glazier, p. 61.
141   "The malignant": Junius Brown, Mower County Transcript, June 3, 1896.
141   "After supper Chaplain McCabe": *National Tribune*, February 12, 1885.
141   "There is not a calmer": McCabe, p.103
142   "I am well": Ibid. , p. 104.
142   "My cold turned into a fever": Ibid., p. 107..
142   "I am still very weak": Ibid., p. 109
142   "Many a poor fellow": Harrold, p. 34.
142   "He took out his little": McCabe, p. 142.
143   "Two hundred and fifty preachers": Ibid., p. 143.
143   "They laid me down": Ibid., p. 144.

CHAPTER 15. TRAPPED IN RAT HELL

145   "Yesterday afternoon": Dow, p. 170.
146   "I witnessed his introduction": Earle, p. 15.
148   "If you would know": Russell, p. 36.
148 "We proceeded in this manner": Rose, p. 8.
149   "Other prisoners used to see us": Ibid., p. 7..
149   "Confined as we were": Caldwell, p. 22.
149   "Sunday, January 31, 1864": Lodge, p. 332
149   "The door had not been nailed up": Johnston, p. 74.
149   "Two days have now been spent": Lodge, p. 332.
149   "The consequence was": Rose, p. 7.
150   "One day, after failing again": Domschcke, p. 39.
150   "On the day that the Rebels": Rose, pp. 7, 8..
150   "A thousand tongues": Moran, "A Thrilling History," n.p.
150   "They asked my advice": Rose, p. 9
151   "To remain in this cold": Johnston, p. 77..
151   "Major Turner, believing": Caldwell, p. 25
151   "'But,' says Turner": Ibid., p. 26.
153   "This story was taken up": Johnston, p. 79.
153   "The cellar was now my home": Ibid., p. 82.

CHAPTER 16. BIG MISTAKE

155   "Captain Gallagher had obtained": Johnston, p. 82.
156   "Some of the workmen": Rose, p. 9.
156   "By sitting in the window": Ibid., p. 9.
156   "It began to be whispered": Caldwell, p. 34..
157   "The guard heard me": Randall, n.p.
157   "There are times when": Johnston, p. 84.

158   "one o'clock A. M.": Rose, p. 10.
158   "At this critical moment": Caldwell, p. 34

Chapter 17. Breakthrough

162   "As midnight approached": Moran, "A Thrilling History," n.p.
162   "His strength nearly gone": Ibid..
163   "McDonald was overjoyed": Ibid.
164   "I had been a prisoner": Ibid.
164   "Those who had been let": Wells, p. 147
164   "Never was my anxiety": Johnston, p. 92.
165   "Freedom was within our grasp": Hamilton, p. 7.

Chapter 18. Breakout

167   "Bright, clear, cool": Dow, p. 173.
167   "A countersign was instituted": Caldwell, p. 35.
167   "The working party": Johnston, p. 95..
167   "Our last meeting": Randall, p. 2.
168   "[The] head needed protection": Wells, p. 151
168   "As the guards were under orders": Hobart, p. 4.
168   "It was a living drama": Ibid., p. 4..
169   "From the upper floor": Domschcke, p. 63..
169   "It was a glorious sight": Bartleson, p. 40.
169   "Picking our way among": Moran personal account, p. 2.
169   "In my anxiety": Ibid., p. 2.
170   "At the mouth of the tunnel": Glazier, p. 83.
170   "A wild excitement": Hobart, p. 4.
170   "knowledge of the hole": Roach, p. 101.
170   "Only one man was allowed": Earle, p. 21.
170   "I pulled myself back": Ibid., p. 21.
171   "the news sent a chill": Moran personal account, p. 2.
171   "Here Col. Streight": Roach, p. 100.
171   "They rushed forward": Caldwell, p. 36..
171   "All noise had ceased": Moran personal account, p. 3.
172   "fighting and raising hell": Glazier, p. 85.
172   "He made no response": Moran personal account, p. 3.
172   "When passing I touched": Caldwell, p. 37.
172   "let my feet down": Moran personal account, p. 4.
173   "it was but the work of a moment": White, p. 4.
173   "righteous retribution": Bartleson, p. 40.
173   "We had to pass through": Wells, p. 155.
173   "As they moved away": Moran personal account, p. 5.
174   "After standing so long": Wells, p. 155.

CHAPTER 19. FIRST NIGHT

175 "We walked two squares": Hamilton, p. 7.

175 "No plan had been arranged": Rose, p. 11.

175 "I slipped out": Wells, p. 156.

176 "We passed out and walked": Earle, p. 22.

176 "My face being very pale": Hobart, p. 4.

177 "As my comrade and myself": Johnston, pp. 96, 97.

177 "We moved quickly": Moran personal account, p. 5.

177 "locked arms and marched out": McCreery, p. 22.

178 "As soon as he called": EVL diary, p. 59.

178 "We heard the jingling of sabers": Fales, p. 7.

179 "A few steps away": Wallber, p. 127.

180 "We made our way": Moran, p. 6.

181 "We came to the Chickahominy": Fales, p. 8.

181 "Our teeth were chattering": Ibid., p. 8.

181 "We soon came to the Rebel camps": Johnston, p. 98.

182 "Among this timber": Ibid., p. 99.

CHAPTER 20. A DAY OF AMUSED EXCITEMENT

183 "On 10 February": Domschcke, p. 64.

183 "For some reason": Glazier, p. 85.

183 "I did this by falling in": Prutsman, p. 22.

184 "Turner counted us": Glazier, p. 85.

184 "At first they suspicioned": Roach, p. 101.

184 "After a careful examination": Moran, p. 47.

184 "Turner appeared in the rooms": Domschcke, p. 64.

185 "was hidden by a large rock": *Richmond Examiner*, February 11, 1864.

185 "The whole thing": *Richmond Daily Dispatch*, February 11, 1864.

185 "The excitement in Richmond": Hale, p. 4.

185 "A thousand and more": Moran, p. 47.

185 "Ecstatic over our comrade's success": Domschcke, p. 65.

185 "Col. A D Streight": *Daily Dispatch*, February 11, 1864.

185 "Dick Turner and a posse": Roach, p. 102.

186 "The next morning I conversed": Cesnola, p. 5.

186 "Meanwhile the report spread": *Richmond Examiner*, quoted in Roach, p. 109.

187 "At the same time": Roach, p. 112.

187 "among the trenches": McCreery, p. 23.

CHAPTER 21. A BARE CHANCE

189 "I became suddenly conscious": Moran, part 3, p. 7.

190 "leveled their carbines at my head": Ibid., p. 8.

190 "got into a dense thicket": Starr, p. 12.

191 "Suddenly a cry": Domschcke, p. 65.

191 "It seems as if the sense": Starr, p. 12.

191   "Turner was lashed into fury": Moran, part 2, p. 8.

191   "Others recaptured were put with us": Starr, p. 12.

192   "Dick Turner's face glowed": Domschcke, p. 65.

192   "those instruments employed": Bartleson, p. 41.

192   "We selected for our first": Caldwell, p. 38.

192   "I should like if I were able": Ibid., p. 38.

193   "Here again we had": Ibid., p. 39.

194   "we crossed with hearts": White, p. 5.

194   "They remembered that we had": Ibid., p. 5.

194   "our suffering was greatly lessened": Johnston, p. 99.

194   "That day I thought our feet": Ibid., p. 101.

195   "where some colored women came": Wells, p. 158.

195   "avoiding all houses": McCreery, p. 23.

195   "The country was alive": Hobart, p. 5.

Chapter 22. Saved by Slaves

197   "It was my turn": Hobart, p. 6.

198   "We are here because": McCreery, p. 26.

198   "After impressing us": Hobart, p. 6.

198   "We gave the negro": McCreery, p. 26.

198   "Finding that our strength": Earle, p. 23.

199   "What intuition or knowledge": Wells, p. 168.

200   "Cap, there is somebody coming": Caldwell, p. 50.

201   "The old uncle volunteered": Ibid., p. 51.

201   "on the fourth night": Johnston, p. 104.

202   "We happened to have a little": Ibid., p. 105.

202   "Again and again we lost our way": Wallber, p. 130.

203   "I had removed my shoes": Ibid., p. 130.

Chapter 23. Pluck and Luck

205   "The water being extremely cold": Hobart, p. 7.

206   "The boat was turned in": Ibid., p. 7.

206   "The officers don't like": McCreery, p. 27.

206   "We gave him one or two greenbacks": Hobart, p. 7.

206   "I had thus given myself": Fales, p. 8.

207   "She brought me a comforter": Ibid., p. 8.

207   "I had not gone far": Ibid., p. 8.

208   "I was just reaching for the axe": Ibid., p. 9.

208   "We had not traveled any": Johnston, p. 107.

210   "we broke away": Ibid., p. 110.

210   "While thus lying concealed": Ibid., p. 112.

210   "looking both before and behind us": Ibid., p. 115.

211   "Night at last came": Calder, p. 47.

212   "when lo! And behold": Ibid., p. 47.

212 "the snow falling rapidly": Earle, p. 24.
213 "hunger, fatigue, and loss": Wells, p. 159.
213 "were likely to perish": Ibid., p. 162.
214 "How long we had lain is uncertain": Ibid., p. 163.
214 "They came up and passed": Ibid., p. 164.

CHAPTER 24. FREEDOM
217 "There were no buildings": McCreery, p. 28.
217 "In a moment they surrounded us": Wallber, p. 131.
218 "They came so close to me": Randall, p. 2.
218 "It is impossible to express": Earle, p. 25.
220 "looking at their coats": Hobart, p. 8.
220 "an old black woman came out": Caldwell, p. 57.
221 "by whom are we halted?": Ibid., p. 58.
222 "Having been furnished with sword": Johnston, p. 120.
222 "Spurring my horse in advance": Ibid., p. 122.
223 "horses already saddled": Wells, p. 165.
223 "one never knows": Ibid., p. 169.
223 "was soon out of sight": Ibid., p. 169.
223 "Colonel Hobart was a man": Ibid., p. 165.
224 "Every paper was full": Earle, p. 25.

CHAPTER 25. ROSE AND STREIGHT
225 "When I attempted to rise": Rose, p. 11.
226 "was hazardous": Moran, p. 48.
226 "My coat was burned through": Rose, p. 12.
226 "But in crossing a small": Ibid., p. 13.
226 "In this cramped position": Moran, "A Thrilling History," n.p.
226 "I quickly looked back": Rose, p. 13.
227 "I found myself this morning": Ibid., p. 13.
227 "Frequently I had to take to the bushes": Ibid., p. 14.
228 "The man in the rear": *Bamburg Herald*, July 2, 1914.
229 "Several of them now seized me": Rose, p. 14.
229 "'Get up, you'll have to come'": *Bamburg Herald*, July 2, 1914.
230 "Rose finally gave up": *Bamburg Herald*, July 2, 1914.
230 "talked as though they would": Roach, p. 109.
231 "I followed Mrs. Rice in to the house": EVL diary, p. 62.
232 "and they thinly clad": Roach, p. 113.
232 "which they found flowing": Ibid., p. 113.
232 "after an hour of peril": Ibid., p. 114.
233 "A negro fortunately discovered them": Ibid., p. 115.
233 "But it was liberty they sought": Ibid., p. 117.

Chapter 26. Make All the Damn Noise You Please

235 "We were received with open arms": Tower, p. 9.

235 "We rolled into Williamsburg": Wallber, p. 133.

236 "Every face registered emotion": Ibid., p. 133.

236 "The officers on board the boat": Tower, p. 9.

236 "expressed the greatest pleasure": Johnston, p. 125.

236 "We found the General well": Caldwell, p. 61.

237 "sent us to a hotel": Wallber, p. 133.

237 "If you imagine a jubilee": Caldwell, p. 61.

237 "met the Hon. E. M. Stanton": Randall, p. 2.

237 "marched to the White House": Tower, p. 9.

238 "We parted, each hurrying home": Wallber, p. 134.

238 "We felt that our sufferings": Randall, p. 2

238 "For years after the war": Forsythe, p. 49.

238 "At the capital there was the usual": Tower, p. 10.

Chapter 27. Aftermath

241 "This escape was hard": Prutsman, p. 23.

241 "The great escapade": Cavada, p. 189.

242 "February 13.—Sixteen more": Glazier, p. 87.

242 "The recaptured officers refused": Moran, "A Thrilling History," n.p.

242 "replied with perfect candor": Ibid.

242 "The cell was about twelve feet": Fales, p. 11.

243 "which seemed like going": Ibid., p. 11.

243 "The excitement was tremendous": Cavada, p. 194.

243 "We could distinctly hear": Ibid., p. 195.

244 "Such a plan for wholesale murder": Glazier, p. 94.

244 "The minute Dahlgren got into": Moran, "A Thrilling History," n.p.

244 "A package of salt": Cavada, p. 192.

244 "To-day the rebels capped": Byers, p. 26.

244 "On the 30th of April": Moran, "A Thrilling History," n.p.

Epilogue. Two Buildings

247 "I prayed in my heart": Hobart, p. 8.

249 After her death: *Richmond Times-Dispatch*, August 11, 1911.

249 These same newspapers would add: *Richmond Times-Dispatch*, January 6, 1959.

Bibliography

Abbott, John S. C. "Capture, Imprisonment, and Escape." *Harper's Magazine* (December 1866–May 1867).

Adams, Herbert. "Neal Dow of Maine: Enemy of Rebels and Rum Lovers." *Civil War Times Illustrated* (March 1986).

Bartleson, F.A. *Letters from Libby Prison.* Edited by Margaret W. Peelle. New York: Greenwich Book Publishers, 1956.

Beaudry, Louis. *Libby Prison Chronicles, Devoted to Facts and Fun.* Libby Prison newspaper, 1889.

Beymer, William Gilmore. *On Hazardous Service, Scouts and Spies of the North and South.* New York: Harper & Brothers, 1912.

Blay, John S. *The Civil War: A Pictorial Profile.* New York: Thomas Y. Crowell, 1958.

Bliss, G. N. *Cavalry Service with Sheridan and Life in Libby Prison.* Providence, 1884.

Boaz, Thomas M. *Libby Prison and Beyond.* Shippensburg, PA: Burd Street Press, 1999.

Boggs, S. S. "Eighteen Months a Prisoner under the Rebel Flag." Self-published, 1887.

Bowman, John S. *The Civil War Day by Day.* New York: Dorset Press, 1989.

Bray, John. "My Escape from Richmond." *Harper's New Monthly Magazine* (April 1864): 662–65.

Bristol, F. M. *Life of Chaplin McCabe.* New York: Fleming H. Revell, 1908.

Brown, Daniel Patrick. *The Tragedy of the Libby and Andersonville Camps.* San Marino, CA: Golden West Historical Publications, 1980.

Buchanan, Lamont. *A Pictorial History of the Confederacy.* New York: Bonanza Books, 1951.

Burrows, Reverend J. L. "Recollections of Libby Prison." *Southern Historical Society Papers* 11, nos. 2, 3 (1883): 83.

Byers, Sam. "What I Saw in Dixie, or, 16 Months in a Rebel Prison." Self-published, Samuel Hawkins Marshall Byers, Dansville, NY, Robbins and Poore, 1868.

Byers, Sam H. M. *With Fire and Sword.* New York: Neale Publishing, 1911.

Byrne, Frank L. "A General behind Bars: Neal Dow in Libby Prison." *Civil War History* (June 1962).

Byrne, Frank L. "Libby Prison: A Study in Emotions." *Journal of Southern History* (February 1958).

Caldwell, D. C. "Incidents of War and Southern Prison Life." Dayton, OH: Self-published, 1864.

Catton, Bruce. *The American Heritage Picture History of the Civil War*. Rockville, MD: American Heritage Publishing, 1960.

Catton, Bruce. *Reflections on the Civil War*. New York: Berkley Books, 1981.

Cavada, Frederick F. *Libby Life: Experiences of a Prisoner of War*. Lanham, MD: University Press of America, 1985. First published 1864.

Cesnola, Louis Palma Di. *Ten Months in Libby Prison*, Pamphlet. Virginia, 1865 Historical Society. U.S. Sanitary Commission, February 15, 1865.

Chamberlain, Capt. J. W. "Libby Prison." *National Tribune*, August 15, 1889.

Cloyd, Benjamin G. *Haunted by Atrocity: Civil War Prisons in American Memory*. Baton Rouge: Louisiana State University Press, 2010.

"Col. Rose's Story of the Famous Tunnel Escape from Libby Prison." Author unknown, Pamphlet. Libby Prison Museum, late 1800s.

Commager, Henry Steele. *Living History: The Civil War*. New York: Tess Press, 1950.

Cowley, Robert, ed. *With My Face to the Enemy*. New York: Penguin, 2001.

Davis, William C. *The Image of War 1861–1865*. Vols. 1–6. New York: Doubleday, 1981.

Davis, William C. *Touched by Fire: A Photographic Portrait of the Civil War*. Vols. 1–2. Boston, MA: Little, Brown, 1985.

Domschcke, Bernhard. *Twenty Months in Captivity: Memoirs of a Union Officer in Confederate Prisons*. Translated by Frederic Trautman. Madison, NJ: Farleigh Dickinson University Press, 1987. First published 1865.

Dow, Neal. "A General behind Bars." Excerpts in *Civil War History* (June 1962).

Drake, N. A. "Coburn's Brigade in Captivity: A Long Journey Full of Hardships to a Life of Misery in Libby Prison." *National Tribune Repository* (November 1907).

Earle, Lt. Charles. "Libby Prison Life and Escape." *The Maine Bugle* 2–3 (1895).

Fairbanks, Pvt. Charles. *Notes of Army and Prison Life 1862–1865*. Bethel, VT: My Little Jessie Press, 2004.

Fales, James M. "Prison Life of James M. Fales, Lieut." Read before the Society, October 12, 1881.

Faust, Drew Gilpin. *This Republic of Suffering: Death and the American Civil War*. New York: Vintage Books, 2008.

Fishel, Edwin C. *The Secret War for the Union: The Untold Story of Military Intelligence in the Civil War*. Boston, MA: Houghton Mifflin, 1996.

Fisher, General B. F. "Life and Experiences in Southern Prisons during the Civil War." *Philadelphia Weekly Times*, May 18, 1887.

Forsythe, John William. *Guerilla Warfare and Life in Libby Prison*. Wymondham, UK: Turnpike Press, 1967. First published 1892.

Frassanito, William A. *Grant and Lee: The Virginia Campaigns, 1864–65*. New York: Scribner's, 1983.

Glazier, Willard Worcester. *The Capture, the Prison Pen, and the Escape*. New York: R. H. Ferguson and Co., 1870.

Hale, Capt. George W. *The Story of the One Hundred and First Ohio Infantry: A Memorial Volume*. Cleveland, Ohio, Bayne Printing Co., 1894.

Hamilton, A. G. "Story of the Famous Tunnel Escape from Libby Prison." Pamphlet (includes list of escapees). Chicago Museum, 1893.

Harrold, John. *Libby, Andersonville, Florence.* Philadelphia, PA: Selheimer Printing Co., 1870.

Harwell, Richard B. *The Confederate Reader: How the South Saw the War.* New York: MetroBooks, 2002.

Higginson, Thomas Wentworth. *Army Life in a Black Regiment.* Reprint, Boston, MA: Houghton Mifflin, 1900.

Hobart, Gen. Harrison C. "War Papers Read before the Commandery of the State of Wisconsin." Vol. 1, p. 394. June 3, 1891.

Hoehling, Mary, and A. A. Hoehling. *The Day Richmond Died.* New York: A. S. Barnes & Co., 1981.

Hugo, Victor. *Les Misérables.* New York: Signet Classics, 1987. First published 1862.

Jimerson, Randall C. *The Private Civil War: Popular Thought during the Sectional Conflict.* Baton Rouge, LA: Louisiana State University Press, 1988.

Jones, David J. "Inside Libby and Out by Leo M. Kaiser." Kentucky Historical Society, October 1961.

Johnston, Capt. I. N. *Four Months in Libby Prison and the Campaign against Atlanta.* Philadelphia, PA: Methodist Book Concern, 1864.

Keller, Allan. *Morgan's Raid.* New York: Collier Books, 1961.

Kent, Will Parmiter. *The Story of Libby Prison.* Chicago: Libby Prison War Museum Association, n.d.

Korn, Jerry. *The Fight for Chattanooga: Chickamauga to Missionary Ridge.* New York: Time-Life Books, 1985.

Lankford, Nelson. *Richmond Burning.* New York: Penguin, 2002.

Larson, Erik. *The Devil in the White City.* New York: Vintage Books, 2003.

Lee, Richard M.. *General Lee's City.* McLean, VA: EPM Publications, 1987.

"Libby Prison." Official Publication no. 12. Pamphlet. Richmond, VA: Richmond Civil War Centennial Commission, 1961–1965.

Lodge, Captain. "Diary." *Journal of the Illinois State Historical Society* Volume 56 No. 2, (Summer 1963).

Long, E. B. *The Civil War Day by Day: An Almanac.* New York: Doubleday, 1971.

MacCauley, Clay. *Through Chancellorsville: Into and Out of Libby Prison.* Providence RI: Rhode Island Soldiers and Sailors Historical Society, 1904.

Mann, Dr. Augustine. *A Grand Army Man of Rhode Island by Wyman.* New York: Graphic Press, 1925.

McCreery, William B. "My Experiences as a Prisoner of War and Escape from Libby Prison." War Paper no. 11. Lecture delivered at Michigan Commandery Loyal Legion, February 6, 1889.

McElroy, John. *Andersonville: A Story of Rebel Military Prisons.* Toledo, OH: D. R. Locke, 1879.

McPherson, James M. *The Atlas of the Civil War.* New York: Macmillan, 1994.

Mitchell, Reid. *Civil War Soldiers: Their Expectations and Experiences.* New York: Viking Press, 1988.

Moran, Frank E. *Bastiles of the Confederacy.* Self-published, 1890.

Moran, Frank E. "Libby Prison: The Tunnel Diggers." *National Tribune*, March 17, 1892.

Moran, Frank E. "A Thrilling History of the Famous Underground Tunnel of Libby Prison or Col. Rose's Tunnel at Libby Prison." Pamphlet. Reprinted from *Century Magazine*, March 1888.

Murfin, James V. *Battlefields of the Civil War*. New York: Colour Library Books, 1988.

Parker, Sandra V. *Richmond's Civil War Prisons*. Lynchburg, VA: H. E. Howard, 1990.

Porter, David Dixon. *Incidents and Anecdotes of the Civil War*, New York: D. Appleton and Co., 1885

Prutsman, C. M. *A Soldier's Experiences in Southern Prisons*. New York: Andrew H. Kellogg, 1901.

Putnam, George Haven. *A Prisoner of War in Virginia 1864–65*. New York: Putnam's Sons, 1912.

Randall, W.S.B. "Libby Prison: The Experience of One of the Successful Tunnelers." *National Tribune*, March 27, 1890.

Ray, Frederick E. *Alfred R. Waud: Civil War Artist*. New York: Viking Press, 1974.

Reynolds, Daniel. *Memories of Libby Prison*. Michigan History Museum 23 (1939): 391-98. Lansing: Michigan Historical Commission

Roach, Lieutenant A. C. *The Prisoner of War, and How Treated*. Indianapolis, IN: Railroad City Publishing House, 1865.

Robertson, James. *The Untold Civil War: Exploring the Human Side of War*. Washington, DC: National Geographic Books, 2011.

Rose, Thomas. "Libby Tunnel: An Interesting Account of Its Construction." *National Tribune*, May 14, 1885.

Russell, Capt. Milton. "Reminiscences of Prison Life and Escape." Vol. 1 of *Military Order of the Loyal Legion of the United States*, 25–38.

Ryan, David D. *A Yankee Spy in Richmond: The Civil War Diary of "Crazy Bet" Van Lew*. Mechanicsburg, PA: Stackpole Books, 1996.

Sclater, W. S. "A Complete and Authentic History of Libby Prison. Pamphlet, Richmond, Virginia: Southern Art Emporium, 1897.

Sedgewick, Arthur G. "Libby Prison: The Civil War Diary by William Armstrong." *Virginia Magazine*, October 1963.

Shrady, John. "Reminiscences of Libby Prison." *Magazine of American History*, July–December 1886.

Smith, Jean Edward. *Grant*. New York: Simon & Schuster, 2001.

Sneden, Private Robert Knox. *The Eye of the Storm: A Civil War Odyssey*. New York: Free Press, 2000.

Starr, George. "In and Out of Confederate Prisons." Paper. May 3, 1892.

Stepp, John W. *Mirror of War: The Washington Star Reports the Civil War*. Englewood Cliffs, NJ: Prentice-Hall, 1961.

Stern, Philip Van Doren. *Secret Missions of the Civil War*. Garden City, NY: Wings Books, 1959.

Straubing, Harold Elk. *The Fateful Lightning: Civil War Eyewitness Reports*. St. Paul, MN: Paragon House, 1987.

Styple, William B., ed. *Writing and Fighting the Civil War*. Kearny, NJ: Belle Grove, 2000.

Szabad, Emeric. "Diary in Libby Prison." *Fraser's Magazine for Town and Country* (March 1868): 385–406.

Tiemann, William F. *Prison Life in Dixie*. Self-published, 1894.

Tobie, Edward P. *A Trip to Richmond as a Prisoner of War*. n.p.: Sidney S. Rider, 1879.

Tower, Major Morton. "Army Experiences of Major Morton Tower from 1861 to 1864." Typescript. Virginia Historical Society, n.d.

Twain, Mark. The Autobiography of Mark Twain vol. 2., P436, University of California Press, 2013.

Varon, Elizabeth R. *Southern Lady, Yankee Spy*. Oxford: Oxford University Press, 2003.

Wallber, Albert. "The Escape from the Libby." In *Twenty Months in Captivity: Memoirs of Union Officer in Confederate Prisons*. Translated by Frederic Trautman. Madison, NJ: Farleigh Dickinson University Press, 1987.

Walls That Talk. Libby Prison. Anonymous pamphlet, 1884.

Wells, James M. "Tunneling out of Libby Prison." *McClure's Magazine*, January 1904.

Wells, James M. *With Touch of Elbow*. Self-published, 1909.

Wheelan, Joseph. *Libby Prison Breakout*. New York: PublicAffairs, 2010.

White, A. B. "Reminiscences of Libby and other Southern Prisons." Pamphlet, 1900.

Wiley, Bell Irvin. *The Life of Billy Yank, the Common Soldier of the Civil War*. New York: Doubleday, 1971.

Wilkins, William D. "Forgotten in the Black Hole: A Diary from Libby Prison." *Civil War Times Illustrated* 15, no. 3. (1976).

Willett, Robert L. *The Lightning Mule Brigade: Abel Straight's 1863 Raid into Alabama*. Indianapolis, IN: Guild Press, 1999.

Wilson, Edmund. *Patriotic Gore*. Oxford: Oxford University Press, 1966.

Index

prisoner counts, 149; Cavada on, 135–36; Chamberlain on beatings, 54–55; Confederacy transporting, 7; death of, 245; Earle and, 42; exchanges of, 32–34, 49, 59, 124–25, 143; food shortages and, 18; Glazier on march, 15–16; hiding, on first night of freedom, 178; international, 52; Libby Prison quarters, 26, 27; Libby Prison searches, 23–26; life as, 1; MacCauley on march of, 11; mail from home and, 134–35; news from, 25–26; newspapers on, 32–33; no planning for, 29–30; parole system, 31–32, 34; railroads for transport, 10–11; Rebel Army abuse of, ix; slaves as, 33; Tobie on plunder from, 9; Tower on farewell to, 13; transporting to Richmond, Virginia, 7–13; Van Lew on, 128; viewing escape, 169; Wells, J. M., on treatment of, 9. *See also* escapees

The Prisoner of War, and How Treated (Roach), 230

prisons, viii; Andersonville Prison, 41, 245, 248; Belle Island Prison, 15, 30; Castle Thunder Prison, 30, 65, 184, 186; Danville Prison, 245. *See also* Libby Prison

Prutsman, C. M: on aftermath of escape, 241; on morning count, 183–84

racism, 56

railroads: for prisoner transport, 10–11; role in US Civil War, 15

Randall, Capt., 213; on bloodhounds, 192; encountering US cavalry, 218; on end of suffering, 238; on Lincoln meeting, 237; on prison breakout, 167; on tunnel breaking through, 156–57

Rappahannock River, 232–33

Rat Hell, 77, 79, 83; guard activity in, 165; guards searching, 155; Johnston in, 151, 152, 153, 164–65; as loathsome, 113–14; Moran on, 172; nights in, 89; recovering from, 132; Rose on, 114; sealed in, 113; trapped in, 145–53; work in, 86

Read, Capt., 67, 70

Rebel Army, 30, 108, 145; abuse of prisoners, ix; Byers on, 33; captures by, 1–6; confronting escapees, 190, 210; death in captivity of, 141; escapees disguised as, 120–22; food and, 18; Glazier on, 8; Hobart on discovering camp,

About the Author

Douglas Miller is an award-winning documentary filmmaker and writer/producer on more than 20 documentaries aired on the History Channel, the Discovery Channel, and Showtime, notably the series "The Color of War," "Modern Marvels," and "Boneyards." He lives in Studio City, California.